LIVES OF THE MASTERS

T0354278

The Second Karmapa Karma Pakshi

TIBETAN MAHĀSIDDHA

Charles Manson

Shambhala

Shambhala Publications, Inc.
2129 13th Street
Boulder, Colorado 80302
www.shambhala.com

Cover art: Robert Fenwick May, Jr.
Cover design: Gopa and Ted2, Inc.
Frontispiece photo © Michael McIntyre
Music notation at page 37 © Dirk de Klerk

9 8 7 6 5 4 3 2 1

FIRST EDITION
Printed in Canada

Shambhala Publications makes every effort
to print on acid-free, recycled paper.
Shambhala Publications is distributed worldwide by
Penguin Random House, Inc., and its subsidiaries.

LIBRARY OF CONGRESS CATALOGING-IN-PUBLICATION DATA
Names: Manson, Charles, author.
Title: The second Karmapa, Karma Pakshi: Tibetan Mahāsiddha / Charles Manson.
Description: Boulder: Shambhala, 2022. | Series: Lives of the masters |
Includes bibliographical references and index.
Identifiers: LCCN 2021020901 | ISBN 9781559394673 (trade paperback)
Subjects: LCSH: Karma-pakshi, Karma-pa II, 1204 or 1206–1283. |
Kar-ma-pa Lamas—China—Tibet—Biography. | Reincarnation. Mongolia—History—
13th century. | China—History—Yuan dynasty, 1260–1368.
Classification: LCC BQ968.A8767 M36 2022 | DDC 294.3/923092 [B]—dc23
LC record available at https://lccn.loc.gov/2021020901

Contents

Series Introduction

BUDDHIST TRADITIONS are heir to some of the most creative thinkers in world history. The Lives of the Masters series offers lively and reliable introductions to the lives, works, and legacies of key Buddhist teachers, philosophers, contemplatives, and writers. Each volume in the Lives series tells the story of an innovator who embodied the ideals of Buddhism, crafted a dynamic living tradition during his or her lifetime, and bequeathed a vibrant legacy of knowledge and practice to future generations.

Lives books rely on primary sources in the original languages to describe the extraordinary achievements of Buddhist thinkers and illuminate these achievements by vividly setting them within their historical contexts. Each volume offers a concise yet comprehensive summary of the master's life and an account of how they came to hold a central place in Buddhist traditions. Each contribution also contains a broad selection of the master's writings.

This series makes it possible for all readers to imagine Buddhist masters as deeply creative and inspired people whose work was animated by the rich complexity of their time and place and how these inspiring figures continue to engage our quest for knowledge and understanding today.

KURTIS SCHAEFFER, *series editor*

Acknowledgments

THANKS ARE DUE to many people and grant institutions who have assisted in the project of researching and writing this work. The project has been a lengthy process, so hopefully I have not omitted any names.

In terms of text research, thanks are due to Burkhard Quessel (British Library) for bringing to my attention Karma Pakshi's memoirs; to the Seventeenth Karmapa Ogyen Trinley Dorje for providing a text on Karma Pakshi's preincarnations; and to Professor Matthew Kapstein for his advice on Karma Pakshi's writings.

For the translation processes, my thanks primarily go to the late Tsering D. Gonkatsang for his patient, diligent, and expert advice. Acknowledgment and thanks are also due to Khenpo Losal, Professor Ulrich Pagel, Thrangu Rinpoche, Professor Charles Ramble, Professor Leonard van der Kuijp, and to Drungyik Tenzin Namgyal.

In terms of writing this book, thanks for advice and information are due to Dr. Cécile Ducher, Dr. Ruth Gamble, Josay Tashi Tsering, Yongey Mingyur Dorje, Dr. Dirk de Klerk, Khenpo Karma David Choephel, Dr. Jann Ronis, Professor Lewis Doney, Dr. Sonam Tsering Ngulphu, Professor Nathan Hill, Catherine Brown, Michele Martin, Kristin Blancke, Michael McCormick, and Michele Laporte.

My thanks for checking on sections of the draft go to Professor Chris Atwood, on the Mongol Empire passages, and to Dr. Roberto Vitali, on the Gya family passage.

Funding for research has come from the Frederick Williamson

Memorial Fund (Cambridge), Faculty Fund (Oriental Institute, Oxford), École Pratique des Hautes Études (Paris), and the Centre de recherché sur les civilisations de l'Asie orientale (Paris).

For the publishing process, my thanks go to Victoria Tubb for her advice on the contract, and to Casey Kemp, Laura Goetz, and Gretchen Gordon for editing.

And all the while, for her patience, encouragement, and support, my heartfelt thanks to Emma.

Karma Pakshi

Introduction

MANY PEOPLE WITHIN the Tibetan Buddhism community—both those born to it and its converts—will be familiar with the name Karma Pakshi (1204–1283). For a more general public, the thirteenth century that he lived in, in a remote area of the Asian highlands known as Tibet, was for Europeans a period of feudalism and the cultural predominance of the Christian church and its monasteries. Several Christian friar schools were founded during this century, in particular the Franciscans and Dominicans, which led rapidly to some friars' missionary work taking place as far afield as China.

The century for China was one of invasions by Chinggis Khan (also known as Genghis Khan) and his descendants, tumultuous years that eventually culminated in some degree of stability with a reunified China under the Yuan dynasty. During the period of Mongolian imperial encroachment into China, Karma Pakshi was probably the only Tibetan ecclesiastic known to preach at the courts of both Möngke Khan and Kubilai Khan in Mongolia and China. He was also the first in his ecclesiastical lineage to be known as Karmapa.

Within the fold of Tibetan Buddhism, the Karmapa lineage of prominent ecclesiastical figureheads is very well known. Each Karmapa is titular head of the Kamtsang branch of the Kagyü sect (also known as Kargyü). The monastery headquarters for the lineage was at Tsurpu Monastery (forty miles northwest of Lhasa) for almost eight hundred years, until its destruction by the cannons and

1

dynamite of the People's Liberation Army in the 1960s. The monastery has since been rebuilt, although a Karmapa has not resided there since 1999. The lineage succession of the Karmapa figureheads has been determined over the centuries by the Tibetan Buddhist tradition of appointing a male child to the position after the death of an incumbent, where the child is considered to be a rebirth of the antecedent Karmapa. The child then usually assumes full authority in his teenage years.

Karma Pakshi is known as being a very early example in Tibetan history of such a child. In his case, his predecessor was a veritable saint: Düsum Khyenpa (1110–1193). As an adult, Karma Pakshi wrote several times that he was "no different" from Düsum Khyenpa, his teacher's teacher's teacher. The "guru great-grandfather," so to speak, had died eleven or thirteen years before Karma Pakshi's birth. Karma Pakshi was the first to self-identify as Karmapa (he used Karmāpa), and eventually Düsum Khyenpa was attributed retrospectively the epithet of First Karmapa. Thus Karma Pakshi is often identified, somewhat loosely, as "the first reincarnate," an emanation of a holy being known as a "trülku" (often commonly rendered as "tulku" from the Tibetan, or "living buddha" in modern parlance).

The "first reincarnate" characterization is convenient and neat, but it would be more accurate to view Karma Pakshi as a major influence in the nascent tradition of reincarnate leaders of the Tibetan Buddhist monasteries, a tradition that has lasted eight hundred years. The meme of reincarnate succession of prominent ecclesiastical leaders was adopted relatively quickly within the Tibetan cultural area, culminating in the seventeenth century with the Fifth Dalai Lama as head of government and the successive heads of government being determined through appointment by reincarnation, a political tradition that continued for three hundred years.

In terms of the development of Tibetan Buddhism, Karma Pakshi was an early advocate within China and Mongolia of Buddhist rituals, philosophy, and meditation practices as interpreted and transmitted through the Tibetan filter. His reputation as such is overshadowed in Chinese history by the greater influence and renown in the Kubilai Khan court of his younger contemporary Pakpa (1235–1280). Indeed, Karma Pakshi's relationship with Kubilai was troubled—but his relationship with Kubilai's elder brother Möngke Khan, the ruler of the entire Mongol Empire at its apogee, was apparently entirely harmonious. The extensive journeys the middle-aged Karma Pakshi made to China and Mongolia, returning with donated riches that would enable his building projects in Tibet, were early examples of what was to become something of a pattern for Tibetan ecclesiastics: missionary tours by monastic leaders in foreign lands made not only for the inherent value of the Buddhist teaching and initiations given but also to accrue sponsorship funds for the development of home monasteries. The pattern continues into modern times.

As a historical figure, Karma Pakshi has been honored in religious artifacts, as can be seen in the numerous scroll paintings (*tangka*s) and statues of him.[1] He also evokes devotion from Buddhist practitioners of his Kamtsang tradition, as he became the subject of a practice "discovered" in the seventeenth century by the First Yongé Mingyur Dorjé, a contemporary of the Tenth and Eleventh Karmapas. The discovered *terma* practice is a guru yoga practice derived from Yongé Mingyur Dorjé's dawn vision of Karma Pakshi giving a short teaching on the nature of mind (from a meditator's point of view).[2] This visionary inspiration came four hundred years after Karma Pakshi's death. Mingyur Dorjé's *sādhana* praxis is still used almost another four hundred years since its revelation and is of central importance to meditators following the Karmapa tradition. When the Sixteenth Karmapa made groundbreaking trips to Europe and North America in the 1970s, a primary recommendation he repeatedly made to Westerners was to practice the Karma Pakshi sādhana. Additionally, in 1968, Chögyam Trungpa Rinpoche was inspired in Bhutan by a vision that included Karma Pakshi. Trungpa's visionary experience became the basis for a practice known in English as *The Sādhana of Mahāmudrā*, which has become a primary practice for Western followers of Trungpa's tradition.

In the following work, much of the material for the Life and Legacy section is derived from Karma Pakshi's memoirs. The memoir collection is known in Tibetan as a *rang namtar*, an autobiographical liberation account, but is more accurately a collection of seven parts, in both poetry and prose, on a range of subjects in addition to the telling of some of his life events. It is not entirely clear which parts Karma Pakshi had a direct hand in composing and which were perhaps dictated to a colleague or disciple coauthor, but nevertheless the works probably originate from his written or dictated account. Two of the sections are described as his "testaments" but are not wills in the sense that a modern reader might understand the term. In the collection as a whole, the memoirs in several parts meander somewhat, which might indicate an orally dictated origin for such passages. For this volume, other biographies and histories have also been consulted, ranging from the Third Karmapa's biography of Karma Pakshi to the modern Tibetan accounts.[3] Readers should be aware that Karma Pakshi refers to himself as Rangjung Dorjé and also his successor is named Rangjung Dorjé.

In the Writings section, the selections of parts of Karma Pakshi's works presented have been chosen thematically—examples of his writing on incarnation, on his meditation teaching, on narratives, on tantras, on consecration, and on a visionary experience of questions and answers with Mañjuśrī; his deathbed song (as presented by Situ Panchen); and an extract from *An Esoteric Great Treasury* (as reported by Situ Panchen), where Karma Pakshi is quoted as giving an overview, in verse, of his lifetime achievements.

Life and Legacy

CHAPTER 1

Early Years

THE GREAT RIVER YANGTZE in China is the third-longest river on our planet. If one starts, in one's imagination, on a bird's-eye journey from the river's wide mouth in the China Sea and flies along the river's course, against its flow, past evidence of human cultivation and cities, up into the hills and then the mountains, twisting and turning through gorges, one would eventually come to the heights of the Tibetan highlands. Farther up along the river's course, imaginatively traveling above fast-flowing, churning waters—where not interrupted by modern electricity dams—one would arrive in the region of Kham in East Tibet. If one were to land beside the river in an area close to the town of Dergé, one might find a riverside community[4] where, eight hundred years ago, a child named Chödzin, later to be renowned as Karma Pakshi, was born.

This child, as an adult, was to become a major influence in the development of the tradition in Tibet whereby the more important Buddhist ecclesiastic offices are passed on to the next generation through the identification of, usually, a male child considered to be a reincarnation of the previous post-holder.[5] Various beliefs in rebirth have been, and still are, widespread across many religions and philosophies, but Tibetan culture is unique in having integrated the belief into the socioreligious administration of cultural centers such as Buddhist monasteries. Indeed, in the seventeenth to twentieth centuries, the succession by rebirth was even integrated into the system of head-of-government succession with the Ganden Podrang

7

rule of the Dalai Lamas (1642–1959). The ecclesiastical succession by rebirth system that permeated official positions in Tibet, and indeed farther afield in Central Asia, was dominant for more than three hundred years. The initial developments of the tradition are often credited to Karma Pakshi's example in the thirteenth century.

A significant feature of the socioreligious context in which this tradition initially developed in Tibet was that in the two centuries prior to Karma Pakshi's time, several monasteries across the Tibetan region had been established and were beginning to flourish. For example, monasteries had begun at Thöling (founded 997), Shalu (1040), Radreng (1056), Sakya (1073), Daklha Gampo (1121), Densatil (1158), Tsel (1175), Drigung Til (1179), and Ralung (1180). Of particular relevance to Karma Pakshi's life are the monasteries established at Katok (1159), Kampo Nenang (1164), Pangpuk (1169), and Tsurpu (1189). This steady gestation of monasteries was a consequence of a revived interest in Buddhism beginning a century and a half after the demise of the Tibetan Empire in the ninth century. The "rekindling the doctrine from dormant embers"[6] was due in part to the activities of royal patrons (Kings Yeshé Ö and Tride Gontsen), Indian missionaries (for example, Atiśa and Śākyaśrībhadra), and Tibetan translator lotsāwas (such as Rinchen Zangpo, Marpa, and Drokmi), to the nascent terma or rediscovered treasures tradition (both Bön and Buddhist), and to the Central Tibetans who had traveled to northeast Tibet to receive and revive the Buddhist monastic ordination tradition (among them Lumé and Lotön). Thus, at the beginning of the thirteenth century, a strengthening Tibetan Buddhist tradition was in the initial stages of engendering a widespread monastic infrastructure, while to the south, over the Himalayas, northern India was succumbing to Muslim invasion forces. In other directions surrounding Tibet, to the north the phenomenal Chinggis Khan was instigating a vast empire whose forces subsequently, during the first half of the thirteenth

century, would overrun Tangut (Xi Xia) and invade Tibet. To the
east, Chinggis's grandson (Kubilai) would eventually unite and
rule over both North and South China during Chödzin's lifetime.
These were indeed tumultuous times for Asia.

Family

Chödzin was born in remote and mountainous eastern Tibet, in
a valley of the river Drichu (upper Yangtze) designated by some
Tibetan writers as "rich in holy dharma,"[7] to his mother Sengza
Mangkyi and father Gyawang Tsurtsa Trangtar.[8] The "Gya" of his
father's name indicates the family clan, associated with the Mukpo
branch of the Dong clan, based initially in the northeast of the
Tibetan cultural area, in the Tuyuhun region (later Xi Xia). The Gya
reputedly suffered a punishing attack by Emperor Songtsen Gampo
in the early seventh century (probably 638) when the emperor was
angered with the progress of marriage negotiations with the Chinese
imperial court. This attack apparently led to the migration of several
Gya, mostly to Central Tibet. Two famously strong Gya brothers,
Laga and Luga, were known to be transporters of the Jowo Buddha
statue to Lhasa as it accompanied Princess Wencheng.[9] Members
of the Gya clan later settled in south central Tibet, particularly
in the Nyang area (encompassing Gyantse and Ralung), and also
came to have lands farther south in the Bhutanese border area.
Several Gya names are known of among the government ministers
in the imperial period. As a clan, they generally seem to have been
reputed to have religious concerns, and indeed to have a penchant
for vegetarianism, both factors relevant to Karma Pakshi's adult
life.[10] His mother's clan, Sing (or perhaps Seng, both clan names),
is unfortunately not well known.

There exist autobiographical writings by Karma Pakshi—some
perhaps recounted to a scribe rather than written by himself—that

are some of the earliest autobiographical writings in Tibetan literary history.[11] However, these texts, seven parts in all, tend to be concerned with his visionary experiences and his discussions about reincarnation, rather more than factual details of people and events, and are largely reticent about his family. There is a reference to the family name—the noble Ü family (*dbu*)—and the area of birth "rich in dharma," but the names of his parents or relatives are not given in his memoirs. Regarding his ancestors, rather more detail is given in an eighteenth-century Karma Kamtsang "golden rosary" account, familiarly known as *A Rosary of Crystal Jewels*, coauthored by Situ Panchen and Tséwang Künchab and published in 1775. In the section on Karma Pakshi's life, it is stated that among his ancestors on his father's side was a certain Tak Namkhai Lhazung, a great-grandson of Emperor Trisong Detsen, who apparently studied with Vimalamitra, Padmasambhava, and the latter's disciple, Nub Namkhai Nyingpo. The timelines relevant for such connections are somewhat improbable. However, the account further states that, being adept in the Vajrarākṣa praxis, Tak Namkhai Lhazung's mastery of mantra enabled him to display the miraculous powers of hanging his clothing on a light ray and "riding" on light rays in the sky. Tak Namkhai Lhazung's half brother had three sons, also Buddhist practitioners. Uncle and nephews traveled as leaders of a community that moved to eastern Tibet, to Kham, retaining the family name of Ü. The account estimates it was eleven to fifteen generations later, covering the intervening four hundred years, that Chödzin was born within this family lineage.[12]

   It was to the same family lineage, yet another five hundred years later, in the eighteenth century, in the same area, at Sato Kyilé Latso near Dergé, that Karma Pakshi's successor as the Twelfth Karmapa, Changchub Dorjé, was born ten incarnations later. The Kamtsang Kagyü *Rosary of Crystal Jewels* account of Changchub Dorjé's life—this section authored by Tséwang Künchab—has much the same outline of the imperial connections of his family as there is for the Karma Pakshi account. The Twelfth Karmapa outline adds that the ancestor of both Karmapas, Tak Namkhai Lhazung (the sky-traveling yogin), had lived in the Chingwa Taktsé palace in Central Tibet, and his grandsons were makers of large statues, echoing Karma Pakshi's connections with the commissioning and creation of statues.[13]

Birth

The child Chödzin was the youngest of several brothers, most accounts giving him as the youngest of three brothers, one account giving four as the total. The numerical discrepancy might be explained by the presence of a half brother named Tsuktor Kyab, mentioned in the fifteenth-century *Blue Annals* history.[14]

Karma Pakshi himself writes of his childhood—without mentioning his family in any detail—that at age six he could read without being taught to do so and at around nine or ten he could read any of the Buddha's teachings, and just by reading a work just once he would understand and fully assimilate the material. He was a precocious child, raised in a Buddhist household. Yet despite his mind being unchanging in meditation, in his own words, like "an unruffled deep ocean," he admits that as a child he did not fully recognize his mind's essence (*ngo ma shes pa*).[15] Subsequent biographers of Karma Pakshi repeat much the same details, with the addition that he would, because of his reading abilities, be sponsored to read texts in other households. Thus he was participating in something of a "merit economy," whereby ritual or reading services create Buddhist meritorious activities sponsored by a local householder. Accounts go on to add that at age eleven, Chödzin set off for Central Tibet to further his studies. Soon after starting his journey, he met another traveler, the Buddhist teacher Pomdrakpa.

Recognition as a Reincarnation

This meeting between an eleven-year-old boy and a middle-aged meditator in about 1215 on a remote mountainside in East Tibet can be seen as highly significant in terms of subsequent Tibetan history and culture. In personal terms for the boy, it is the occasion when first intimations of recognition occur that young Chödzin was a reincarnation of Düsum Khyenpa, a revered meditator who had been born and active in the Kham area and had died in Central Tibet more than ten years before Chödzin's birth. The propitious encounter on a hillside between Chödzin and Pomdrakpa, and their consequent relationship as pupil and master, could be considered an important factor in developing and establishing the reincarnate ecclesiastic tradition in Tibet—the so-called tulkus or living buddhas phenomenon that became widespread among Buddhist societies of Central Asia.

Karma Pakshi himself does not give much detail about the meeting, other than stating in his autobiography that Pomdrakpa told him, "You are someone with karmic propensity, aren't you? Since meeting you, many pure visions have occurred."[16] More detail is given in accounts by the Third Karmapa, Rangjung Dorjé, probably written about a century after the event, that the meeting occurred at Shabom, close to Selko Monastery where Pomdrakpa had been practicing and experiencing tantric visions for the past sixteen years.[17] According to this later account, at the time of their meeting Pomdrakpa appears to have been impressed by the youngster, asking him, "Young practitioner, where are you going?"

Chödzin replied, "I come from Sato and am going to Ü," which also could be read, perhaps fancifully, as a symbolic "I come from higher ground and go to the middle."

The master said, "You would be a wonderful student of mine—do not go anywhere, but stay." Later, that night, during a public religious initiation requested by a Sherap Lodrö, Pomdrakpa had an inspiration. He spoke to Chödzin alone after the gathering had dispersed: "Tonight, directly opposite where you were sitting, Düsum Khyenpa and all the Oral Lineage (Kagyü) appeared clearly. Your karmic tendencies are wonderful."

Subsequently, when on the way to Selko Monastery they were below the Shelmur hill between Selka and Shoko, Pomdrakpa said, "Today an appearance of Düsum Khyenpa filled the whole sky, so you are a very fortunate one. Do not go elsewhere, and practice in accord with my teaching." Thus the young Chödzin, born to a family with Nyingma connections, would come to be taught under the aegis of a developing Tibetan Buddhist lineage, known in its early days either as the Kargyü (White Lineage) or Kagyü (Oral Lineage). The lineage derived from the extraordinary exploits of Marpa the Translator in the eleventh century in bringing tantras and meditation instructions from India and Nepal.

Master and Disciple

Pomdrakpa was a practitioner who had many visionary experiences in connection with tantric rites and meditations. Born in eastern Tibet in 1170, he does not seem to have met in person the saintly Düsum Khyenpa, who retrospectively became known as the First Karmapa. Düsum Khyenpa, born in 1110, had left East Tibet in 1189 for Central Tibet to develop Tsurpu Monastery at 14,100 feet (4,300 meters) above sea level in the Drowo Lung valley about forty miles by road northwest of Lhasa. Düsum Khyenpa had first visited the Tsurpu area thirty years earlier, after which he returned to his homeland in East Tibet. After establishing the monastery in 1189, he died there in 1193.

Despite Pomdrakpa probably not having met Düsum Khyenpa, the Pomdrakpa biographies do report he had several visions of

Düsum Khyenpa, before and after the meeting with young Chödzin. When Pomdrakpa was fourteen years of age, he had had his first vision of Düsum Khyenpa, shortly after meeting one of Düsum Khyenpa's principal students, Drogön Rechen (1148–1218), at a place called Bob Gargang in East Tibet. Drogön Rechen later ordained Pomdrakpa as a monk, and for some time transmitted to him tantric meditation initiations and realization, "like father and son."[18] During this period, Pomdrakpa had a vision of Düsum Khyenpa instructing him to stay in one place: he subsequently resided at Selko Monastery for sixteen years, gaining meditative experience and visions.

In turn, once Chödzin had agreed to study with Pomdrakpa, he received novice ordination from the master. Karma Pakshi's memoir gives some information on the spiritual instruction he received as a teenager from Pomdrakpa.[19] The work quotes directly Pomdrakpa's remark on meeting the future student, as given above, that he was someone with special karmic propensities and that the meeting had engendered visions. The teacher then gave instruction on two subjects: "the *dohā* songs of the Great Brahmin Saraha" and the connascent *mahāmudrā* meditation instructions of Gampopa (1079–1153), Düsum Khyenpa's main teacher.

The first subject, "the Great Brahmin dohā songs," refers to the Indian yogin Saraha's famous song trilogy known as *Song for a King*, *Song for a Queen*, and *Song for the People*. The dating for Saraha's life is not definitive, but he is known to have lived in India about four hundred years before Karma Pakshi. Sahara is an important figure for the mahāmudrā meditation lineage of the Kagyü tradition, which maintains that Saraha was the first human in the transmission lineage deriving from the celestial Buddha Vajradhāra. Once Saraha's written works had traversed the Himalayas, Tibetan versions were included in the eventual Tengyur canonical collection of commentaries on Buddhist scriptures and teachings. It seems that the three dohās were of particular interest to Tibetans, and of them especially the longest dohā, the *Song for the People*. Elsewhere in his autobiography, Karma Pakshi refers to Düsum Khyenpa as being in essence the same as the Great Brahmin Saraha in terms of them both being symbols of immutable truth, and he quotes a couplet from a song he attributes to Düsum Khyenpa:

The lama is the Great Brahmin;
His oral instructions are the Mahāmudrā.[20]

The tradition of Saraha's teaching that Karma Pakshi refers to is possibly the tradition passed on from Tipupa in India to the yogin Rechungpa (d. 1161) and then to Düsum Khyenpa, although it may have come via the Marpa lineage, through to Milarepa and Gampopa to Düsum Khyenpa, or indeed a mixture of both traditions.

A poem (a *gur* song) ascribed to Karma Pakshi, with the title *Melody of Transcendent Dharmakāya*, seems relevant to this period in his life:[21]

The identity of samsara and nirvana throughout time,
The primordial uncreated nature—
Transcendent Saraha,
A supreme being,
Directly delivered the instructions of the oral lineage.

In the *dharmakāya* mandala of one's own mind,
Nondual mind and appearance are a shimmering reflection—
When a yogin of the wisdom realm
Does not shift from a realm of being effortless
In all going, moving about, lying down, and sitting,
They are called a yogin with absolute conviction—
Spoken from Saraha's wisdom.

Even the multitude of appearances have one essence,
Like waters merging into an ocean—
All phenomena of the experiential world
Are a perfect nirvana pure land.

Indeed the quantity of appearances has one essence
When there is mastery of the non-meditation state.
With uniquely immaculate dharmakāya,
Yogins who have realized the essential meaning
Are said to have completed their activity.

This short melody of transcendent dharmakāya
Is the realization of Śavari[22]—
Let us give the advice to fortunate beings!

The second subject of instruction that Karma Pakshi received
from Pomdrakpa was the introduction to the connascent mahāmudrā
taught by Gampopa—the meditation instructions and accounts of
meditation experiences brought from India by Marpa and then
transmitted to Milarepa and on to Gampopa, who combined the
instruction with his Kadampa training and later taught Düsum
Khyenpa. A song by Karma Pakshi can be seen as relevant:[23]

Within a mandala of clear wisdom
Abides the master of self-arising realization:
Is this not the Dakpo eminent doctor, Gampopa?
May the holy one bless me.

The essential value in these quarrelsome times
In the northern snowy country
Is to eliminate the darkness for the six classes of beings:
Is that not mahāmudrā?

The Dakpo eminent doctor's blessing,
A *nirmāṇakāya* benefiting beings,
He maintained the capital of the Oral Lineage:
Is this not Düsum Khyenpa?

In the tracks of the master,
The vajra yogin has been born,
Transmigrating in the world
With unimaginable fortitude
And practicing yogin disciplines:
Is this not a yogin without desire?

In unlimited pure lands everywhere,
Explaining phenomenal existence as mahāmudrā,
Overwhelming the lesser vehicle yoga:
Does he not practice the Mahāyāna?

In unbiased pure lands
The desire-free yogin lives,
Acting without adopting or rejecting:
Is this not the great equanimity?

A manifestation that has completed the two
    accumulations,
A rain of needs and wants,
Gifts distributed without desire and unimpeded:
Is this not the proper type of clinging?

In a song of seven somersaults
The desire-free yogin
At the seat of the lama master
Will sing of experiences that have arisen.

Karma Pakshi's autobiography remarks that as a result of the instructions received from Pomdrakpa, he came "to know and realize in an instant the infinite wisdom that is self-cognizant of one's ignorance about all phenomena within samsara and nirvana."[24] When he related this experience to Pomdrakpa, he asked the teacher, "Is it like that?" Pomdrakpa replied, "Despite the essence being unending, since deluded ignorance in beginningless samsara is ever present, it is necessary to teach the cycle of points about the subtle energies and the mind within the expanse of non-meditation." Pomdrakpa went on to state that such instruction is sufficient for practitioners such as themselves, but it is necessary to use a more graduated approach for teaching the varying grades of trainees, and to know how to modify various faults that arise in Buddhist practice.

His memoir records that Karma Pakshi therefore received all the instructions of the lineage, and in particular it mentions the "four points on introduction to the four kāyas."[25] This instruction later became Karma Pakshi's preferred teaching to give publicly, which he used during his travels in his middle age, when he taught both Kubilai Khan in China and Möngke Khan in Mongolia. He sometimes refers to the teaching in terms of "three kāyas," or even five, all referring to aspects of buddhahood. It would seem that this teaching was his core message for those interested in what he had to say. In his autobiographical writings Karma Pakshi mentions the teaching by name many times, in glowing terms, but does not elaborate extensively. However, a text by a Rangjung Dorjé, assumed to be the Third Karmapa, gives detail on the subject, and this latter text was commentated on extensively by the Eighth Karmapa in several volumes.[26] Briefly, the practice is a simple meditation (that is, a direct instruction that may be simple in words yet difficult to achieve for busy minds) in conjunction with a breathing and *trulkhor* yogic exercise to aid the meditation.[27]

The timeline of events for any travels of the master and student during the period of instruction and practice with Pomdrakpa is not clear. Karma Pakshi himself mentions he had a "non-meditation" mahāmudrā experience in the Namrak hermitage near Selko Monastery in the Kowo area.[28] A middle-length biography (*A Deity's Great Drum*) by the Second Shamarpa, Kachö Wangpo, completed before 1405, gives some details of the meditation and visionary experiences the young man had, but with scant data regarding dates or locations.[29] Later accounts generally are not specific on the timelines for Karma Pakshi's visions, dreams, and experiences, and also the locations of the events are not always given. Some of the visions experienced during Karma Pakshi's development as a meditation master are presented in chapter 2 (pages 24–27) herein, covering the period from his boyhood through to a lengthy retreat period in his adult years.

Monastery Education

As to Karma Pakshi's monastic education, it largely took place at Katok Monastery (established in 1159 and situated between the towns of Dergé and Batang in East Tibet). The head of the monastery from 1192 until 1226, Tsangtön Dorjé Gyeltsen (1137–1226), had developed a considerable reputation as a teacher. Tsangtön was the main disciple of Dampa Deshek, the founder of Katok. It seems that at some point Pomdrakpa had become doubtful of Tsangtön's reputation and decided to visit Katok to see for himself. On meeting Tsangtön he was duly impressed and received initiation and teaching. This must have occurred before Tsangtön's death in 1226 and may well have occurred considerably earlier: there is no mention of Chödzin, the youthful Karma Pakshi, meeting Tsangtön, so it is likely that Pomdrakpa went to Katok before he first met Chödzin in the latter's eleventh year (in 1214 or 1216). Indeed, Chödzin and Pomdrakpa's first meeting at Shabom may have occurred when Pomdrakpa was on his way back from Katok, but this is only conjecture.

There being no evidence to surmise that Chödzin met Tsangtön Dorjé Gyeltsen, he probably went to Katok sometime after 1226, in his early twenties. He had been advised by Pomdrakpa to study at Katok Monastery, established sixty years earlier and now under the leadership of its third abbot, the illustrious Jampabum (1179–1252). Chödzin received full monk's ordination from Jampabum and was given the ordained name Chökyi Lama (also recorded as Darma Lama). In the Katok tradition, there is a story that as Chödzin first approached Katok on a horse, as the monastery came into view, he had a vision that the whole area had become the body of the deity Vajrasattva.[30] His horse bowed and left a hoofprint impression in the rock, so that location became known as the "horse-bowing" place. It is also recounted in the Katok tradition that the young man once flew "like a bird" across the valley to a forested hillside to leave a full-body imprint in a rock there.

More conventionally, Chökyi Lama's time at Katok may well have been a receptive period of studying, under the aegis of the scholarly abbot Jampabum. Jampabum's writings are not currently available, but a short history of Katok states that he ordained thousands of monks of Central Tibet, Amdo, Minyak, Jang, and Gyelmorong, teaching them monastic regulations, the "middle way" philosophical positions, and Buddhist analysis, all in terms of sutra exegesis.[31] Regarding his knowledge of tantra, Jampabum was learned in the more recently translated tantras of the Sarma traditions, such as Cakrasaṃvara, Hevajra, and Kālacakra. For the older tantras preserved by the Nyingma tradition, he disseminated principally the "three classes of *mdo-sgyu-sems*," a phrase that references the Mahāyoga, Anuyoga, and Atiyoga classifications. For Mahāyoga, he taught the *Guhyagarbha* in particular, and also *Eight Classes of Magical Net*. In terms of Anuyoga, he taught the *Sutra of All Intentions* and so forth of the five primary sutras. As for the "Great Perfection" (Dzogchen), in terms of three classes of Mind, Space, and Instruction, he knew the five earlier translations of Mind Class tantra; the thirteen tantras of the later translations (Sarma), the Space Class of Dorjé Zampa's tradition; and the Instruction Class seventeen tantras. Jampabum is described as having merged into one stream the flow of teachings of Padmasambhava, Vimalamitra, and Vairocana—dharma heroes of the eighth-century Tibetan Empire—and he preserved the So, Zur, and Nub traditions, to disseminate and develop as the Katok tradition.[32]

Within this context, Chökyi Lama presumably was exposed to a rich mixture of Nyingma scholarship while at Katok. Although Karma Pakshi's memoirs do not elaborate on the years of study, the tantra expertise he witnessed at Katok may have been a major influence on the young man's Buddhist studies. It is notable that when, in middle age, he wrote a lengthy tome referencing more than seven hundred tantra texts, his *Limitless Ocean of Excellent Explanations of the Limitless Ocean of Buddhist Doctrine*,[33] half the tantras mentioned therein could be designated Nyingma tantras, the other half Sarma tantras. This seems to indicate Karma Pakshi's interests in both Nyingma and Sarma traditions. However, it is worth remarking, even at risk of simplistic analysis, that in Karma Pakshi's autobiographical writings the names such as Padmasambhava or Vimalamitra of the Nyingma tradition are referenced only a couple of times, whereas Saraha, crucial to the Sarma tradition, features at least a dozen times. Such name referencing might loosely indicate a stronger interest in the Sarma side of his praxis. Certainly, in a manuscript text of more than forty songs attributed to Karma Pakshi, several of which are interspersed throughout this biography, there are at least a dozen references to Saraha and mahāmudrā.

However, the *yidam* personal deity practice (Jinasāgara, known in Tibetan as Gyelwa Gyatso, or in the West as Red Avalokiteśvara or

Red Chenrezik) and the protector practice (Mahākāla, or Bernak-chen) that Karma Pakshi became known for were originally both from Nyingma lineage sources. It is noteworthy that in his memoirs, after quoting a statement attributed to Düsum Khyenpa about the Great Brahmin Saraha (as given on page 15), Karma Pakshi remarks that "although Dzogchen and Mahāmudrā are a pair of different names, they are in essence one."[34] It was such remarks that probably led in the seventeenth century to Karma Chakmé's assertion, when writing about the "union of Dzogchen and Mahāmudrā," that Karma Pakshi's writings are about the union of Mahāmudrā and Atiyoga.[35]

Likewise, the accounts of Karma Pakshi's intensely personal visionary experiences, in keeping with his immersion in both traditions, feature both Nyingma and Sarma deities. The next chapter addresses the rich period of approximately twenty years following his study at Katok, when he developed his yogin practices of meditation in remote areas of East Tibet.

CHAPTER 2 ·

Meditation Development

THE PERIOD OF upbringing and education for Chökyi Lama—not named Karma Pakshi until his middle age—seems to have gone on until well into his twenties. After showing much promise as a Buddhist practitioner in his childhood, and then spending his teenage years with Pomdrakpa, he had gone to Katok Monastery to be ordained by Jampabum. At some point he left the monastery with its opportunities for doctrinal studies, and as a mature adult spent time as a yogin practitioner on a remote hilltop about 150 miles south of Katok, in an area near Batang. Accounts of this time in his life are not so much concerned with the dates of activity, yet do occasionally give a sense of the locations where his meditational experiences occurred. The information given in the literature, from his own memoirs to the eighteenth-century *A Rosary of Crystal Jewels* by Situ Panchen,[36] is usually not much more than stating that Karma Pakshi witnessed a vision or had a visionary dream or a meditative experience. Premonitions, omens, and miracles are also mentioned.

Karma Pakshi's own accounts of his meditative experiences are not always presented in sequential time, whereas the main accounts by other authors usually are. Three such accounts written fairly close to his lifetime are the biography written by his successor, Karmapa Rangjung Dorjé (1284–1339), followed by the *Red Annals* in 1363, and then a more extensive biography written before 1405 by Kachö Wangpo, the Second Shamarpa.[37] Naturally, these three accounts probably stem from Karma Pakshi's own telling of his inner experiences, oral and literary. The most extensive and informative secondary accounts for the meditative experiences are found in the biographies by Kachö Wangpo and Situ Panchen (eighteenth century), so they are primarily relied on here for the next period in Karma Pakshi's life, up until he left for Central Tibet in about 1249. It is the period when Karma Pakshi received his training, put it into practice, became a noted yogin, attracted students, and developed a burgeoning reputation. His reputation eventually brought him to the attention of Kubilai Khan, the warrior prince marauding along the western flank of Song China as he conquered the kingdom of Dali farther south.

During this period of his life, Karma Pakshi mostly stayed in Kham in East Tibet, except for some time on pilgrimage farther south into the northern area of the Dali kingdom. Following the approximately fifteen years of his education with Pomdrakpa and then in Katok Monastery, he went south to Kampo Nenang (a monastery retreat founded in 1164 by Düsum Khyenpa) and then spent a total of eleven years nearby at the remote Shar Pungri hill. Then he went on pilgrimage about two hundred miles even farther south in order to circumambulate the sacred mountain of Kawa Karpo (Meili Xueshan, 22,112 feet), towering between the parallel upper reaches of the Mekong and Salween rivers.[38]

After the pilgrimage, he traveled about four hundred miles northwest to Karma Monastery (a monastery retreat founded 1185 by Düsum Khyenpa, located close to the upper Mekong River) for a few years before he made his first journey even farther west, into Central Tibet, to travel to the monastery at Tsurpu.

Visions

After a lengthy and concerted effort in his practice of the instruction on "introduction to the four kāyas," which, as described in chapter 1, was introduced to Karma Pakshi in his youth, at some point Karma Pakshi had a realization relating to the true nature of phenomena, which he expressed using the simile that "everything appears like an image in a mirror."[39] His memoir further states that he witnessed infinite peaceful and wrathful deities speaking Buddhist teaching, with multitudes of colors appearing spontaneously. All this was likened to when hail hits a pool of water and bubbles appear immediately yet then disappear, so for him the sensory experiences—due to the subtle energy and mind (*lungsem*) practices he was engaged in—were not objectified.

His account continues by saying that while he was in solitary retreat in the Namrak hermitage of Selko Monastery, engaging in his subtle energies practice (somewhat akin to *prāṇāyāma*), he had the experience of non-meditation within a mahāmudrā context.[40] Subsequently, his master taught him further yogin practices in the Nāropa tradition. Karma Pakshi admits that although he had not yet fully realized all the instructions, his self-aware gnosis meant that he had not even a hair's tip of non-understanding or non-awareness. Being in solitary retreat, he had no students to communicate with, so it was like, as he puts it, a situation where several musical instruments without any players make no sound—a silent orchestra, so to speak. He realized "mastery of total knowing and total spiritual awareness," which, he states, is how he came to be known as Omniscient Self-Arising Vajra (Künkhyen Rangjung Dorjé). It is noteworthy that many Karmapas thereafter have the term *dorjé* in their formal name. Karma Pakshi uses the name Rangjung Dorjé for himself more than fifty times in his memoirs, with a variety of epithets preceding the name. He only once refers to himself as Karmāpa Rangjung Dorjé, toward the end of his "second testament."

For this period of Karma Pakshi's life, other accounts have embellished the tale with further detail and comments. For example, when Karma Pakshi was practicing the breathing exercises and meditation connected with the "warmth" (*tummo*) practice, he was able to spend time outdoors in the dead of winter, naked except for a single cotton cloth. In interludes between these meditation sessions, he would often see "Jetsunma," a reference to Vajrayoginī, an important female meditation deity for the Kagyü tradition used in the visualizations for the practices concerned with the inner subtle energies and one's mind. Also, several later accounts state that Karma Pakshi had visions of Buddhist heavenly pure lands with accompanying female spirits or *ḍākinīs*. At one time, for an entire day, he experienced a vision of a mandala of the fierce dharma-protectors creating thunderous sounds of HŪṂ and issuing a prediction to Karma Pakshi that he would achieve extraordinary far-reaching spiritual activity.

Intensive meditation practice periods can lead to unusual dreams of Buddhist deities or buddhas. Karma Pakshi does record several times throughout his memoirs that dreams occurred, but he does not mention any for this period. However, some of the later accounts give information on visionary dreams for the same period, so perhaps these vignettes come from an oral tradition. Karma Pakshi apparently had a vision at the retreat at Selko of the compassion deity Avalokiteśvara, with eleven faces and with the Buddha Amitābha as the head crest. With the sound of the deity's mantra, OṂ MAṆI PADME HŪṂ, multicolored lights radiated out to all sentient beings, to purify them all, and the lights then merged into Karma Pakshi, whereupon four ḍākinī spirits appeared and said, "The time has come to give this teaching to all." However, he did not teach on the subject of singing the *maṇi* mantras until he had gone farther east to Pungri.

In a later dream, the sky was suffused with red light, and Jetsunma (Vajrayoginī) appeared, as red as coral, clothed in white bone ornaments, with an entourage of four ḍākinīs, standing on a base on top of corpses, and holding a curved knife, a skull bowl, and a tantric lance. Jetsunma spoke to Karma Pakshi, saying, "The Jetsunma yogini is the source of all the tantras."[41] Apparently, he thought that this referred to a statement by Milarepa that due to Jetsunma the seven hundred doors of the four classes of tantras are opened.[42]

Another dream is replete with symbolism: in a broad, red valley in which flowed a torrential river, a woman stood on the bank. He asked her from where the river flowed. She responded, "It has come from the head of this valley, and this flow of alcohol that you see is yours. It has flowed for a long time."[43] He then went to the head of the valley and saw that the flow came from a giant *kapāla* skull bowl. Above in the sky, he witnessed a red-bodied Jetsunma, ornamented and surrounded by sixteen red goddesses facing her and with a resounding cacophony of *ḍamaru* drums. She stated that Karma Pakshi had enhanced the instructions of the lineage, and she prophesied that the realization of the lineage would come to him.

The Death of Pomdrakpa

Having spent about five months in retreat at the Gotsangdrak hermitage near Selko, Karma Pakshi interrupted the retreat idyll because of the impending advance of Mongol forces. It is to be recalled that in the 1230s, after Chinggis Khan had died in 1227, southern China was still under Song dynasty rule, as it was not fully conquered by Mongol forces until 1279. However, as early as 1227 Mongols had proceeded to advance into the northern Sichuan area. It may be one such destructive Mongol advance southward that Karma Pakshi refers to in his memoirs.[44] As a consequence, both the master Pomdrakpa and his student moved farther south to Markham. Pomdrakpa's master, Drogön Rechen, had years earlier prophetically advised Pomdrakpa not to move to Markham. According to Karma Pakshi, in that area people were mistaken in their views, perhaps meaning that faith in Buddhism was not prevalent.

Pomdrakpa fell ill, and a conversation he had with his student was reported in later histories.[45] Therein, speaking of impending death, Pomdrakpa tells his student that he should continue the doctrine of Düsum Khyenpa, as far afield as Tsurpu. A verse of song by Pomdrakpa is quoted:

If you wish to be set free and liberated
From samsara's ocean of suffering,
The blessing of the supreme lineage
Is to be sought by associating inseparably with the master.[46]

The student asks, "Where are you going?" to which Pomdrakpa replies that he would be reincarnated in Tuṣita heaven to be with Maitreya, a future Buddha. Karma Pakshi was encouraged to direct prayers and worship to both Maitreya and Pomdrakpa together. Karma Pakshi's memoir states that Pomdrakpa, in his final testimony, tells his student, "Because it will be necessary to practice henceforth, for whoever knows what to practice or not practice, perfecting the intention of the Oral Lineage (Kagyü) is the way of connecting between lama and student."[47]

Karma Pakshi's memoir remarks that at the time of Pomdrakpa's death several signs of spiritual accomplishment manifested at various levels—at ground level, in the air, and in the sky above—and as a consequence the local people, whom he had earlier described as holding non-Buddhist views, were now pleased and amazed. Karma Pakshi declares in his memoir that his master magically emanated luminosity identical to Saraha's.

After the death, Karma Pakshi moved about a hundred miles farther south to Tsorong Monastery in the area of Menkung, which lies due west of Kawa Karpo. He admits that at Tsorong he was somewhat despondent about the loss of his master. Several of the visionary experiences he wrote of at this time are concerned with fierce protection deities. At one time, at Tsorong, the protector deities Dorjé Paltsek and Damchen Tseura, at the head of a group of local deities from the Bubor area (Litang), came to invite him to their area farther northeast.

Also while at Tsorong Monastery, Lekden Gonpo Bernakchen manifested to Karma Pakshi in a vision. The protector deity carried a sandalwood staff, stamped his feet, and made three drawings on the ground with the staff. The memoir states that Karma Pakshi took this to be an omen to not stay and instead to proceed eastward, giving his interpretation of the three drawings on the ground:

> Merit as stable as a mountain;
> The lineage illuminating like the sun and moon;
> Renown spread like the sky.[48]

Speculatively, this interpretation by Karma Pakshi might indicate that the drawings were of a mountain, the sun and moon, and perhaps an encompassing circle for the sky, but why this visionary experience was interpreted as a recommendation to proceed eastward is not clear.

The move away from Tsorong may have been triggered by his despondency at the death of his master, and perhaps also the local people with "wrong views," as he puts it, made his stay uncomfortable. In any case, the fearsome deity stamping his feet on the ground is credited with having caused an earthquake in the area. Later, Karma Pakshi stuck a written statement on the door of Tsorong Monastery, saying, "You all do not need me—I will not return; who knows whether a master of all throughout the world will come?"[49] It would seem that he had had enough and was primed to leave. The episode of the pillar is echoed in a later incident, as will be seen when, much farther north, Karma Pakshi posts a different statement on the pillar of a monastery.

Retreat Years

Karma Pakshi left Tsorong and proceeded northeastward with a small party of students but no other companions, crossing the Mekong and Yangtze rivers (at some points in this region the two great rivers are only about thirty miles apart). He kept to his ascetic practices and commitments while traveling. On occasion people who were sick or had a disability would pass by, and he found that just by touching them with his whip (presumably he was traveling by horse) he would cure them and give them courage as they went on their way. Word must have spread, because eventually many would gather "like rain"—he writes that he transmitted his blessing to all who wanted it, and he became famed as a *siddha*, an adept in spiritual practices who had developed special powers.

Situ Panchen's *A Rosary of Crystal Jewels* states that Karma Pakshi came to Kampo Nenang Monastery, which Düsum Khyenpa had founded in 1164, southwest of Litang. Here Karma Pakshi saw in a vision Düsum Khyenpa within a rainbow-like palace among Cakrasaṃvara deities. He also dreamed that a local Buddhist cleric erected a bejeweled throne and asked Karma Pakshi to be seated on it. Karma Pakshi took this to be a sign of unifying the Nyingma and Sarma traditions. Then at dawn, while he was meditating, he had visions, lasting a week, of the body and pure realms of the buddhas of the ten directions.[50]

He went a bit farther north toward Shar Pungri, a rounded mountain northeast of Batang in an area inhabited by the Go, one of the ancient clans of Tibet. Karma Pakshi describes Pungri as a place where gods, spirits, and ḍākinīs gather like clouds in the sky and where previously the yogin Lama Nyaksé (1140–1201) had meditated. Karma Pakshi may well have felt a close affinity to Lama Nyaksé. A text ascribing authorship to a disciple (named Yeshé Gyeltsen) of the Third Karmapa Rangjung Dorjé purports to record information provided orally by Karma Pakshi. A large part of this work focuses on giving a sequence, with some biographical details, of seventeen preincarnations of Karma Pakshi, one of whom is Lama Nyaksé (a shortened form of Nyakdré Sébor). In a short passage about the Lama Nyaksé preincarnation, the text has a succinct vignette:

The one renowned as Nyakdré Sébor,
Born in Markham Gang, an excellent place for nomads and
   farmers,
Through the might of his seeing the immovable protector
   Krodharāja
There is the ability to move and destroy even the supreme
   mountain.
He shaved his hair and beard,
Changed his clothing's color and wore saffron.
After getting rid of his household goods
He kept discipline as an ascetic
And lived in the glory of the vows.
He traveled to towns and the countryside
Relying on alms activity for his food
Performing rites for mental stability in all the pure places and
   staying there—that was a life born as the masterful yogin
   Nyakdré Sébor.[51]

Nyaksé was born in Kham and went to Central Tibet as a youth and studied with Pakmodrukpa Dorjé Gyelpo (1110–1170). He became a wandering ascetic and then returned to Kham, eventually founding a monastery south of Chamdo, called Legön Chökyi Podrang, and attracted students. By remarking on the connection at remote Pungri to Lama Nyaksé, Karma Pakshi may have wished to emphasize the ascetic, yogin aspect of his own activity at this time, as he entered into a lengthy period of retreat at Pungri: as much as eleven years in total.

At Pungri, Karma Pakshi experienced several visions. He does not mention his age when the Pungri retreat started, but it is likely that he was in his late twenties. His earliest vision at Pungri seems to have been of hordes of gods and worldly spirits who "made the earth vibrate and even shook the sky" and were subjugated by a demonstration of a shower of flashing lightning bolts.[52] Karma Pakshi in his memoir says he then thought that if peaceful and wrathful deities—taken to be signs of manifesting deep meditation (*samādhi*)—had not spontaneously appeared, that would have meant there was no need for a teacher in several regions. This may hint that he was thinking of being useful as a teacher for regions farther afield, as indeed eventually happened.

For the lengthy sojourn in Pungri, after trading several pieces of coral for barley and provisions, Karma Pakshi began his retreat, making this statement:

> To have stabilized the vows
> Is the life force of mahāmudrā;
> To have accomplished the gathering of the two accumulations
> Is knowledge that "knowing one liberates all."

He resolved, as he puts it, to engage in continual practice of the above four points, the eternal cycle of the true nature of existence, in accord with the saying,

> Keeping in mind all sentient beings
> Attracts the minds of all sentient beings.

In a song ascribed to Karma Pakshi, he also mentions the "knowing one liberates all" attainment. The song's colophon describes the song as "A Song of Preserving the Life Story of Rinpoche Karmāpa,"[53] where the attainment features in the section about Marpa:

We are the children of the glorious Vajradhāra:
He showed us the Vajrayāna esoteric practice.
Preserving the life and liberation account of Tilopa
Causes spiritual powers of an ocean of ḍākinīs to descend
    upon us.

We are the children of Lord Nāropa:
He causes the spiritual powers of the *virās* to descend
    upon us.
Preserving the life and liberation account of Marpa the
    Translator
Increases our knowledge of "knowing one liberates all."

We are the children of Lord Milarepa:
He raised the victory banner of the Oral Lineage doctrine.
Preserving the life and liberation account of Dakpo Lhajé
Demonstrates the mahāmudrā of apparent existence.

We are the children of Düsum Khyenpa:
He was like a great coursing of the river of the Practice
    Lineage.
Preserving the life and liberation account of Drogön Repa
Benefits beings through the fourfold activities.

We are the children of the precious lama:
He has maintained the Kagyü seat.
The worldly and divine spirits
Bestow incomparable blessing.

As the retreat went on at Pungri, when Karma Pakshi taught about the meditations connected with breathing, the Go people of the region and their children were naturally attracted, and his teaching about gathering the "two accumulations" (virtuous merit and wisdom) helped in terms of karma to accumulate wealth offerings and food—Pungri was becoming a viable retreat location. Monk practitioners were also attracted, eventually as many as five hundred, who spread out over the mountain as Karma Pakshi developed his practice of, as he puts it, recognizing the "four kāya bodies," a term for relating to buddhahood by way of four aspects, involving a meditation practice on mind and the subtle energies.

In later biographies, he is credited with having written during this period a treatise named *Seeing the Pure Realm of Buddhahood*, but the work itself has not been definitively identified.[54] At some point he sensed that the emissaries of the Ma-Gön "sibling" protectors (Mahākāla and Śrī Devī) had spread out to bind by oath the eightfold group of gods and demons in the region,[55] and Karma Pakshi writes in his memoir that he therefore demonstrated clearly his activity as far away as China and Jang (roughly, the western Yunnan area). He was realizing the extent of his dharma influence far and wide yet still maintaining meditative isolation at Pungri. He attributes the manifold appearances of peaceful and wrathful deities to his having set in motion his teaching on the "introduction to the four kāyas."

Compassion Meditation
and Mantra

In addition, Karma Pakshi seems to have engaged especially in Avalokiteśvara practice, as he reports several visions of this deity associated with compassion practice, in particular the Jinasāgara tantric aspect of Avalokiteśvara. Indeed, in later tangka portraits from the eighteenth century onward, his personal meditation deity (*yidam*) is painted in the sky behind him as red Jinasāgara (Gyelwa Gyatso) in tantric embrace. His visions are not always of the red version of the deity: at times he witnesses a white or blue or yellow Avalokiteśvara. As a further indication of the link with the deity of compassion, in the *Red Annals* (completed 1363), the author Tselpa Künga Dorjé wrote that a wisdom ḍākinī taught Karma Pakshi a special tune for singing the famous six-syllable maṇi mantra (OM MAṆI PADME HŪM) associated with Avalokiteśvara. Tradition has it that Karma Pakshi promulgated the tune, which came to be used widely in communal singing of the mantra. In a slightly more elaborate account written by the Second Shamarpa a generation after the *Red Annals*, an esoteric-wisdom ḍākinī appeared in a dream, surrounded by an ocean of dancing ḍākinīs, and said to Karma Pakshi, "You do not know how to recite the maṇi mantra." He asked, "How should one recite it?" whereupon four ḍākinīs sang the tune in unison. The wisdom ḍākinī then said, "If subsequently one uses this tune for the mantra, then all who hear it will be greatly blessed, and it will be of great benefit to beings." In a song attributed to Karma Pakshi, named in the colophon as "Melody of Karmāpa's Intention," he extols among several "necessities" the maṇi mantra and its benefits:[56]

In a mandala of four immeasurables,
I, a yogin with paired aspiration and application,
The stallion of *bodhicitta*
I ride throughout the world—that is a necessity.

In the mandala of fourfold *e waṃ*,
The yogin of the completed fourfold empowerments,
With a victory banner empowering maturing and liberating,
I lead the fortunate—that is a necessity.

All buddhas in all times
As miraculously compassionate Avalokiteśvara
With the six-lettered superb speech mantras
Act for the benefit of beings—that is a necessity.

Nondual samsara and nirvana,
The identity of immaculate dharmakāya,
Ultimate mahāmudrā,
I will accomplish buddhahood—that is a necessity.

For those adorned with multiple fears,
I pacify all the poisons—
What is called the four types of activity
Will protect the teaching—that is a necessity.

This short melody of five necessities—
The universal yogin,
With oral advice for the fortunate,
Sang it below the eastern mountain.[57]

The singing of the maṇi mantra in communal settings is a tradition whose origins have been credited to Karma Pakshi's vision,
but the simplified tune that is currently promulgated widely is
apparently not the same as the tune received by Karma Pakshi. In
the twenty-first century the late Lama Norlha—known as a skillful
chanter at Pelpung Monastery—at this author's request did sing the
tune in the tradition of Karma Pakshi. From the recording (made
in 2006), the contemporary composer Dirk de Klerk notated the
tune as shown on page 37.[58]

Karma Pakshi states in his autobiography that he stayed on the
Pungri mountain for eight years, whereupon on several occasions

om____ ma ni pe_____ me_____ hung

om_____ ma__ ni pe____ me hung____ hri

© Dirk de Klerk

either Avalokiteśvara or a buddha or Buddhist protector deities exhorted him to travel in order to benefit sentient beings. However, he decided not to do so just yet, and stayed for another two and a half years, engaging in meditation practice and teaching, in particular, on his lungsem meditations on mind and subtle energies. It would seem that it was here at Pungri he developed the teaching on lungsem he extolled to others, in connection with his teaching on "introduction to the four kāyas." He later taught this extensively in China and Mongolia, to everyone from ordinary folk to emperors at court.

After Retreat

After about eleven years at Pungri, in his early forties, Karma Pakshi went south to the Kampo Nenang and Kolti monasteries near Mount Genyen (6,204 meters at its summit). Both monasteries had been destroyed by "fighting forces"—the forces are not identified, but may well have been Mongolian, as their forces had been intermittently continuing their campaigns against the Song in western China. He directed his visionary and ascetic energies, in combination with breathing and retention of breath, toward uplifting the derelict places, claiming that when he breathed out the places shook. On a practical level, he repaired Kolti Monastery, in particular the golden ornamental roof, and developed the two monasteries, both building them and teaching the local residents. He spent three summers and winters in the area before heading yet farther south on pilgrimage to the sacred Kawa Karpo Mountain, rising majestically above the region between the parallel upper Mekong and Salween rivers.[59] Karma Pakshi spent a summer and winter in the Kawa Karpo area and, according to his successor Karmapa Rangjung Dorjé, had a vision of the sacred mountain as a palace of wisdom deities and worldly spirits. Karma Pakshi apparently wrote a pilgrimage guide for circumambulating the area; however, a guide text by Karma Pakshi has not yet been identified.

After the pilgrimage, traveling north, Karma Pakshi went to Karma Monastery near the upper Mekong, north of Chamdo, which had been founded by his predecessor Düsum Khyenpa in 1185. Having developed as an accomplished meditator, he was now gradually taking on the mantle of Düsum Khyenpa, much as master Pomdrakpa had requested him to do, by visiting the monasteries associated with the predecessor in eastern Tibet. During his sojourn at Karma Monastery, which lasted for a winter and a summer, after a session of lungsem meditation, Karma Pakshi had a premonition of long life, and had a vision in which a "white man" appeared, asking him to erect a statue of Maitreya, which he eventually did for the monastery. This seems to be the first instance of Karma Pakshi either creating or overseeing the creation of a statue. Later, such work became a fairly regular activity for him at the monastery temples he was associated with.

While at Karma Monastery, Karma Pakshi apparently composed a song. Judging from its content, the song may well have been composed during this sojourn rather than his later visit to the monastery after his travels to China and Mongolia. The colophon to the song describes it as "A Song of Lama Karmāpa's Leonine Steadfast Certainty":[60]

In a mandala endowed with the five wisdoms,
Guiding sentient beings, O Lords of Dharma,
I pray to the tantra masters.
Faithfully, I ask for blessing.

South of Karmā Monastery,
An especially noble place of practice,
Yogin of the *dharmadhātu*,
I sing a melody of the basis, path, and fruition.

Ema! Deluded sentient beings,
Living for such a long time in the samsara of the three
    realms—
A continual mix of happiness and suffering—
Such pitiful sentient beings!

Through the cause and effect of previously accumulated
    karma
Now I have obtained a precious human body
And renounced according to the Buddha's teaching—
Having the ornament of morality does totally overwhelm!

With the precious jewel of the practice lineage,
One absorbs the essence, meets the lama master,
Completes the four empowerments instructions of the oral
    lineage—
The unrivaled activity is totally overwhelming!

In the palace of the four cycles
Lives the king of breath and mind together;
His ministers, unifying the two accumulations, surround him—
His mastery of all is totally overwhelming!

The stainless dharmakāya is beyond conceptualization,
The sun of indivisible wisdom rises,
So a variety of benefit for sentient beings occurs—
The spontaneous fruition is totally overwhelming!

In all activity of day and night,
In this life, the next, and the *bardo* between,
My continuous stream of diverse nirmāṇakāya emanations
Has manifested as beings—totally overwhelming!

The unbiased yogin
Sings a short melody of his realization of certitude;
The fortunate ones who are to become trainees—
May their paltry purity fully flourish in one life!

At some point while at Karma Monastery, when performing a *torma* ritual for young monks visiting from the Shangshung area in southwest Tibet, the visitors requested Karma Pakshi to come to Tsurpu Monastery in Central Tibet, which had become dilapidated. It had been more than sixty years since Düsum Khyenpa's death at Tsurpu, and in that time, as far as is known, there had been five abbots managing the monastery, two of them for just a few years and the other three for probably more than a decade each.[61] The Second Shamarpa, writing more than a century later, stated in his biography of Karma Pakshi that the monks of Tsurpu Monastery had resorted to drinking alcohol. Both the buildings and their monastic inhabitants seem to have slid down a path of decline.

In response to the repeated requests by the Shangshung monks that he come to Tsurpu, Karma Pakshi decided to set off west in about 1249, taking the southern route to Lhasa, perhaps because he considered that taking the more northern journey westward was liable to violent interruption by marauding Mongol forces. Still in his middle age, he was about to embark on significant further consolidation of the transfer from his reincarnation predecessor of the responsibilities of leadership and management of monastery communities and properties.

CHAPTER 3

Teaching, Traveling, and Building

AFTER SPENDING much of his adult life devoted to meditation practice in the Kham area of East Tibet, Karma Pakshi began to make use of his spiritual maturity. This would lead to the fruition of his career in the roles he developed as a Buddhist missionary, a spiritual adviser to the emperor of the greatest land empire in world history, and as a healer and a peacemaker across Tibet, China, and Mongolia. After the death of his master Pomdrakpa, during the period of his meditative retreats in East Tibet, he was developing a reputation as a teacher. When the retreat period ended, he was initially involved in repairing and developing the monasteries founded by Düsum Khyenpa, the predecessor retrospectively titled the First Karmapa: Düsum Khyenpa's own works do not contain the Karmapa epithet. In Karma Pakshi's memoirs, he refers to himself as Karmapa many times, with variant spellings, and less frequently as Karma Pakshi. Thus it would appear that Chökyi Lama, to refer to Karma Pakshi's ordained name, was the first in the lineage to be entitled Karmapa—it is not clear whether this was before or after he became known as Karma Pakshi.

Names

When the Karmapa epithet first occurred is not stated in the early records. At the time when Pomdrakpa first identifies the boy Chödzin, the eleven-year-old Karma Pakshi, to be associated with

Düsum Khyenpa, it is not reported in Karma Pakshi's memoirs that Pomdrakpa uses the term Karmapa. Rather, the connection to Düsum Khyenpa comes through Pomdrakpa describing his visions to the boy, when he refers to Chödzin as "someone having karmic propensity" (*las 'phro*). Whenever there is reference to Karmapa in the memoirs, the spelling is usually given as *karmā pa*, and mostly with the qualifier "well-renowned name." In most instances in the subsequent Tibetan histories the title is given as *karma pa*.

It may well be that the title Karmapa derives from the name of the important monastery Karma Monastery north of Chamdo, founded in 1185 by Düsum Khyenpa and repaired and enhanced by Karma Pakshi a century later in the mid-1240s. This monastery became an important Karma Kamtsang center in East Tibet for the Karmapa tradition, although at the time of Düsum Khyenpa and Karma Pakshi, they both spent more time at the Kampo Nenang Monastery south of Litang. Indeed, the Kamtsang title of the Karmapa tradition within the Kagyü sect derives in part from the Kampo toponym. In turn, it may be that the Karmapa title derives from the name of Karma Monastery.

When in 1249 Karma Pakshi was about to set out from Karma Monastery to Central Tibet, encouraged by two young monks from the Shangshung area and by visionary exhortations to go west to Tsurpu, he remarked that the northern route was full of Mongols and non-Buddhists. Just over twenty years earlier, Mongolian rampages had resulted in the destruction of the Tangut Empire (Xi Xia) in 1227. Chinggis Khan had died in August 1227 while on this campaign. The Mongolian warriors' attentions had then turned to Song dynasty China and elsewhere, reaching as far as the eastern flank of Europe—areas now known as Poland, Austria, Hungary, Croatia, Serbia, and Ukraine. Tibet itself was invaded by Mongol-led forces in 1239, bringing death and destruction as far into Central Tibet as Reting Monastery (founded 1057, 140 miles north of

Lhasa). Drigung Monastery (founded 1179, 83 miles northeast of Lhasa) seems to have avoided destruction in 1240 because of an unusual hailstorm.

Curiously, an account from the fifteenth century—the *Dharma History*—has it that on his journey to Central Tibet in 1249 Chökyi Lama traveled on the northern route, and when he arrived at Drigung Monastery he gained the name Karma Pakshi.[62] This may be an error: perhaps the author (Tséwang Gyel) had confused Karma Pakshi's first east–west journey with the trip made almost twenty years later, when he again traveled from East to Central Tibet after completing his tours in China and Mongolia. If indeed Chökyi Lama did acquire the name Karma Pakshi at Drigung, it would make sense if this followed his adventures in Mongolia, given that Pakshi is a loanword from the Mongolian for "teacher" or "master." However, it might have been thought peculiar if he had acquired this partly Mongolian epithet in a Tibetan region that within the last thirty or so years suffered at the hands of Mongolian raids. Nevertheless, one can imagine that as Karma Pakshi arrived in Drigung on his return from extensive travels in China and Mongolia, with tales of initiating imperial masters in Karakorum (Möngke and Ariq-Böke) and pacifying the enmity of Kubilai in China, that his role as a teacher of important Mongols led the Drigung monks to refer to him as Karma Pakshi. Or it may be that the epithet was acquired in Mongolia, perhaps at the court of Emperor Möngke, where Karma Pakshi taught and initiated the emperor and several members of the court. Indeed, the title may either refer to "the teacher from Karma," meaning the monastery location, or, more humorously, as a pun on both the place-name and the Buddhist doctrine on karma, which presumably Chökyi Lama discussed at court during his missionary visits. One could imagine the humor of the Karakorum court or of the Drigung monastics referring to the unusual, magical monk traveled from afar as both "teacher from Karma" and "teacher of karma" in one name. Therefore, it is plausible that the title originated as a nickname used in the Mongol courts or in Drigung Monastery and then became a badge of acknowledgment for his followers. Karma Pakshi's memoirs refer infrequently to Pakshi, or Pagshi, so he may not have been enamored of the term himself. It may or may not be significant that in his memoirs the name Pakshi only occurs in several of the text titles of the sections of the memoirs. Within the texts, the term "Pagshi" occurs just five times in passages linked to Möngke Khan or Kubilai Khan, and once when Karma Pakshi is returning from China, yet he freely uses the epithet Karmāpa to refer to himself in his memoirs, so it seems to be his preferred term for self-reference. Thus it might be that the epithet Pakshi, or Pagshi, was, in his terms, only considered relevant to his activity in Mongolia and China.

Regarding two recently available manuscripts, in one text that purports to report Karma Pakshi's spoken information on his pre-incarnations, the writer uses the term Karmapa, and in the other text, a collection of the songs attributed to Karma Pakshi, the term Karmāpa is used—neither text uses the name Karma Pakshi within the body of the text, although the name Pakshi is used on the title pages of both items.[63]

First Journey to Tsurpu

Karma Pakshi's memoirs remark that on his journey to Tsurpu for the first time (1249), in the countryside before arriving at Lhasa, he saw evidence of the destruction wreaked by the Ling and Beri people from East Tibet, in addition to that of the Hor Mongol attacks of 1239–1240. Karma Pakshi's accounts do not give much further information on his passage to Lhasa beyond stating that he passed through the Kongpo area; the biographies of Karma Pakshi by the

Third Karmapa and Second Shamarpa do mention a visit to Drigung during which Karma Pakshi had a vision of ḍākinīs dancing.
Once he had arrived at Lhasa, he went to make offerings in
front of the sacred Jowo Śākyamuni statue, brought to Lhasa in the
seventh century by Princess Wencheng of China when she came to
marry the mighty Songtsen Gampo, first emperor of Tibet. Karma
Pakshi had a vision in which light emerged from the statue and
dissolved into his chest, an event later attributed by the Third Karmapa as a sign of his predecessor's success in spreading the Buddhist
dharma.[64] En route to the Tsurpu valley about forty miles northwest
of Lhasa, there seems to have been several unusual storms and an
earthquake, interpreted in Karma Pakshi's memoirs as signs of his
subjugation of the local spirits.

Arriving at Tsurpu, multiple visions of Düsum Khyenpa manifested to Karma Pakshi, which he took as an encouraging sign for
the continuation of the lineage. However, at the time of his arrival
more than half a century after the death of Düsum Khyenpa at
Tsurpu, the monastery was apparently in a somewhat ruinous state,
and several monks had taken to drinking. Düsum Khyenpa had
first visited the area briefly in the 1150s during his first period of
residence in Central Tibet, and then returned in his late seventies to
establish a monastic base in Central Tibet, up the Tölung valley.[65]

After the founding and construction development of Tsurpu
Monastery by Düsum Khyenpa, on his death in 1193 the monastery
community was led for a few years by Lhola Yakpa, a masterful
meditation student of Düsum Khyenpa. Next in charge, according
to The Blue Annals completed by Gö Lotsāwa in 1478, was the local
monk Rangjung Sangyé, followed by one of Düsum Khyenpa's
primary disciples, Gyawa Gangpa, from Gya. The latter was succeeded by two further monks from the Gya area, Gyatso Lama
and Rinchen Drak. Several of the abbots managing the monastery

between Düsum Khyenpa's death and Karma Pakshi's arrival were students of the founder, and were followed by local associates of the students, continuing until the dissolute situation Karma Pakshi came to find. Thus, the succession had not been a matter of family blood relations or intuited reincarnation. During the next inter-regnum period, between Karma Pakshi and Karmapa Rangjung Dorjé, the successive head managers of the monastery were relatives within Karma Pakshi's family; hence, this latter period exhibited quite a change in succession policy from the previous Karmapa interregnum. In that first interregnum, from First to Second Kar-mapa, the first five abbots managed affairs for a fifty-six-year period before Karma Pakshi arrived from East Tibet in 1249 to take over. The transition process itself is not mentioned in any detail by the early accounts, neither the transferal of property rights nor any transferred recognition of a titular position of "Karmapa." The later Situ Panchen account (eighteenth century) couches the transition from the interregnum period to Karma Pakshi's period in terms of the female deity Palden Lhamo telling Karma Pakshi—just after he had arrived at Tsurpu—that if he taught for two days it would improve the situation with the dissolute residents. After Karma Pakshi had accomplished this task, apparently Palden Lhamo was pleased and announced that Karma Pakshi was the holder of the Düsum Khyenpa lineage, and that she would assist in its protection as long as the Buddhist teaching remained.[66]

In a song credited to Karma Pakshi, described in its colophon as "The Tsurpu Lama's Song about the Vajra-like Palace," he was effusive about Tsurpu as a site for meditators:[67]

When the siddha lama
And those who have been blessed
Pray with devotion to the ḍākinī,
Bless us so there is no flux of gathering and separation.

The nirmāṇakāya's abode in the Tibetan region,
In the northern Land of Snow,
Its glaciers like crystal stupas,
Is the palace of Avalokiteśvara.

In the forests of the upper central mountains
At the glorious site of Tsurpu,
Because it is unchanged for ever,
Is the palace of the siddhas.

The temple for both oneself and others
Is a palace of Three Jewels:
Buddha with his bodhisattvas,
And all the *vīra*s and ḍākinīs.

In imagination and reality, physically born
And completely perfecting the two accumulations,
The nirmāṇakāya acts to benefit beings
In a palace for fortunate students.

In the sky of one-flavor realization,
The sun of the multitude of miraculous powers shines—
To mature and liberate the world
Is the palace of essential truth.

The yogin free of birth and death
Acts to benefit beings in the ten directions—
Eternal and everlasting,
It is a palace for self-liberation in samsara.

Having no rival among the many,
Like some great central Mount Meru,

Surrounded by a host of buddhas and his bodhisattvas,
This is the palace of the supremely powerful.

With these melodious seven short stanzas,
The yogin practicing his discipline
In Tsurpu of glorious Orgyen
Has sung of his experiences,
Giving the advice of great meditators.

Karma Pakshi wrote little of the six years he spent in Central Tibet
based at Tsurpu before he left for China, except to say that he
"matured and liberated" people spiritually and made famous the
name and teachings of Düsum Khyenpa. His successor the Third
Karmapa wrote of numerous visions Karma Pakshi had in the six-
year period. In many cases the Third Karmapa gives an interpretation for a vision—for example, a vision in a dream at Tsurpu of
"innumerable buddhas" was a sign of Karma Pakshi's mastery of
enlightened activity; a vision of the twelve Tenma goddesses near
what is now known as Mount Everest (Qomolangma) was a premonition for Karma Pakshi of conflict and unpleasantness to come,
which proved to be the case in his relations with Kubilai Khan.

Invitation from Prince Kubilai Khan

When at Tsurpu in about 1254, Karma Pakshi received a "golden
letter"—an emissary bearing a golden Mongolian pass—sent from
Prince Kubilai, grandson of Chinggis Khan. Möngke Khan (1209–
1259), head of the Mongolian Empire since 1251, was Kubilai's elder
brother by six years. At Möngke's command, Kubilai had been
leading since 1253 a section of the military campaign against the
Southern Song dynasty by taking a route south through western
Sichuan to the Dali kingdom, southwest of Chengdu. The Dali

kingdom was subjugated by the Mongol forces in 1254, and Kubilai, according to *Yuan Shi* dynastic records, had returned north by
1256. In this campaign against Dali, Kubilai would have passed
through northern Dali, and in that area is the sacred Kawa Karpo
Mountain that Karma Pakshi had visited in the 1240s. The region
is not so far from the area widely known to present-day tourists to
contain the nominal "Shangri-La."[68] At some time on his campaign
Kubilai seems to have received reports of the extraordinary Chökyi
Lama with his visions and healing powers. Perhaps Karma Pakshi's
local reputation was still strong even after an absence of five or six
years. So, the campaigning warrior prince "invited" the faraway
monk to visit his court. As Karma Pakshi puts it, "Prince Gobla
(Kubilai), due to his previous karma and aspirations, had heard
that the renowned Karmāpa displayed many signs of having special
powers so he sent a golden-pass envoy."[69] The invitation may have
been more a command rather than a request, as Mongol warrior
princes and their emissary "requests" were not to be trifled with.

However, Karma Pakshi in his memoirs expresses doubts about
whether to go: "At the time of the invitation, I was in some doubt
as to whether to go or not go."[70] Perhaps his thinking was that
such a journey would mean interrupting his work of preaching,
building, and repairing, and in addition the risks of dealing with
the fiercely military Mongols must have seemed great. As far as
is known, Karma Pakshi had hitherto not been involved in any
political activity with ruling forces—indeed, he and his teacher Pomdrakpa had two decades earlier moved south to Markham to get
away from Mongol dangers. As for this tricky invitation, just as with
other major decisions made in his lifetime, it was a vision that helped
him make up his mind. A serpentine, *nāga*-like combination of the
deities Vajrapāṇi and Nanda—"miraculously undifferentiated," as
Karma Pakshi puts it—displayed ethereally like a rainbow to say,
"All your teaching and activity will be completed."[71]

In a song attributed to Karma Pakshi, he reflects on his activity. The song's colophon refers to it as a song about "impartial benefit for sentient beings" and "the teaching persisting for a long time":[72]

O Lord of the Dharma, protector perfect Buddha,
I maintain the three vajra vows.
I pray to the tantra teachers—
Bless us, supreme Buddha and bodhisattvas.

Living blessed by tantra teachers,
The yogin who has completely perfected the two
     accumulations,
Not tired of rebirth, acting for the benefit of beings—
Amazing! Is he not a great person?

With totally pure prayers,
Influenced by worthy trainees,
In the Buddha pure land of Pungri
Beings who see, hear, or remember me
Are established within one lifetime on their enlightenment
     path—
I have established a seat of the Kagyü lamas.

The great meditator is like a roaring herd of lions,
He is like a king controlling a mandala of pleasures,
The karmically fortunate one acts to liberate absolutely all
     beings
From the pain of the three poisons
And has established them on the path of spontaneous bliss.

An inconceivable variety of activity—
Nowadays I think, "Is my activity finished?"

Until I reach the outermost limits,
I perpetually guide beings.

The practice lineage, like the huge coursing of a river,
Arises from a great meditator as the fundamental source—
Because of living for a long time with the doctrine,
I am not hindered by the envious.

For this yogin, an excellent tantric practitioner,
At the regal residence at Setrom
An experience occurred, so I sang this—
May it inform the jealous.

Encouraged by the omen of Vajrapāṇi and Nanda, Karma Pakshi
sent the envoy off and made his preparations to leave. This must
have been somewhat disconcerting for the people then living at
Tsurpu and its environs, the monastery only recently having been
revived due to the presence of its charismatic master. However,
Karma Pakshi writes that he had a meditative experience of Palden
Lhamo—a female deity who also was often an inspiration to Düsum
Khyenpa—with her huge entourage. Palden Lhamo said to him,
"You still have time to achieve your many works, so leave behind
your assets for your residency and send out your wise experience."
So Karma Pakshi followed the advice, distributed his wealth locally,
and set off for Kham and Hor.

This was quite some decision. Tibetan ecclesiastical engagement
with the Mongols had occurred earlier, for example at the point of
the sword or flaming torch in the 1240 and 1252 invasions that pen-
etrated the northern areas of Central Tibet, or *vide* the protracted
journey northeast made by the renowned intellectual Sakya Paṇḍita
along with two child nephews, who eventually arrived at Liang-
zhou in 1246 to conform to the summons by Göden Khan. Sakya

Paṇḍita met with Göden Khan in 1247 and remained in the Liang-zhou area until his death in 1251. Later Tibetan histories—notably the sixteenth-century *Feast for Scholars*—would have it that by 1252, under the leadership of Möngke Khan, the Mongol rulers deter-mined at a convocation that each of the major khans would be asso-ciated with a particular Tibetan Buddhist sect.[73] Of the four sons of Tolui, Möngke was to be associated with the Drigungpa. Kubilai was at first to be with the Tselpa Kagyü, yet he famously switched to supporting the Sakyapa (Pakpa) due to his wife Chabui's influence. Hülegü was with the Pakmodrukpa; Ariq-Böke, with the Taklungpa Kagyü. Even if these neat sectarian alliances were genuinely a delib-erate policy, they were not always kept to. Not long after Möngke had overseen the arrangement, Kubilai, during his military travels southward through western Sichuan and back to his homeland in the north, issued his invitation to Karma Pakshi.

Kubilai was moving fairly rapidly in this period: he set off from his northeastern China appanage territories in September 1253. With military forces he completed the lengthy journey to Dali, relatively quickly subjugated the kingdom of Dali, and then began to return northward in August 1254. Karma Pakshi's writings mention no date for the meeting with Kubilai, but subsequent Tibetan accounts usually give the year as 1255. As to the location of their meeting, according to the *Red Annals* Kubilai was "in the borderlands," and they met at Sertö in the Rongpo area, which has been posited as being located near Kanding.[74] However, that would have entailed Karma Pakshi passing through his homeland territory in Kham, which he makes no mention of in this context. He does recount that en route the people he met were impressed with his Buddhist teaching, and eventually he met the prince at his nomadic palace (in Mongolian, his *ordos*).[75] It might be more likely, given that Kubilai had left Dali in the late summer of 1254, that the meeting was farther north, in Qinghai province.

Meeting Prince Kubilai

The initial meeting between warrior prince and meditator monk seems to have gone well. Karma Pakshi's memoirs mention that when he arrived at the prince's encampment, there was great respect and veneration shown, so Karma Pakshi taught Prince Kubilai and his family about the Buddhist enlightened attitude (the bodhisattva approach), blessing their minds and thus lessening their sufferings and making them content.[76]

Kubilai Khan's powerful mother (Sorghaqtani Beki, c. 1190–1252) was a Christian of the Church of the East, and Kubilai had favored hitherto Chinese Daoist or Buddhist advisers and administrators, and then later used several Muslim administrators: the princely court must have had a very diverse gathering of religious allegiances and influences. Karma Pakshi does not go into particular detail about how he was received among the court but states that "with a Lord of Secrets (Vajrapāṇi) stare" he vanquished the infidel debaters with their wrong views, which suggests a highly demonstrative performance during a debate or discussion.[77] This does not seem to be have been a formal debate, as became better known in the debates of 1255–1256 (at Karakorum) and 1258 (at Kaipingfu, also known as Shangdu or Xanadu), but more like a competitive discussion between religious advocates at the Kubilai encampment. Karma Pakshi claims that as a consequence of his skill in such discussions, the Buddhist doctrine gained in influence, and indeed the warrior prince and his queen, Chabui, invited him to stay with the court.

However, omens of impending warfare and conflict appeared to Karma Pakshi, and a vision gave him warning. After he had invoked Avalokiteśvara in his Buddhist practice, the deity told him, "Do not stay here for a long time. I foresee much greed and anger will occur. Go to the wider plains farther north, where you will be respected by everyone."

Leaving Prince Kubilai

Karma Pakshi decided—again a significant decision made due to a visionary experience—to not stay with Kubilai's princely court, to the khan's disappointment. This decision to leave led a few years later to vengeful imprisonment, torture, and exile for Karma Pakshi at the orders of Kubilai. Throughout his lifetime, Karma Pakshi was wont to pay close heed to the admonitions and advice seen and heard in his visions. So, instead of remaining at the princely court, where his proselytizing activity seems to have been going well, he went to see a pro-Buddhist, virtuous local ruler, in a fortified town within an area named Gha, referring to the Xi Xia area (also known as Tangut or Minyak). Arriving there, still in 1255, evidently a manifestation of the fierce pair of Mahākāla-Mahākālī protection deities, a resplendent Vaiśravaṇa with a golden, bejeweled elephant, plus many ḍākinīs rendered the local people awestruck. The protector deities requested, "In order to produce an ocean of Buddhist dharma, please stay here awhile and build a great temple." Within four months—in 101 days—Karma Pakshi organized the building of a temple named Trulnang Trulpay Lhakhang (Miraculously Manifest Temple). During the construction process, he was visited in several visions by such Vajrayāna deities as the sixty-two-deities mandala of Cakrasaṃvara, a group of seven buddhas, and Avalokiteśvara and Tārā, all swirling overhead like clouds.

At some point the goddess Kurukullā communicated to Karma Pakshi that he should now leave, so he set forth north again, this time to the town of "Ling-ju," now known as Lingwu. At Ling-ju there seems to have been several problems for Karma Pakshi, with the jealousies of philosophers, and indeed demonic forces (*māra*), "falling like lightning." A host of ḍākinīs appeared, led by a vajra ḍākinī effulgent and transparent as a rainbow, who said while playing a ḍamaru drum,

Have no fear, no worries, yogin.
I am a deity with power over existence;
I subjugate the greatest powers.

This blessing by the ḍākinī, according to Karma Pakshi, led to a
transformation of attitude within the town and its region, so "enemies became kinsmen, obstacles arose as siddhis, and I benefited
people in spiritual maturing, salvation, and empowerment."[78] His
reputation as a peacemaker seems to have been notably enhanced.

At early dawn on the first day of the twelfth month of the Hare
Year (February 6th, 1256), a vision of a shining white Brahmin,
wearing a conch-shaped turban, appeared to Karma Pakshi, stating, "I have come from the North—do not stay here, but go forth
to there." Karma Pakshi took the advice and headed north toward
the fort of Kamju, which he gives as being part of a fortified wall,
presumably part of a section of the so-called Great Wall of China
and therefore close to the Gobi Desert. Here he witnessed a "yellow
woman" carrying a vase, her body glowing with light and moving
everywhere unimpeded, something of a ghostly apparition pene-
trating walls. She offered him a jewel, saying, "I shall act as your
benefactor in this region, so this will be of widespread benefit to
people," and then disappeared like a rainbow.

Two months later, on the first day of the second month of the
Dragon Year (April 5th, 1256), the mountain deity Nyenchen Tan-
glha and the border-protecting Tenma female deities presented
themselves, telling Karma Pakshi that if he rode his horse back to
Tibet, they would be of service to him. So, Karma Pakshi headed
back toward Tibet, to the Tsongkha area (near Xining), where for
twenty-one days multicolored rainbow lights swirled in the sky, and
a scented rain fell constantly. A vision of a white man wearing a silk
robe, his body huge and emanating light, said, "I am a white sky
deity. You must go north." Then a welcoming party of Mongolian

messengers arrived to escort Karma Pakshi, providing a rapidly moving escort. The escort of fast riders might refer to the Mongolian imperial relay horse-riding system used for conveying postal material. Although the system had not yet been fully introduced to Tibet itself, it was extant in many areas controlled by the Mongol khans.

Evidently Karma Pakshi had attracted the attention of Möngke Khan and his court based in Karakorum on the grasslands of Mongolia. To meet with the request to go to the imperial court, and to fulfill the admonition of the "white sky deity," Karma Pakshi, in his early fifties, set out to make the journey across the Gobi Desert.

CHAPTER 4

Meeting Möngke Khan

THE INVITATION to visit Möngke Khan came to Karma Pakshi when the emperor was the current reigning "Khan of Khans," the Khagan, of a huge empire extending from Korea to Eastern Europe, a vast enterprise across Asia. Möngke himself had been leading marauding forces in Eastern Europe fifteen years earlier, taking a major role in Mongol invasions of Crimea and Hungary (1240–1241). For Karma Pakshi, the journey from the Xining area northward entailed crossing the Gobi Desert area to Dalanzadgad, approximately eight hundred miles depending on the route, and then about another 350 miles to the Karakorum area, Möngke's imperial capital.

En route to Karakorum, Karma Pakshi recounts that the imperial envoys saw for themselves the various miraculous signs he displayed, such as causing poisonous insects of the area to fall to the ground. The memoirs summarize these events as being a blessing for the earth and his first manifestation of the signs of "ordinary siddhis" or preternatural powers.

It was when Karma Pakshi got closer to the imperial capital, according to his memoirs, that a revelation occurred to him that there was a significant connection to be made between Möngke Khan and the tale of one of Düsum Khyenpa's previous lives. Düsum Khyenpa had recounted to his own disciples a typically Buddhist tale that in an earlier life, in the western continent Bountiful Cow, he had been born as an elephant in a royal herd belonging to a malicious infidel king. The elephant had contrived to crush the king

59

to death, in order "to rescue from the lower realms this king who was acting like a despot."[79] According to several early accounts of Düsum Khyenpa's remembered previous incarnations, the malevolent king in subsequent lives became a disciple, eventually becoming Düsum Khyenpa's sponsor, Gönpawa. Karma Pakshi's memoirs also outline the tale, with some embellished details that the evil king was riding the large elephant (Düsum Khyenpa's preincarnation) while seated on a throne decorated with cloths, surrounded by other elephants carrying the royal family and soldiers. The lead elephant rolled over, and the other elephants charged, thereby trampling and killing the malevolent king and his entourage.[80]

As Karma Pakshi journeyed to the capital of the empire, he intuited that the king killed by an elephant had been reborn as Möngke Khan and that because of the emperor's habits of previous lives he "maintained the tenets" of Christian and Daoist masters. Certainly, Möngke's court accommodated family members and officials of a variety of religious persuasions, however it does not seem that Möngke was as yet a follower of any particular masters. Möngke is famously known for being open to a variety of religious philosophies, as indicated by the report provided to King Louis IX of France by the Flemish Franciscan monk William of Rubruck. Rubruck wrote that in his final audience with the Khan, in May 1254, the warrior emperor remarked (as interpreted to Rubruck by an East Syriac Christian interpreter), "But just as God has given the hand several fingers, so has he given mankind several paths."[81]

The court and its environs at Karakorum were certainly awash with clerics of East Asian philosophies and religions ("sky worshippers," Tenggeri followers, Confucians, Daoists, Buddhists), in addition to receiving Muslims, Jews, and the Christians of the East Syriac, Orthodox, Armenian, and Catholic traditions, all received as envoys, missionaries, and debaters. The court environs must have been a veritable mélange of professionals concerned with religious truth, morality, and ritual efficacy. Indeed, Möngke's family had several Christian adherents among its number, especially on the female side—his own mother was a Christian. Möngke himself had appointed in 1252 a Kashmiri Buddhist, Namo, in charge of all the clerics. It would seem that in gaining the interest of the emperor in any one religion, one would face quite some competition. Indeed, the reported "fingers of the hand" analogy could be seen as a sociopolitically useful response, designed to obviate interreligious conflict and jealousies. Ongoing arguments and violent actions had taken place, in particular between the Daoists and Buddhists in China, with a Mongolian dimension of the disagreements and jealousies derived some years earlier from the favoring of the Daoist priest Qiu Chuji by Chinggis Khan in 1222.

When Karma Pakshi arrived in the region of Karakorum in 1256, the imperial court was encamped at Shira-Ordo, less than twenty miles southwest of the capital. In terms of the context of the politics of religion at the court, the controversies between the Daoists and Buddhists had erupted in 1255, with an imperial debate set up to help resolve the issues. The Buddhist side had been led by Namo and the Shaolin Monastery leader. Karma Pakshi makes no direct mention of either the debate of 1255 or the disputes about resolving it, which were still ongoing in 1256.

During the annual, seasonal tour of imperial encampments, Möngke was probably at Shira-Ordo in July and August.[82] It was in this area, in high summer a decade earlier, that another missionary monk, Giovanni da Pian del Carpini of the Franciscan Christian order—an order established in Italy in 1209—had arrived, a short time before Güyük Khan (cousin to Möngke) had been elevated to the position of Khan of Khans. For the emperor immediately previous to Güyük, Ögedei (Möngke's uncle), this location was routinely used as the "summer camp" before the autumnal sojourn farther south, near Lake Gashuun Nuur. It is reasonable to assume the traditional itinerary was continued when practicable by Möngke, until 1257 when he set off for his campaign in Song dynasty China, where he died in 1259. Evidently the itinerant courts were very impressive to foreign visitors. A decade earlier, Carpini had been sent as an emissary of the Pope Innocent IV's policy of *remedium contra tartaros*. Carpini's eventual report to Pope Innocent IV, in Latin, has a description of the white *ger* tents at Shira-Ordo ornamented with gold and brocades—one tent reputedly large enough to hold two thousand people—and containing plentiful quantities of silks, furs, and gems. In 1256, when Karma Pakshi rode north across the desert to meet Möngke Khan, the Mongolian Empire was approaching its apogee: "un empire panasiatique, eurasiatique, international, mondial."[83]

Imperial Audience

Arriving at Shira-Ordo, Karma Pakshi's intuition regarding Emperor Möngke's prior incarnation in the king-and-elephant episode seems to have become coupled in Karma Pakshi's mind with an understanding of a prophecy made by Düsum Khyenpa about the latter's future rebirth. The prediction was reportedly made by Düsum Khyenpa in response to a query by students about future rebirths, his response written up with varying degrees of detail in three separate, near-contemporary accounts: by his students Galo and Bhikṣu Kumara Bodhi, and by Dechungwa (who had consulted two other students for their memories of their master). All three accounts quote the master as saying he would first be reborn in northeast India, in Kartika. He went on to add that also he would be reborn in Lhodrak, in South Tibet, the site of the "seven places of achievement," presumably referring to seven significant sites for Buddhist practitioners in the Lhodrak area. Additionally, both Galo and Bhikṣu Kumara Bodhi's accounts state that Düsum Khyenpa had said he would also take rebirth for the sake of one disciple. This must have been somewhat puzzling to anyone committed to the bodhisattva ideal of altruistic work over multiple lifetimes to bring *all* beings to enlightenment. Indeed, the prophecy was apparently somewhat enigmatic to Karma Pakshi until this time.[84] Dechungwa's account varies slightly in saying that Düsum Khyenpa had stated he would next take rebirth in the East, where his current patron, Gönpawa, would be reborn as the king.

So it would seem that Karma Pakshi, as he approached the nerve center of the vast Mongolian Empire, made a connection between the tales of preincarnation as an elephant and also of future rebirth for the sake of one disciple, taking the connection to mean that his life's fulfillment was for the sake of the Mongol emperor—the likely connotation being that conversion of such an emperor would in effect be beneficial, from a Buddhist perspective, for many millions of people. As Karma Pakshi puts it, "by the force of their connection with previous karma," the royal family present, including the emperor's younger brother Ariq-Böke and his queen, and their entourages, paid great homage, out of faith and inspiration, to the visiting meditation master.

The memoirs also recount that as Karma Pakshi had first approached the "palace tent" of the emperor at Shira-Ordo, meteorites and lightning fell like rain, seeming to the visitor to be something of an army of deities and spirits. Whereupon he, with "the roar of Hayagrīva," overwhelmed the hordes and bound them by oath, thus becoming victorious over the māra obstacles. Karma Pakshi manifested bodhicitta and gave the emperor his "Avalokiteśvara stare," while a rainbow and light shone after the storm.

Once Karma Pakshi had gained his first audience with the "earth-protector king," the emperor commanded, "I am the ruler of the world—get rid of my obstacles!"

Karma Pakshi replied, "Tonight, I will think about it a bit"—a somewhat brave reply to make in front of a warrior emperor. In the morning of the next day, Karma Pakshi again had access to Emperor Möngke and gave his recommendations, as recounted in verse:

> Indeed, in this imperfect world,
> Never will there be a king like you,
> Whatever any astrologers have said.
> I myself—Karma Pakshi—
> Seek to counteract your obstacles.
>
> Benefit the Buddha's teaching and all beings,
> Distribute food and wealth throughout the kingdom,
> Repair the residences of the lamas,
> And make sky offerings with no sense of loss.
> Again and again I ask you to set free
> The criminals kept in the prisons.[85]

The advice is that, in order to ameliorate the perceived "obstacles," the emperor should initiate a program of social welfare, religious sponsorship, and judicial amnesty.

In particular, the memoirs also recount that for three days the Great Brahmin Saraha surrounded by eighty-four siddhas and innumerable yogins filled the northern sky, all the characters dancing. With the dissolution of the manifestation, the "royal guardian of the earth" (Möngke Khan) was freed, in Karma Pakshi's terms, of the "subject-object perception of duality," and the lesser nobles and their subjects became relaxed in their minds. The memoirs then state that ever since this episode, any visual depiction of Saraha surrounded by the eighty-four siddhas is of great blessing.

According to Karma Pakshi's memoirs, his demonstration of omens and miraculous visionary manifestations at the royal court was overwhelming, to the point where the royalty present—even the titular heads Möngke and Ariq-Böke—eventually decided to take up the teaching of the Buddha.[86] Consequently, there seems to have been a distribution of goods to all people in the area from the royal treasury—one of the several social-benefit themes of Karma Pakshi's influence on the emperor—upon which a disembodied voice was heard saying of the emperor, "You are greathearted and generous!"

Further, it is claimed that this "king of the world" kept to the Buddhist vows for a month, after which he developed the altruistic attitude of bodhicitta. According to Karma Pakshi, it would seem that Möngke was following Buddhist guidance with quite some commitment. The visiting meditation master then bestowed "the four empowerments" (tantric initiations named the Vase, Secret, Wisdom, and Word empowerments) and gave guidance on "introduction to the four kāyas," Karma Pakshi's signature teaching on meditation.[87]

It may seem incongruous that the imperial warrior—scourge of populations from Kyiv to Karakorum, who just a few years earlier had many in his wider family executed for their plotting and "disloyalty" as he manipulated his way to the position of Great Khan during the process of switching the imperial succession from the Ögedei family branch to the Tolui branch of the heirs of Chinggis Khan—should himself be engaged seriously in such peaceful Buddhist activity. By 1257 Möngke was making preparations for the invasion and conquest of Song China. Further afield, in 1258, under his reign over the empire, the citywide massacre at Baghdad led by his brother Hülegü put an end to the Caliphate, a fateful event so catastrophic in human terms that it resounds right into the twenty-first century for the extremists seeking to restore the Caliphate.

Nevertheless, as can be seen from William of Rubruck's account of his own meetings and discussions with Möngke in 1254, it does appear that the warrior emperor had a thoughtful interest in religious matters. The involvement with Karma Pakshi may have been partly due to the "entertainment" of miraculous manifestations, and partly also to the practicality of gaining the aid of supernatural forces for his imperial projects, as well as any personal interest he may have had in religious matters.[88] Whatever his motivations and attitudes with regard to the disparate activities as both warrior and Buddhist initiate, it certainly seems that Möngke did not suffer religious hypocrisy lightly, as evidenced by his reported conversations with William of Rubruck on the Christian day of Pentecost in 1254 (May 31st): "To you God has given the Scriptures and you Christians do not observe them."[89] Yet the emperor himself does not appear to have seen discrepancy between his warmongering activities and his interest in the advice and requests for social policies by the recently arrived Buddhist monk.

Social Policies

The Karma Pakshi memoirs have it that in addition to opening the treasury to distribute goods to people of the area, the emperor ordered his treasury officials to make sure the holy structures of the Buddhists, other religions, and the "sky worshippers" had funds for upkeep and repair, thus accomplishing religiously virtuous activity. For the duration of his first sojourn with the emperor, Karma Pakshi claims that due to his influence there were thirteen occasions when there was amnesty for prisoners—perhaps many were criminals, but one suspects that also foreign prisoners of war and ransom-guarantor prisoners were among the releases. Möngke had been known to grant amnesty before Karma Pakshi's arrival, notably after the multiple purges of disloyal nobility at the start of his reign. Nevertheless, the frequency of the releases claimed for this period later in the reign is remarkable. The memoirs have it that in "Gurum" (Karakorum) it was Möngke himself who enacted the procedure of release, and that he personally established a "Pakpa" temple (probably meaning it was dedicated to Avalokiteśvara). Möngke commanded temples and stupas to be repaired over the region and commissioned numerous new statues of Buddhist deities. As Karma Pakshi's memoirs put it, the good virtue was "inconceivable and indescribable."

Another aspect of claimed influence on imperial court policies was the adoption of vegetarian sensibilities, at least for a limited period. In his memoirs, Karma Pakshi recounts that after the major, three-day manifestation of Saraha, and the ensuing initiation into the bodhisattva vows and the special "introduction" teaching given to the emperor, it seems that Möngke kept in mind the Buddhist teaching and added to an edict (*jasaq* in Mongolian) a requirement that there should be no killing of animals, which according to Karma Pakshi held for a period of eleven months—the time limitation perhaps referring to the period between Karma Pakshi's first meeting with the emperor and the emperor's preparations for war in China in the following year.[90] The edict also stated, according to Karma Pakshi, that each person should keep their own professed religious and moral tenets. The latter injunction chimes with Möngke's apparent concerns about ecclesiastical hypocrisy, as reported by Rubruck about his final discussions with the emperor.[91] The requirement to abstain from killing animals may have been in accord with doctrinal exhortations by the Daoists and Buddhists present at Karakorum, all likely to have vegetarian inclinations, so the prohibition may not have been entirely due to Karma Pakshi's intervention. However, the claim made does indicate that Karma Pakshi himself probably had a predisposition toward vegetarianism.

A dietary prohibition, or at least a strong disapproval, also common to several religious codes is that against alcohol. In contrast to both Carpini's and Rubruck's accounts making several references to Mongol drinking customs and habits, Karma Pakshi makes none. However, Karma Pakshi's memoirs do remark on his own miraculous imbibing of alcohol. When he was at "the palace of

Alaga"—possibly the Avarga base (near present Delgerhaan) that Chinggis had used, where Möngke went from June to July of 1257 to pay respects to his warrior grandfather before beginning the campaign to conquer South China—Karma Pakshi gave a blessing of tantric empowerment to several princes, who then witnessed a vision of the deity mandala. At the palace, in the presence of several "fortunate princes," Karma Pakshi's memoir claims that he drank the palace dry of its store of alcoholic beverages.[92] He does not seem to have become inebriated, stating that for himself there was no fundamental concept of drunkenness—that it was like "water merging into an ocean."

After finishing the alcohol, the empowerment mandala of Cakrasaṃvara appeared in a vision, and Karma Pakshi led the participants in the "maturing and liberating" initiation. One wonders whether he actually drank dry the stores of a Mongol palace—truly a superhuman feat, given what is known of imperial drinking habits—or perhaps what is meant is that one of the four sections of the famous drinking fountain at Möngke's court was emptied dry. The fountain had been created by the Parisian master craftsman Guillaume Boucher when he was at Karakorum. It is not clear whether the drinking fountain was portable, but it would not seem impossible that, being metallic, it could be dismantled or folded to be taken on any journey with the itinerant imperial court. In any case, the "drinking dry" of some of or all the alcohol in the palace was an unusual, if not miraculous, feat, and probably especially impressed the court members accustomed to drinking heavily.

Karma Pakshi's ability to "mature" and "liberate" his audiences pertained to a wider public than just the immediate court. He claims his edifying discourses and instructions were understood in as many as "360 languages," so the hearers were able to gain liberation into heavenly realms.[93] The mass edification led to the subjects being inspired to, in Buddhist terms, give up the ten unvirtuous actions and aspire to the ten virtuous ones.[94] He remarks that in turn this adoption of moral commitments would help spread the Vajrayāna teaching and practices he extolled. More prosaically, at this time at the Mongol court he also taught widely his tune for singing the six-syllable Avalokiteśvara mantra, derived from his earlier vision at Pungri of the ḍākinīs who taught him the tune. Such communal chanting of a short mantra would communicate easily across any number of languages. Thus, in contrast to the difficulties experienced at Kubilai's court after Karma Pakshi's premonitions of conflict, the tour in Möngke's kingdom was seen as a highly successful mission, and Karma Pakshi's memoir acclaims Möngke as a great dharma king (*dharmarāja*).

Warfare

Despite the Buddhist interests and the generous social policies that may have derived from the amicable association of the two men, the warrior and the meditator, nevertheless the emperor did not abdicate his role as a fearsome conqueror. In early 1257 Möngke began his preparations to conquer southern China to further the campaign southward begun by his grandfather more than a third of a century earlier. So he spent June and July of that year visiting Chinggis's old palace sites in Mongolian territory, honoring the great campaigner who had died thirty years earlier. After returning to Karakorum, in the next year Möngke and his forces moved across the desert to reach the Liupanshan Mountains by May 1258. Eventually, Möngke's army for this campaign may have numbered as many as 600,000.

It is not clear whether Karma Pakshi was traveling with the military hordes once Möngke had set off south. It is likely that Karma Pakshi was with the Möngke court during the homage visit to Chinggis's old camps (near Delgerhaan, 140 miles southeast of

Ulaanbaatar), hence the account of the alcohol-drinking episode at the Alaga palace. But once Möngke had returned to Karakorum for the summer of 1257, it is unlikely the warrior and thaumaturge traveled together on the route march south. Certainly Karma Pakshi does not mention being present at court when in early 1258 at Karakorum the brothers Möngke and Kubilai effected a tearful brotherly reconciliation after a contretemps over Kubilai's tax-raising arrangements in northern China. For Karma Pakshi to have been present at the imperial court when Kubilai visited might have been awkward for both of them, although on the other hand a reconciliation between the two might have been effected, but the memoirs are silent on either possibility.

A Karma Pakshi song speaks of the emperor—its colophon describes the song as "The Spontaneous Activity of Lama Karmāpa".[95]

Knowing all from the unmanifested realm,
O lamas of the siddha lineage,
Look on me with eyes of compassion—
Pray bless me for all time.

The yogin who has completed the two accumulations
Acts to mature and liberate, with a variety of methods,
As a servant to those of the Oral Lineage,
In the green northern Land of Snow.

In the pure land of the precious southern region,
In the palace of the supreme place
The yogin of spontaneous activity
Effortlessly benefits beings.

In the Buddhist pure realm of Pungri,
The *dharmatā* yogin, being a hermit,

Healed the pains of suffering
Of all six types of beings.

At the time of an increasing moon I went to the spacious
    plain—
Naturally liberated from desire and anger, I move on,
At the same time universally benefiting beings.

At the treasury of the *cakravartin* emperor,
Surrounded by princes and ministers,
The unimpoverished yogin
Wonders whether they are naturally liberated
From subject-object duality.

In these degenerate times of conflicting doctrines,
The unconfined yogin
Spontaneously, without seeking to do so, benefits others.
Worthy of praise, unmatched by others,
Fearlessly, he wonders whether the turquoise dragon has roared.

In the pure land of southern samsara,
Their universal compassion benefited beings—
O Buddha and bodhisattvas, without exception,
Pray bless us eternally.

Karma Pakshi's memoir states that after the first period spent with
Möngke, he was at some time (undated) in "the Chagatai capital"—
presumably referring to Almaliq (near present Yining/Ghulja in
western Xinjiang), approximately 1,200 miles from Karakorum.
Due to his activities there, "needs and wants fell like rain," and he
associated his visit with the abundant blessings of Buddha Ratna-
sambhava.[96] Elsewhere in the memoirs he does refer to traveling in

the "Ili River area," which is near Almaliq. At Almaliq in the years 1257–1258, the nominally ruling Khan was Mubarak-Shah, who at the time was a minor. In effect, the Chagatai regions were ruled by his widowed mother, Orqina Khatun, a granddaughter of Chinggis Khan. Karma Pakshi does not give any reason for his traveling so far afield, but it may have been at the recommendation of Möngke Khan, or perhaps of Oghul-Qaimish (one of Möngke's queens who was aunt to Orqina), or indeed of Orqina's sister, Elchiqmish, one of Ariq-Böke's main wives. Mubarak-Shah eventually converted to Islam, and his mother was known to be sympathetic to Islamic ministers. Karma Pakshi recounts that non-Buddhists in the area gathered around and developed faith and respect toward him, but he does not mention engaging in any teaching of the royal family during this sojourn—he may not have been as royally welcome as he had been at the Karakorum court.

Visionary Dreams

During the return from the Chagatai capital, heading southeast, Karma Pakshi had some visionary experiences that were important in the later period of his life. The memoirs have it that when he was in the Ili River area, which runs west into Lake Balkhash, he seems to have become somewhat despondent about the turbulent times and says that the area he was operating in was "under the influence of demonic hindrances," that the world was at war, "like a great forest of conflict between the gods and jealous gods."[97] His memoir says that he felt he must have committed many bad actions in past lives, with the consequence that now he must live in such a time and such a place.

This mood led to him spending time in prayer and meditation, "invoking the Buddha's holy mind" and making generous gifts, such as bolts of cloth, to local people. After a week of such devotions, one night he had a dream of a huge statue of Śākyamuni Buddha, ten arm spans high (about fifty to sixty feet) and "as bright as the sun in the sky." As the light radiated from the statue, Karma Pakshi heard a voice resonating with the command, "Before too long, after you have gone to Tibet, erect a single statue of Buddha like this one, and the trickery of demons will be pacified so that the kingdom will become happy." He thought to himself, "At a time of such domestic and foreign conflict, when I have eventually arrived at Tibet, where is this deity statue to be made?" The response was, "Because you are blessed by the Buddha, his bodhisattvas, and the worldly protectors, pray without any doubt whatsoever, and it will be made." Karma Pakshi certainly took this advice seriously, and some years later he had a statue of similar size made at Tsurpu, despite considerable difficulties.

After the initial dream of the statue by the Ili River on his southeasterly journey from Almaliq, Karma Pakshi is likely to have traveled along part of the northern Silk Route. At one time, in the area of what he designates "the huge Aras mountain range," he had another significant dream in which he was alone on the peak of a black mountain that rose above the clouds. As he was slowly falling, a winged white horse arrived, which he mounted. The miraculous horse appeared to have hooves like human hands, so it was able to reascend the rocks. Horse and rider reached a pleasantly wide and open plain on the mountain, whereupon Karma Pakshi said, while still in the dream,

> Excellent horse, you are like a golden goose;
> I, an excellent man, am like Prince Siddhārtha—
> I will liberate you from great fear.[98]

As he and the horse rested, he heard emanating from light that shone everywhere a voice saying, "Furthermore, when all the hordes of corporeal and incorporeal spirits have appeared before you as māras, it will become terrifying. Matured by that, you will become fully victorious." It would seem to be a premonition of misfortunes and triumphs to come.

A while later, when he had reached the Hor and China border, again the local situation troubled Karma Pakshi: he wrote that it seemed that he had come to a city ruled by the terrifying Yamāntaka (Defeater of Death), where all the people were wailing with great cries of fear, at a time "when rage, tyranny, and danger abounded."[99] He responded by praying to Palden Lhamo with the invocation,

> Unique mother goddess, Palden Lhamo,
> Pray bestow liberation from terror
> And bestow the accomplishment (*siddhi*) of a deathless life span;
> I shall protect the teaching of the teacher
> And lead the six classes of beings on the path—
> Mother, the time has come, *samaya*!

Whereupon he heard in response,

> Have no fear, yogin, have no fear—
> I will liberate you from terror!

Then the Brahmin Saraha appeared, accompanied by deities, and this vision overwhelmed and eliminated all fear locally. Perhaps reminded of the earlier dream and admonition to help spread peace and well-being through building the statue, at this time Karma Pakshi wrote a formal letter, to be sent to Tibet, in which he proclaimed that a huge statue, ten arm spans high, should be built and be named Ornament of the World, and that he would return to ensure the task was completed.[100]

Toward Tibet

The journey farther east meant that he arrived at a place Karma Pakshi refers to as Kecu, where he spent eight months. Kecu could refer to Kucha, or to Turpan, both on Silk Routes. During this period at Kecu, Karma Pakshi had a vision of Mañjuvajra and the mandala of Cakrasaṃvara—he saw a "mist of deities" appearing over the whole of China. Hearing the deities teaching the tenets of the various cycles of the Buddhist teachings, he was inspired to write the *Limitless Ocean of the Doctrine*. The Limitless Ocean epithet (*rgya mtsho mtha' yas*) was used for a series of titles that became the major component of the extant literary works of Karma Pakshi.[101]

The memoirs are not forthcoming on the process of the journey crossing the Taklamakan Desert, perhaps along its eastern side and then along the Gansu Corridor, but it is stated that Karma Pakshi met up again with Möngke Khan in the Xi Xia region. Möngke and his army had arrived at the Liupanshan Mountains area in the summer of 1258. It is likely that Karma Pakshi arrived toward the end of the summer, a summer of drought. Karma Pakshi again blessed Emperor Möngke, with a Heruka empowerment, whereupon a *yoginī* vision miraculously manifested with a group of ḍākinīs to say or sing,

> Said to be blessed by three siddhas
> And performing the dharma siddhis,
> Distinguishing clearly the infidel and Buddhist tenets,
> You have promulgated the Buddha's teaching,
> O wonderful yogin master!

In this mountainous area, the local river had dried up with the summer drought. The emperor spoke to Karma Pakshi: "All the people are experiencing thirst. What is to be done about it?" With a large army present, it must have been a serious situation. Karma Pakshi's memoirs state that he flexed his hand, whereupon the nāga king Lord of Mantras was seen to come rolling in on clouds of steam. Karma Pakshi requested rain of him, whereupon conch-white snow fell over the entire area. The people of the kingdom developed faith, saying, "Śākyamuni is true!" and offered many jewels and much gold for Karma Pakshi to develop his projects in East and Central Tibet.

At some point, Karma Pakshi asked Emperor Möngke for sponsorship and received one thousand *dre* measures of silver, which he then used to build and repair temples in the Xi Xia area—the claim is that he used the silver for three thousand projects.[102] Karma Pakshi's memoir states that the emperor and he, in the borderlands of China and Xi Xia, were patron and priest,[103] an arrangement that later became important between Kubilai and Pakpa.

However, the time had come for the warrior and thaumaturge to part ways. Karma Pakshi had a vision of Düsum Khyenpa riding a blue lion, traveling in the sky surrounded by siddhas. The Düsum Khyenpa of the vision said to Karma Pakshi that the spread of the Buddhist teaching would decline, and therefore he was requesting Karma Pakshi to return to Tibet. Consequently, Karma Pakshi said to the emperor,

I will not stay. I will go to Tibet—
I should accomplish great deeds there.

Möngke's reaction was apparently conciliatory, in that he was pleased and sympathetic, and gave to Karma Pakshi a large seal and possibly a golden robe.[104] Möngke then headed farther south, dispatching a wing of armed forces to successfully attack and retake Chengdu, but then he himself became stalled in besieging Chongqing and died near the city, in the oppressive southern heat of

August 1259. Karma Pakshi's memoirs have a very short obituary remarking that the emperor had exhausted his unfavorable karma—illustrated in the story of Düsum Khyenpa's preincarnation as an elephant that crushed a malevolent ruler—and was now, along with his court, on the "path of purity."[105]

In something of a reflection on the highlights of his own life, Karma Pakshi, in a song attributed to him, refers to a few places and times he found especially useful for practice—included is the period he spent with Möngke. The colophon states that the song is about unrivaled places of practice:[106]

In the palace of the unmanifested realm,
O Master, completely perfected five kāyas,
If I pray continuously,
Bless me for all time.

In the border region of both Ü and Tsang—
A nirmāṇakāya abode, pure land of the Buddha—
Are the holy, special places of practice.
The medicine deity, Jomo Gangkar,[107]
Is surrounded by an uncountable horde of medicine deities.

For the cakravartin king
Surrounded by a group of ministers
In a marvelous, amazing practice place, like a northern Orgyen,
The vīras and ḍākinīs amass like clouds,
The spiritual powers, special and ordinary,
Were gained in an instant—
An especially holy, excellent place was found.

Ema! Wonderful! In this way,
I have known just one dharma practiced here

From the sutra and tantra taught by the Buddha:
Knowledge of "understanding one liberates all" has
  flourished.

The instructions on these important points have been
  collated
Like a heap of precious jewels[108]—
May the very heart of the buddhas
Be made the true mentality of oneself and others.

The sun of infinite realizations has shone—
Pure clarity, as if in an endless sky.
The most esoteric Vajrayāna,
Its essence extracted is the special dharma of Nāropa,
Is like a great rolling river of practice lineage.

Even when there are not any tantric practitioners,
The tantra practitioner lion stands proudly in the snow—
He is given immeasurable spiritual powers.
Indisputable lama master of all time (Düsum Khyenpa),
I, the yogin who has followed you
With mind pure as the sky,
I have unified the two accumulations that are like a galaxy of
  stars.
I am an ordained monk who has attained self-control.
May fortunate students know this!

In the pavilion of the crystal white snow
I have spoken—the indescribable yogin
Sings a melody with no lack of courage—
May the multitudes of vow-keepers be satisfied!

CHAPTER 5

Captured by Kubilai Khan

WITH THE DEATH of Möngke in the late summer of 1259, the position of Khan of Khans for the vast Mongolian Empire was now open. By June 1260, two of Möngke's younger brothers, Kubilai and Ariq-Böke, had separately had themselves "crowned" as successor Khan of Khans. The elevation of Kubilai occurred in May in Kaipingfu (later named Shangdu, site of Coleridge's famed Xanadu) with the backing from afar of his brother Hülegü, then engaged in warfare against the Mamlūks in the Galilee area. The younger Ariq-Böke was elevated in June in the homeland, Karakorum, supported from afar by his cousin Berke Khan, who at the time was busy invading and ravaging southeast Poland. The fraternal rivalry led to a period of internecine hostility among the Mongols (the "Toluid Civil War"), until Ariq-Böke's acquiescence in 1264.

Karma Pakshi does not write on the details of the imperial conflicts, and his information on the personal episodes that he does recount of the period is somewhat sparse. He himself seems to have been busy using the donated wealth for his missionary and reparation projects in the areas of China northeast of Tibet (which he refers to as "borderlands"), either commissioning statues, stupas, and buildings, or even getting manually involved in the projects himself. He saw these religious projects as accomplishing enormous benefit for sentient beings at a time when moral virtue was diminishing.

However, Karma Pakshi does record that Kubilai issued a "fierce edict" against him, which may well have been a death warrant.[109]

The issue at hand, as posited by later Tibetan historians, may have been that Karma Pakshi was seen as something of an accomplice to Ariq-Böke, now Kubilai's rival, and so was seen as an influential enemy by association. Yet Karma Pakshi may not have seen Ariq for quite some time, since he had left Karakorum. Another factor in Kubilai's antagonism toward Karma Pakshi may have been the perceived slight against Kubilai in 1256 when, after the initial harmony, Karma Pakshi elected to leave Kubilai's entourage—the dish of revenge was now sufficiently cold on Kubilai's plate to be consumed. The Tibetan historical work the *Red Annals*, written almost a century after the event by a retired Tibetan official who had served in the Yuan court of the fourteenth century, alludes to this perceived slight as being the reason for the deadly order.

Karma Pakshi's memoirs are not explicit in prose about the warrant and his eventual capture but treats the events in allusive verse. Perhaps intimating his own thoughts about why the warrant was issued, in the section of his memoirs entitled *Effulgent Light Annihilating Poison*, he seems to ascribe the reason for his arrest as being that

According to the legal tradition of the infidels,
The bearded one was said to be an evil spirit.[110]

Evidently, he felt that it was the fault of court advisors who saw him as an evil spirit that had influenced Kubilai's decision. This verse marks an unusual instance where Karma Pakshi refers to his own appearance—"the bearded one." Early portraits from the thirteenth century have him portrayed with a goatee, and thereafter portraits in paint and sculpture also show him with the goatee. Early histories do not have further elaboration on the beard, but some accounts from the twentieth century have it that Karma Pakshi was hung up by his beard during his imprisonment and torture by Kubilai's forces. The tale has it that Karma Pakshi then cut his beard

off and issued a curse that just as his beard had been cut, so the
Mongol's royal family line would be cut short. This episode of the
cut beard and the curse does not appear in earlier records: the story
may have been invented or may have emerged from an oral retelling
passed on over the centuries, to be written down much later. The
curse, if made, was hardly successful: Kubilai lived another thirty
years, and his family lineage ruled China for a hundred years. Yet
such a curse may well have been very unnerving to the royal court
if its meaning and import had been translated, taking into account
that perhaps some of the Yuan court's undoubted fascination with
Tibetan Buddhist teachers and their rituals and rites may have been
due to familial fears and concerns about childbirth and fertility.[111]
The tale would certainly make for a suitably dramatic interpretation
in opera or film. In modern times, the episode of the beard and
the curse is sometimes used as an amusing tale explaining why no
subsequent Karmapas have had a beard.

Yet another interpretation of the reason Kubilai turned so vehe-
mently against a former religious advisor is given in the sixteenth-
century history *Feast for Scholars* by Pawo Tsuklak Trengwa. The
account therein runs that previously when Karma Pakshi had been
in favor at the prince's court, from 1255–1256, and had given an initiation, some of the nobles had not "received the vase" in the process
of a Vajrayāna tantric empowerment. This had caused anger, so the
nobles had told the prince to evict Karma Pakshi, which Kubilai
did with an uttered "Pe!" When Karma Pakshi had gone outside
the empowerment room, he had had something of a heart attack,
which may have been a contributing factor in his decision to leave
the Kubilai court—the omens were not good. Several years later,
the nobles' resentment of Karma Pakshi apparently had not been
forgotten. Festered resentment among the courtiers may have con-
tributed to the reasons why, after Möngke's death, Karma Pakshi
was arrested—or at least why an attempt at arrest was made.

Capture and Torture

The capture of Karma Pakshi has several interpretations in the historical accounts, giving the dramatic failures of hundreds of soldiers to capture or kill the miraculous adept, who seems to have been unaffected. The *Red Annals*—written in 1363 by a retired Tibetan dignitary, Tselpa Künga Dorjé, who had been at a court of the Yuan dynasty, following in the footsteps of his father and grandfather as administrators at court—briefly recounts that the soldiers had tried to burn Karma Pakshi, drown him, throw weapons at him, and poison him, to no avail. Subsequent historians follow much the same account, occasionally adding the additional trial of being thrown off a cliff. The *Blue Annals* makes the observation that two of Karma Pakshi's disciples, Yeshé Wangchuk and Rinchen Pel, died from being burned during these trials, but gives no further detail.[112]

Karma Pakshi's account is more visionary, and he accentuates the positivity of his immunity from being harmed and his triumph over adversity. He sees the confrontation in these terms:

> Looking properly at this situation,
> See the retinues of protectors and guardians of Buddhism
> Enjoying red meat and blood!
> See in front of Palden Lhamo
> Red *rakta* swirling around!
> See the heated and stricken trainees,
> Terrified and panicking.

Karma Pakshi asserts that in this dire situation his realization and thus his freedom from fear—"the fearless nirmāṇakāya"—made him like "a powerful lotus king" who overwhelmed malevolent gods and spirits, binding them with oaths of obedience, likely an oblique reference to Padmasambhava. Indeed, he states that he had risen over sixty miles into the sky—"two hundred *li* above the impure earth"—when the imperial messenger named Elagan had arrived with the edict.[113] The poetic "flying" may well be a metaphorical elevation above the turbulent times, for, as he put it:

Sentient beings have become sinful,
The bad karma times have been irksome—
Much slander and sarcasm are proclaimed,
So hailstorms fall throughout the region.

Instead of getting involved in such negativity, he states that he feels compassion toward impure sinners and that for such a samaya-vow-keeping yogin the hordes of fierce protective deities are on his side. Consequently,

At that time this yogin said,
"A yogin who realizes the dharmakāya,
Is at all times pure by nature,
He has no fear of the fire and water elements."[114]

He also states that this courage and freedom had been achieved through his mastery of meditation on the subtle energies, so that he is free of enemies.[115] The defiance made Kubilai extremely angry, yet the executioner felt powerless and agitated by the anger displayed. Karma Pakshi was unmoved.[116] Instead, inspired by masters of his lineage, he proceeded to sing a lengthy prayer for the prevention of "untimely death." At the end, rainbows swirled, and many people present developed faith in him. The emperor was again annoyed—one is reminded of another infamous confrontation between royalty and cleric from the twelfth century in English history, "Will no one rid me of this turbulent priest?" In that instance, the outcome was assassination of the cleric. In this case in China, the tragic outcome was rather different: the executioner committed suicide. Then further tragedy occurred when the fierce female deity Palden Lhamo appeared with forty-four thousand soldiers, declaring support for Karma Pakshi and causing a violent storm:

> The triple-faced black goddess of tempest
> Summoned terrifying messengers,
> Creating lightning and wind that filled the three realms.
> They threw down from the sky a rain of insanity and sickness
> As earth, stone, and mountain rocks—
> All the tents and wagons were smashed
> Like scattered bird feathers.

In the ensuing chaos, people lost their lives, others were struck down by illness, and some were just terrified. Faith in the Buddhist master, who was defying execution, was awakened. Such a miracle, Karma Pakshi wrote, had not been seen or heard of before by anyone.

Exile

After the storm, Kubilai mitigated the imperial death sentence to exile, a punishment used by Mongol rulers in China. Karma Pakshi gives the location of his exile as Ke'u Je'u, a place on the banks of a sea or large lake. Later Tibetan biographers refer to the bank as a barren area, treeless and with little vegetation, so it may have been a beach on present-day Bohai Bay, not so far from Kubilai's eventual capital at Dadu (Yenching, later Beijing). However, at the time of Karma Pakshi's internal exile, Dadu was not yet developed as a capital, and Kubilai's capital was Kaipingfu, known as Shangdu after 1263 and as Xanadu in Coleridge's celebrated nineteenth-century incomplete poem: *Kubla Khan, or A Vision in a Dream*: "In Xannadù did Cubla Khan..."[117] It was from Shangdu that Karma Pakshi

left for Tibet after eventual reconciliation with Kubilai.[118] Approximately seventy miles north of Shangdu is the large lake Dali Nur
(Lake like a Sea), an inland saltwater lake now part of the Hexigten
Global Geopark. The area around the lake is known for its volcanic
rock terrain. An area beside the southern side of the lake is now
known as Kehu Guri, a name not entirely dissimilar to Ke'u Je'u, so
it may be a reasonable candidate for the location of Karma Pakshi's
exile.[119] Karma Pakshi also states that for some months he was on
an island, and indeed Dali Nur Lake has some small islands.

In the inhospitable region of exile, while staying for three months
on an island in a lake, Karma Pakshi caused a "cool and fragrant
rainfall," which delighted all people in the area. He records that
he spent in total two years by the lake, and he may well have used
much of the time to write, expanding his Limitless Ocean series.
For example, after having a vision of a yellow Mañjuśrī in which
twenty-one doctrinal questions were debated with the deity, Karma
Pakshi wrote *Questions to Ārya Mañjuśrī: A Limitless Ocean of Questions
and Answers*, a lengthy text dealing with the twenty-one questions
for debate, primarily on the subject of valid cognition (*pramāṇa*).[120]
The vision was of yellow Mañjuśrī with eleven faces, a thousand
hands, and a thousand legs, with each hand holding a bowl in
which was seated a buddha, resplendent with golden light. The
vision of Mañjuśrī appeared for a considerable time and said to
Karma Pakshi, "In the future, you will command as far as from
China and Minyak (Xi Xia) up to the ocean, blessing these lands
with your connascent gnosis wisdom, and I too shall bless them
for eternity." Karma Pakshi wrote that, due to his own "perfection
of self-arising gnosis," he thereafter became known as Omniscient
Rangjung Dorjé.[121] It may be recalled that he also refers to himself
in such terms for the period when he was in solitary retreat as a
young man, when he had no students—this episode may be illus-
trating that he had become more widely known by the epithet. He

states that later, while returning to Tibet, he wrote the Mañjuśrī
vision statement on one of the pillars in the miraculous Trulnang
Trulpay Lhakhang temple he had founded some years earlier in
Xi Xia, so that the people of China could see a record of the pronouncement even though they had not been able to see and hear
the vision.[122]

After the two years in exile by the lake or sea, Karma Pakshi proceeded to a place he called Chongto, which is likely to have been
Zhongdo, the old Jin dynasty capital a little southwest of the site
where Dadu was yet to be established. He was probably summoned
by Kubilai, who seems to have continued in his mistrust and antagonism toward Karma Pakshi. At this meeting, two years since their
catastrophic previous meeting, Kubilai had Karma Pakshi locked up
in an "Avalokiteśvara temple," with the doors nailed shut and three
guards in shifts watching over the temple—there was no chance of
escape.[123] The imprisoned yogin proceeded to manifest ḍākinīs and
deities within the temple. The manifestations could be seen from the
outside his prison, as the walls had apparently become transparent.
Such miraculous events seem to have affected the Khan. As Karma
Pakshi's memoirs have it:

> Then, when seven nights had passed,
> I had made the royal ruler of the earth happy—
> Taking up my lotus feet to his crown,
> He expressed words of joy.
> Everyone who had been jealous said,
> "*Ema!* Is he not a wondrous great man?"
> All the great meditators, holders of the practice lineage—
> Do they not maintain the Kagyü seat?
> All the ordained sangha together—
> Do they not spread the teachings of Śākyamuni?
> All the mantrins who have amassed power—

Have they not recited the great protective teaching?
All the furious vīra heroes—
Have they not pacified and tamed?
All the buddhas and their bodhisattvas who have bodhicitta—
Have they not planted the dharma banner?
The valuable advice of the profound aural lineage
Brings out the best in everyone.[124]

Kubilai had had a significant change of heart. So he set free his prisoner, telling him, "Wherever you wish to go in Tibet, please perform Buddhist prayers for me." With that, Karma Pakshi set off on the lengthy return to his homeland in East Tibet, and then a farther journey to Tsurpu, which in all took eight years.

Details of the return journey are sparse in Karma Pakshi's memoirs. It would seem that from Zhongdu he passed through a place he gives as Hun Chil, where he perceived that local troubles were being caused by the fierce female *mamo* deities: their "quarrelsome breath" spread like thick clouds over the area, creating epidemic diseases. Karma Pakshi heard buddhas speak, and a blue Medicine Buddha manifested in a cloudless sky, radiating light to heal the sick populace. The light rays also blessed the local wells and ponds. When people drank the water, all sickness was removed from the area, and the buddhas said, "Misery is eliminated!" The people were amazed and became devout toward him. It would seem that there was an understanding that clean water was crucial to eliminating the epidemic, so the disease may have been typhoid or cholera.

A song credited to Karma Pakshi opens with an address to the Medicine Buddha, and although it is not specific about where he composed it, the final verse does refer to being "below the snow mountains," presumably meaning lower ground such as China. The colophon refers to the song as "Lama Karmāpa's Revocation of Inferior Samsara".[125]

Unique refuge for all beings,
O Medicine Buddha, cleanser of the suffering of sickness,
The medicinal[126] precious lama—
I pray to you, grant your blessing.

Sentient beings of the three realms of samsara,
Wandering again and again across the ocean of samsara—
May they go immediately to the plain of great happiness!

Due to karma and result purified over lifetimes,
I have gained precious human birth;
I have used the power of the ten-syllable mantra
For immediate liberation beyond samsara!

Entering the door of the Buddhist doctrine,
In hearing, studying, and meditating on it I have purified my
    being.
I will fully accomplish the potential of this life—
Immediate reversal of attachment to the world!

I follow after the lamas of the lineage,
Yet even in continuous practice of *samādhi*
I am involved in noisy dullness and excitement—
May I immediately travel to the transcendent plain!

I have grasped the harm of great effort in desire and consumption,
And its reliability and deception, as taught by the lama:
Despite so much flux of ebb and flow
May I immediately keep in mind the Kagyü main seat!

To become a buddha in one lifetime—
Incomparably spontaneously natural

Precious jewel of all beings—
May I immediately accomplish the embrace of my purpose!

This short melody of the five "immediates"
Was composed by a yogin self-liberated from samsara
Below the snow mountains place of practice—
May faultless qualities be perfected!

Farther toward the China–Tibet border, at Shing Kun (Lintao, south of Lanzhou), again obstacles from the gods and demons were perceived, so Karma Pakshi rode a wild horse onto the plain, whereupon a vision of a great nine-headed *heruka*, Padma Wang-chuk, manifested dancing in the sky, with three loud neighs, and the spirits were overwhelmed. For this event, the twentieth-century author Rinchen Pelzang of Tsurpu wrote that when the spirits of China, Mongolia, Tangut, and Uighur were subjugated, they were bound with the verse:

The powerful yidam subjugated apparent existence;
The anger of the Mongolian heretic king has been tamed—
Fire, water, poison, weapons, and the elemental powers
     vanquished,
We supplicate at the feet of Karma Pakshi.[127]

Thereafter, Karma Pakshi traveled on into Kham, where, according to later historians, before proceeding to Central Tibet he commissioned at the Karma Densa Monastery a statue of Maitreya, a buddha of a future era, and then in the Nenang Monastery a statue of Dīpaṃkara, a buddha of a previous era. The wealth accumulated on his travels was being put to use for creating statues. Karma Pakshi had sent ahead, a few years earlier, instructions to begin work at Tsurpu on the huge Śākyamuni statue he had dreamed of. Once created, there would be a trio of buddha statues from three eons for a triad of monasteries.

As he approached his seventies, it was time for the returning traveler to use the wealth gained in the past sixteen years or so of traveling in order to enlarge and improve Tsurpu, thus ensuring it would be established as the major Karma Kamtsang monastery.

CHAPTER 6

Return to Tsurpu

THE VENERABLE meditation master returned to Tsurpu in the early 1270s after more than a decade and a half away. After leaving Tsurpu in 1255, Karma Pakshi had traveled as much as ten thousand miles by horse and foot—first eastward to leave Tibet, then northward to the imperial capital in Mongolia, then over to the Almaliq area, then crossing northern China from Almaliq to the Xanadu area, and eventually back to Central Tibet. In his travels, he had suffered imprisonment and maltreatment by Kubilai Khan's forces. Three of the Toluid brothers, grandsons of Chinggis Khan and leading characters in the vast Mongolian Empire—Möngke, Kubilai, and Ariq-Böke—with their queens and courts, had heard and appreciated Karma Pakshi's teaching and advice. He had also repaired and established Buddhist buildings, commissioned statues, and inspired multitudes of people. He had set off to return to Tsurpu in the Tölung valley with donated riches and several books he had authored while on his travels and during his enforced isolation. En route, he passed through and spent time in his homeland, East Tibet.

East Tibet

In the twentieth century, in 1951, Namkhai Norbu made a traveling diary record of his own travels among nomads of eastern Tibet. In 1965 Hugh Richardson encouraged him to publish, and within the eventual 1983 book was a transcription of a devotional song sung by nomads.[128] The ballad is largely about Karma Pakshi's adventures and travails in China and Mongolia. In the Tibetan there are forty-three lines. The first verse is as follows:

> For each great person, for everyone,
> He turned the dharma wheel in China:
> The man who encouraged Chinese people to dharma
> Is the yogin Karma Pakshi—
> To the Lord Karmapa I pray!

The ballad continues to describe his childhood and then segues abruptly into the tortures he endured in China:

> He turned his horse's bridle down toward China.
> Offerings swirled like a snowstorm—
> To the Lord Karmapa I pray!
> When he was hurled from a white rock,
> Spontaneously he became the king of birds, the vulture—
> To the Lord Karmapa I pray!
> When flung into blue water,
> Spontaneously he became a natural waterbird—
> To the Lord Karmapa I pray!
> When thrown into a pit of thorns,
> It would become a cushion of smooth white silk—
> To the Lord Karmapa I pray!
> When thrown into a red fire,
> Spontaneously he became red Agni the god of fire —
> To the Lord Karmapa I pray!
> When put inside a small cell,
> Spontaneously it became a multi-door stupa—
> To the Lord Karmapa I pray!

When put in a dark room,
A sun of divine light rays shone—
To the Lord Karmapa I pray!
When flung into a pit of insects,
The large insects danced around him
And the smaller insects swirled around him reverentially—
To the Lord Karmapa I pray![129]

Seven centuries earlier, on the lengthy journey home from Xanadu, Karma Pakshi had passed through his homeland Kham, the region where Namkhai Norbu took note of the song of praise sung by nomads of the area. The Karma Pakshi memoirs do not elaborate about his temporary homecoming in Kham, but the erecting of statues in the region does feature; presumably the commissions were enabled by his wealth obtained in China and Mongolia. In Kampo Nenang, he commissioned a statue of Buddha Dīpaṃkara, known as the Buddha for the previous eon. In the last stage of the journey within eastern Tibet before heading farther west to Central Tibet, at Karma Monastery he erected a large statue of Maitreya, the Buddha for the next eon. A large statue of the Buddha for this eon, Śākyamuni, was yet to be created.

"Ornament of the World"

Karma Pakshi's main concern on returning to Central Tibet, in his seventies, seems to have been to follow the injunctions he had received in far Northwest China from an oneiric vision of a huge Śākyamuni Buddha, about sixty feet tall, a dozen years before his return to Tsurpu. The dream figure had told Karma Pakshi to build a statue in Tibet in order to ensure happiness within the country. After the dream, he had written ahead from the area around Kecu (Kucha or Turpan) a public letter to the community at Tsurpu

Monastery in Central Tibet to start work on the statue. It would seem that in the letter a person expert in statue-making, a skilled "pakshi" (master), living in the Penyul area north of Lhasa, was commissioned to do the work.[130] To oversee the work, Karma Pakshi sent his disciple Dengom with seven mule-loads of wrought gold and instructions to get the copper required for the alloy from copper mines in Central Tibet. The location of the mines is given as Rampa, which may allude to mines at Tölung Rampa, not far from Tsurpu. A reference to the manufacture of the statue appears in the sixteenth-century *Feast for Scholars*, stating that the ore used came from the Rampa Zangkung mine.[131]

When Karma Pakshi arrived over a decade later at Tsurpu the work on the statue was not yet done, and took another three years to complete. The practicalities of such a project must have been exceptionally difficult, given the local resources and contemporary technology. For instance, a predominantly copper casting would require temperatures of over 1085°C (1984°F) to melt the copper, and about half that to melt zinc to make an alloy. The melting of the copper required a greater temperature than that generated by a wood fire—possibly a charcoal fire would be adequate, but more likely there was the need for coal, which had to be accessed and transported. Despite the complications of such a project, Karma Pakshi was determined to fulfill the instructions of his dream-vision, and he had funds available from gifts accrued on his travels. The creation of the sixty-foot statue was of considerable importance to him: the dream had been experienced during his week of prayer for peace by the Ili River when he had been despondent about the conflicts in the world. He posited that creating the statue was a virtuous project that would enable the spread and increase of the Buddhist doctrine, which in turn would facilitate and preserve peace and stability in Tibet. He referred to the statue as the Ornament of the World, something of a precursor of a modern title such as

World Heritage Site, which it would likely be called nowadays if the statue had survived the years of the Great Proletarian Cultural Revolution (1966–1976), which had been so destructive for Tibetan religious institutions.

In addition to the locating, assembling, and processing of resources, the huge statue's practical construction must have been a tremendous task, given the engineering capabilities of the time and the region. Karma Pakshi states that the Buddha in his dream was ten "arm spans high." If an outstretched arm span of a man is from five and a half to six feet, that would make the dream figure about sixty feet high. It seems Karma Pakshi decided to construct one of the same size. Hugh Richardson's estimate—on seeing the actual statue in 1948 and 1950—of sixty feet corroborates the approximate height given in the Karma Pakshi memoirs.[132] The monastery site was attacked by cannon fire and with drilled explosives in the Cultural Revolution, and eventually the statue was destroyed and so unfortunately is no longer visible. Richardson had no photos of it among his photographs of Tsurpu.

Ornament of the World was not the only large buddha statue built in Tibet during the thirteenth century. Sixty years earlier, in about 1212, a gilded copper Maitreya had been completed at Tropu Monastery, roughly two hundred miles west of Tsurpu. After twelve years of preparation and manufacture, it stood at a reported eighty cubits, or approximately 120 feet, so is likely to have been a standing statue, or else seated in the "Western style" on a throne with legs arranged vertically, both postures common to Maitreya statues. The statue was destroyed in the early eighteenth century during a Dzungar Mongol invasion.

By way of comparison with a currently intact metal statue created in the thirteenth century, the well-known Kamakura Daibutsu Buddha statue in Japan, completed in 1252, is thirty-three feet high and estimated to weigh 120 tons. Rudyard Kipling published in 1892 a poem about the widespread appeal and influence of the Kamakura statue, containing the lines

> And down the loaded air there comes
> The thunder of Thibetan drums,
> And droned—"*Om mane padme oms*"—
> A world's width from Kamakura.

He ends the poem with

> Is God in human image made
> No nearer than Kamakura?[133]

Kipling presumably did not know of the great Tsurpu statue, almost twice the height of the Kamakura Buddha, yet the final lines of his paeon, with a substitution of place-names, could equally refer to Tsurpu's giant statue.

Another ancient, huge metal Buddha created in preindustrial times and still extant is the Nara Tōdai-ji Daibutsu seated buddha statue finished in 752 C.E., just under fifty feet high and estimated to weigh 250 tons. It is of comparable height to Ornament of the World, although both of these Japanese statues are less high than Ornament of the World was.[134] Both Japanese statues were cast, but records from the past do not make clear how Ornament of the World at Tsurpu was made. It is likely that the statue was created either by hammering metal sheets (repoussé) or by using the lost-wax method of casting.[135]

Using either technique, the statue was probably created in sections and then assembled, which would chime with a well-known tale that indicates there were problems with the assembly. The story repeated in several histories is that when the statue was initially placed in situ, it appeared to be leaning to one side, whereupon

Karma Pakshi sat in meditation in front of it and leaned to one side to emulate the statue. The master, using a meditation technique involving holding the breath, then righted himself vertically, and the statue also miraculously straightened. This vignette first appears in writing in the *Feast for Scholars* history—Karma Pakshi himself does not refer to any such corrective straightening.[136]

Obstacles and Blessings

Karma Pakshi's memoirs do, however, contain a whole section— eight folios in length—devoted to his observations and thoughts on the Ornament of the World statue. The section is entitled "Biographical Account of Building the Ornament of the World Great Deity."[137] The account briefly alludes to the expense of creating the huge work, funded by the wealth gained in his extensive travels. At some point while building the sculpture, a light shone from the top of the "throne"—probably referring to either the top of the decorative bas-relief often found behind a buddha statue, or to the top of the platform the statue was to be seated on—and there were earth tremors for two days over the whole region. The tremors were interpreted as an omen of the negative forces of demons and heretics instigating obstacles to the artists' work and causing dissension. The tremors affected the structural integrity of Tsurpu's pillars, and several monastic artists were killed. The influence of the negative forces seemed to have entered the hearts of the whole team of artists and craftsmen, Buddhist and non-Buddhist, because, according to Karma Pakshi's account, they began to quarrel among themselves. The disputes spread from the work crew to the group involved in providing food for the monks at the monastery, so the discontent had spread from the workshops to the kitchens. The situation was initially resolved by one of Düsum Khyenpa's nephews, unnamed, who encouraged the disputants to take up and practice wholesome

Buddhist attitudes rather than engender conflict. The memoir also remarks that the whole region at that time abounded with conflict and numerous calamities.

Karma Pakshi's personal response to the troubles and conflict was to manifest a mandala of the tantric deities Hayagrīva Vajrarākṣasa and Yakṣa Vajrarākṣasa. From within the visionary mandala, for seven days he fed all the negative forces of the region, and from the miraculous effulgence of his profound meditation the demons were overwhelmed so that the entire valley and all the mountains of the Tsurpu area—the earth, stones, vegetation, and woods—were blessed as a mandala of Vajrarākṣasa, bringing peace and stability. During his meditation, Karma Pakshi beheld light rays emanating from Hayagrīva Vajrarākṣasa to shine on a large rock outside the monastery—he saw the boulder clearly, from a distance. He understood this miraculous display as a consecration of the rock, identifying the rock with the name Soring Zamka. The memoir states that because his unshakable meditation had merged into the rock, anyone seeing, hearing of, or remembering the rock will be expurgated of their own sins and receive blessings. While the Vajrarākṣasa deity was visible on the rock, people troubled by sickness caused by spirits, leprosy, mental illness, and depression came to worship at the rock and were relieved of suffering and harm. The memoir recommends that if people were to later pour water over that consecrated rock, drink the ablution water, and circumambulate reverentially for as much as a week, then such actions would be a very effective purification of even the most serious of sins and would lead to an enhanced spiritual outlook, better health, and the knowledge that suffering can be ameliorated.[138]

One of the songs ascribed to Karma Pakshi is addressed to Hayagrīva. The colophon refers to the song as "Quintain Vajra Verses on Invoking the Commitments of the Protectors":[139]

O masterful Hayagrīva deity,
From the southwest direction, please establish a form
For the bodhicitta yogin
Presently residing at the Kagyü seat—
Now is the time to bless this illusory existence.

O Jinasāgara Avalokiteśvara,
From the dharmatā realm, please establish a form:
The yogin with miraculous compassion
Presently guides the six classes of beings on the path—
Now is the time to hoist a victory banner of maturation and
    liberation.

O yogin with hosts of ḍākinīs,
From the Khecara realm, please establish a form:
The yogin who keeps to ascetic practices
Presently guides fortunate ones on the path—
Now is the time to bestow the two types of spiritual powers.

O Heruka with hordes of vīras,
From the supremely powerful realm, please establish a form:
The fearless yogin
Presently acts for the teaching—
Now is the time to remove the multitude of obstacles.

O mighty Protector-Protectress siblings
With hordes of vow-keepers, please establish a form:
The yogin who will accomplish the Vidyadhāra state
Has overwhelmed the deities and spirits of apparent
    existence—
Now is the time to accomplish the four types of activity.

O loyal deities and spirits of the apparent world,
From a place of samaya vows, please establish a form:
The yogin keeping the supreme vows
Will accomplish a variety of activity in every direction—
Now is the time to act as a servant and emissary.

In the upper south area, at a place called Karmā,
A seat of the Oral Lineage has been established:
Due to all that has gone before,
May the hosts of lamas, meditation deities, and ḍākinīs
Hold us with their compassion and give us their
    blessing

Consecration

The importance of consecration is emphasized by Karma Pakshi both for the obvious religious benefits of the sanctification of an object and thus its effects on a worshipper, but also for the effects the larger projects have on the surrounding environment—both the local geographical area and the society of its inhabitants.[140] He makes the point that when people who have doubts about Buddhism, or even have no faith, come in the presence of an artifact endowed with consecration blessing, it can be seen how such people are influenced to develop their good qualities and eventually attain spiritual accomplishments:

When people are involved in faith and blessing, then if someone relies on faith, devotion, and conviction toward an artifact endowed with consecration blessing, there is no doubt that, instantaneously, the good qualities and accomplishments have imbued their consciousness.[141]

After all, he continues, if such a statue was nothing more than the bits and pieces of its materials of manufacture, then it would be inconceivable that the finished article could aid in spreading appreciation of the Buddha's teaching and thereby make people happy, yet that is what happens. Moreover, Karma Pakshi adds that the blessing of the consecration emanating from the Ornament of the World statue, along with that of a group of five other buddha statues he commissioned at Tsurpu, enhanced and increased the nutrients of the soil in the local area, resulting in good harvests of grain, especially barley.

However, Karma Pakshi does not shy away from reporting that despite his statue projects there were also untoward natural events and even disputes between people in the area. Some of the statue makers died while working on the projects, as did a benefactor, and there were arguments and conflict. He makes the point that the Buddha had often been quoted as saying that wherever good works are being done, there also the obstructive forces of Māra will appear, attempting to harm the influence of the precious dharma. Yet the positive influence of such excellent statues, properly consecrated, prevails, as Karma Pakshi concludes in verse:

> Unaffected by an army of obstructive negative forces,
> The supreme statue and the five types of victors
> Have become the glory of all the world—
> People who see, hear of, or remember them
> Are themselves blessed and consecrated
> To fully conquer the warrior (Māra).
> So, with quintessential gnosis,
> The supreme statue—the spontaneous manifestation
>   of three kāyas—
> Will give rise to continual spiritual activity:
> The improvement and protection of all people.[142]

Another section of the memoirs mentions in passing that at Tsurpu Karma Pakshi commissioned a total of nine statues: the above-mentioned six, plus statues of Düsum Khyenpa, of Avalokiteśvara, and of the ancestral Tibetan "holy emperor" Songtsen Gampo (seventh century). The latter imperial figure was apparently completed in a somewhat miraculous fashion: "magically manifested like the one Padmasambhava had erected at Samyé Monastery."[143] Incidentally, elsewhere in his writings, Karma Pakshi makes almost no reference or allusion to the eighth-century Padmasambhava.

In Ü–Tsang

So for some years after the return from China, Karma Pakshi was busy with organizing sculptures and buildings to further establish Tsurpu, to make it a grander monastery and also to instill blessings in the minds of followers and in their environment. He seems to have succeeded in constructing the lasting physical basis for an institution that was still young, where the buildings had "been in ruins" when he first arrived fifty years after Düsum Khyenpa's death. Once the projects were proceeding smoothly, he would have had time to travel in Central Tibet. However, his memoirs remark that when he arrived back at Tsurpu from the extensive travels, he had a vision of Vajradhāra accompanied by hordes of *ḍāka*s and yoginīs and the Brahmin Saraha: "above, below, in between, spread everywhere without overlapping one another, legs in *vajra āsana* posture, arms in earth-touching mudra, resounding with the echoing sound of mahāmudrā."[144] Karma Pakshi took this vision as a sign that he should not travel any more.

A song attributed to Karma Pakshi, which he composed for his student Darma Sengé, is addressed to Saraha and references Vajradhāra, so it may be relevant to the vision of Saraha. The colophon of the song refers to it as "Perfect Completion of the Five Kāyas":[145]

The *dharmakāya* complete pervasion throughout samsara and
    nirvana,
O unlimited Saraha,
I pray there will be no flux
Of gathering and separation—
Pray grant the blessing of maturing and liberating.

The blissful *saṃbhogakāya*, supreme spontaneous bliss,
O unchanging Master,
Within a realm of great bliss, I pray:
Pray grant everlasting blessing.

The immeasurable *nirmāṇakāya* hosts of clouds congregate
With everlasting, inconceivable activity—
I pray to the supreme Brahmin:
Bless me forever.

O buddhas and bodhisattvas of the ten directions,
Dharma lords having excellent qualities,
And lamas of outstanding qualities:
I pray to you, grant your blessing.

In limitless pure lands of all directions,
The incredible multitude of activities,
A cascading rain of the meaningful essence:
Bestow on me the spiritual powers of the four kāyas.

Inseparable emptiness and compassion,
O Vajradhāra, completely perfected five kāyas
Unchanging for all time:
Bless us fortunate ones.

The meaningful essence in an age of strife
Is like the sun shining in the sky—
To the one who matures and liberates the six types of beings,
Pray bless us freely.

To the blissful *dharmakāya* Master
I pray continuously:
May every being of the six types
All rapidly attain buddhahood!

Visitors

Although he interpreted the vision of Vajradhāra and Saraha and others as an injunction for himself to not travel away from Tsurpu, Karma Pakshi had some notable visitors during his final few years. Firstly, later accounts record that in 1277 Karma Pakshi and the famous Pakpa (1235–1280) met in Tsurpu, possibly after Pakpa had successfully organized, in the same year, a convocation of Buddhist teachers and sangha at Chumik Monastery, fifteen miles southwest of Shigatse. At that time, Pakpa held the position of Imperial Preceptor (*ti shih*) to Kubilai Khan and was on a visit to his homeland. It is not clear if Karma Pakshi and Pakpa had met earlier in China. Pakpa had been summoned to Prince Kubilai for the first time in 1253, at the age of eighteen and while still a novice monk. They met in the Liupanshan area before Kubilai had left for his Dali campaign in September of that year. Pakpa did not go on the campaign south to Dali, although in 1254 he did travel in Kham. After Kubilai had returned northward from Dali in late 1254, it is possible that in 1255, when Karma Pakshi was invited to court and arrived to see the prince, he may have met with Pakpa among the traveling court circles in the borderland areas of northeast Tibet and western China. Karma Pakshi records that he himself did not stay long at the Kubilai court because he had a premonitory vision of Avalokiteśvara telling him that trouble at the court lay ahead, and he should move farther north. One might surmise that Pakpa and Karma Pakshi met at this time, but there is no mention of their direct interaction in these earlier years.

Later, Karma Pakshi was traveling far and wide: farther north to Karakorum, west to Almaliq, and back to Liupanshan in north China (1256–1259), and by 1260 Pakpa had risen in the Kubilai court in Xanadu (the court transferred to Dadu (Beijing) later on). Pakpa was appointed a state preceptor (*kuo shi*) at the age of twenty-five, after Kubilai had declared himself Khan of Khans in May 1260. Tibetan histories have it that the gifted young man had already granted Kubilai and members of his family and court the Hevajra tantric initiations. For the initiations, the protocolar question of the preeminence of princely warrior and younger ecclesiastic during the empowerment arose—who was to sit in place of honor, the secular warrior or the religious officiant? The difficulty had been settled diplomatically by Kubilai's principal wife, Chabui, when she suggested that during religious ceremonies the cleric should take precedence, and for secular meetings the prince would supersede. So Pakpa was accepted, in certain instances at least, into the very center of the imperial court. It may be that despite Pakpa's position as an important religious figure in the court, it did not warrant him to be influential politically in the arrest and attempted execution of Karma Pakshi in the 1260s, and likewise he may not have been involved with the eventual release. Pakpa's influence in these high dramas of Karma Pakshi's life is not clear.

However, at the time of their meeting in 1277 in Central Tibet, whatever their previous interactions, at Tsurpu they sat as equals— "on level seats"—according to the *Red Annals*.[146] During the visit Karma Pakshi was said to have remarked to Pakpa that "Before, when I was chaplain to Möngke Khan, I thought of you as the bodhisattva Priyadarśana." The bodhisattva allusion may be a reference to a bodhisattva mentioned in the *Lotus Sutra* who was known for doing a body-sacrifice practice. Unfortunately, there is no record in the Karma Pakshi memoirs of any earlier meeting with Pakpa to help explain. If an earlier meeting did happen, then referring to Pakpa in 1277 as a notable bodhisattva of the past indicates that even if there had been any difficulties between the two men when in China, years later there were no prior antagonisms to remark upon. Both men can be seen historically as influential figures for subsequent Tibetan ecclesiastic orientation toward imperial Mongolian and Chinese sponsors—both lamas had initiated an emperor into Vajrayāna practices, and both had been honored by two of the most remarkable warrior emperors in world history.

A second important visitor to Tsurpu during Karma Pakshi's elderly years was Orgyen Rinpoche, a renowned master of esoteric Buddhism who also spent much of his life traveling far and wide.[147] This short, three-day visit proved to be crucial to the development and subsequent continuance of the Karmapa lineage. Orgyenpa, born in 1230, was in 1282 on his way eastward from Sakya to the Yarlung Valley. After crossing the Tsangpo River, he decided that completing the journey farther east to Yarlung would not be beneficial just then, and so he turned north toward Tsurpu. According to Situ Panchen, writing in the eighteenth century, Karma Pakshi's clairvoyance ability led him to say to the people around him, before Orgyenpa had arrived, "Kyé, you gossipers of Tsurpu—the siddha Orgyenpa, like a pillar between earth and sky, is indeed on his way!" On his part, Orgyenpa said to his companions, "The Karmapa monks are very busy. Let us stay here." The visiting party rested behind the top of a mountain and then traveled by night, perhaps seeking to test Karma Pakshi's clairvoyance. Karma Pakshi used his clairvoyance to see the ruse and sent a welcoming party in the morning. He then met Orgyenpa by the Maitreya statue in the Tsurpu complex. The two got on well, and at one point Karma Pakshi asked Orgyenpa to sing the song he had sung in the Asura Cave in Pharping (Nepal), possibly his "Thirteen Non-Necessities Song."[148] The visit lasted just three days, during which time Karma Pakshi passed on instructions on the cycle of teaching derived from Nāropa—the "mixing and transference" cycle for death meditations—and also on Karma Pakshi's own "introduction to the three kāyas" teaching. Karma Pakshi also granted a Red Avalokiteśvara (Jinasāgara) initiation for Orgyenpa. At one point in the initiation, Karma Pakshi placed a bowl of barley on Orgyenpa's head and stirred the barley with a ritual stick: it is thought that at this point a significant mind-to-mind transmission took place, ensuring the continuity of the Karma Pakshi lineage.

In later histories it is also stated that Karma Pakshi gave Orgyenpa a black hat, ostensibly to pass on to Karma Pakshi's successor incarnation. This hat was not the celebrated black "Vajra Crown" that was given in the fifteenth century by Emperor Yong-le of China to the Fifth Karmapa.[149] It is likely to be a hat derived from a Tangut or Mongol design, as seen in several tangkas dated to the thirteenth and fourteenth centuries in which a Karmapa is depicted as wearing a black hat with golden trimmings. Some later accounts refer to a black hat given to Karma Pakshi by Möngke Khan, in which case the hat would likely have been one of Mongolian design. In Karma Pakshi's memoirs, he makes reference to a hat "emblazoned with gold" (the overall color is not specified), calling it a symbol of the unchanging dharmatā, worn by Düsum Khyenpa because he was in essence equally as accomplished as the Great Brahmin Saraha:

The lama is the Great Brahmin.
His oral instructions are the mahāmudrā.[150]

In thirteenth-century portraits of Karma Pakshi and Düsum Khyenpa, they both usually wear black hats embellished with gold-colored decoration and a diamond-shaped emblem at the front, with slight variations. However, the transfer of any physical hat to Karma Pakshi, or indeed from him to Orgyenpa, is not recorded in Karma Pakshi's memoirs.

The successor Karmapa, Rangjung Dorjé, wrote a biography of his own master, Orgyenpa, which does state that a black hat was placed on Orgyenpa's head by Karma Pakshi.[151] Another Orgyenpa disciple, Sönam Özer, wrote more fully of his master's visit to Tsurpu—he may have been there with his master at the time of the visit—stating that a black hat was placed on Orgyenpa's head. In this latter biography, Karma Pakshi was reported to have said to Orgyenpa at the time, "We two for many lifetimes have been master and disciple, and you must look after me again. I will be your student in the sunny south, so now I will for the sake of all beings give the Jinasāgara empowerment and the essence of the six-syllable mantra and the 'introduction to the three kāyas.'" Whereupon he repeated again and again, "May the activity of the practitioner the Vajra King Orgyenpa be accomplished!"[152] Thus, Karma Pakshi is reported to have given to Orgyenpa an indication of a future reincarnation and the direction of the area in which he would be reborn.

A third example of visitors to Tsurpu—not so elevated in social or religious status as Orgyenpa—was an itinerant potter by the name of Tönpa Chöpel and his wife Jomo Yangdren. In addition to being a craftsman, Tönpa Chöpel was knowledgeable in the *dohā* religious songs, Nyingma rituals, and pacification tantras. The couple came from an area on the snow line in Mangyul, southwest from Tsurpu, toward the border of Nepal, north of Kathmandu. Their party from this locale was on pilgrimage and had included Tsurpu on the itinerary in order to pay respects at the new, huge statue—its reputation must have already spread far. Karma Pakshi met the party at an upper part of the Tsurpu valley, where the path curves like a bow, and asked Tönpa Chöpel to stay behind briefly. Karma Pakshi then plied him with some high-quality gifts of clothing and food and said, "It is necessary that you loan me a dwelling place."[153] Tönpa Chöpel was somewhat puzzled, and when he told companions about the episode later, they laughed at him because, being an itinerant potter, they said, he had no home, so how could he loan one? It was in the following year that his wife Jomo Yangdren gave birth to a child. Five years later the child was recognized and confirmed by Orgyenpa to be Karma Pakshi's reincarnation. It would seem that in asking for a "loan of a dwelling place" Karma Pakshi had been laying preparations for his impending transition from one life to another.

Death

The Karma Pakshi memoirs do not, of course, cover the events of his death, but his approaching demise is mentioned in a short untitled text, described within as a second "testament," that was written at Tsurpu, probably close to the time of his death in the winter of 1283.[154] He had had a premonition about the "separation of body and mind" some twenty-five years earlier when he had been with the Mongol emperor, Möngke. As his memoir records, despite his expertise in the vase-breath techniques and his control of his energies, at that time with Möngke he had several "omens" of the separation of body and mind—he thought he would soon die, while in his fifties. His response was to send a messenger to Tsurpu, instructing people there to build a stupa structure that emulated the grand Śrī Dhānyakaṭaka stupa in India.[155] For the stupa project he sent valuables that had been given to him from the imperial treasury, in order to create the meritorious conditions to obviate the signs of death. From a Buddhist viewpoint, engaging in virtuous activities improves the practitioner's prospects in terms of karma, which can mean prolonging the precious human life. As Karma Pakshi did not die at that time, he later gave instructions to place in the stupa some bone relics of Düsum Khyenpa.

Further premonitions of demise influenced Karma Pakshi to become energetically engaged in "turning the wheel of oral teaching." Despite several such indications of mortality, he maintained a fearless attitude and prayed to the lamas, yidams, and protectors—in particular to the fierce goddess Palden Lhamo:

> O, universal mother-goddess, glorious goddess,
> The Buddha's teaching has been protected by me.
> As a guide I have led the six classes of beings—
> Bestow on me the siddhi of deathless life![156]

The two themes in this verse of protecting and promoting the Buddha's teaching hark back to the opening passage of Karma Pakshi's second testimonial text, when he recalls that his first teacher, Pomdrakpa, had made two testimonial statements shortly before his death: that Karma Pakshi would both raise the banner of the Buddha's teaching and proclaim the greatness of the practice-lineage teaching. The spreading of the teaching was seen by Karma Pakshi partly in terms of projects such as the creation of the Ornament of the World statue and other religious statues and structures in central and eastern Tibet, and partly in terms of the visionary manifestations witnessed by other people to whom he would then give a teaching on causes and conditions.

During his later years at Tsurpu, Karma Pakshi had several more indications of the separation of body and mind, which he expressed in terms of *māra* obstacles causing his own brief illnesses and the sickness of two of his horses. He had concerns about after-death existence, in particular whether he would later be reborn in a heavenly existence, and about the timing and circumstances of his death: "I hoped to achieve my longing for the various heavens and had endless concerns about separation—about knowing what the timing would be and what circumstances of death would appear."[157]

To counteract these thoughts of impending demise, over a forty-day period he perfected, as he put it, his identity as the mandala of wrathful and peaceful buddhas. This may refer to a Guhyagarbha practice that is associated with the Tibetan Buddhist interpretations of experiences after death, which were later explored in depth in Karma Lingpa's fourteenth-century writings on the death and rebirth process (bardo), nowadays popularly known as The Tibetan Book of the Dead. The site for this forty-day retreat may have been the cave (now surrounded by a building) in the hill above Tsurpu where Karma Pakshi was reputed to have done a "dark retreat."

When he taught about his experience of identifying with the mandala to other people, manifestations and dreams would occur to them. The externalized manifestations visible to others caused the witnesses to think that he was seriously ill, and even his closest disciples said it was wrong for him to be doing a rite with such consequences. Out of their concern, they plied him with "endless noodles and tea."[158] In the testament, Karma Pakshi says he recalled a statement he ascribes to Milarepa:

Frightened of fear in ephemeral life,
I established the interconnection between breath and
  mind.[159]

Karma Pakshi's testament elaborates on this by saying that without breath there is no life: "When the breath in the nostrils cannot go back and forth, so-called Death comes immediately," and thus mastery of meditative breathing techniques is important to a practitioner. He later extols in the testament the virtues of his teaching and practice of the "introduction to the four kāyas," which includes breathing and yoga instruction.[160]

In 1282, the Year of the Horse, Karma Pakshi had something of a health crisis, described as being "like the destruction of an old house moved and shaken up," an apposite simile for people from regions susceptible to earthquakes. His testament puts it that despite his expertise in controlling his mind and energies through the practice of vase-breathing, several omens of deterioration of his bodily four elements occurred, a decline "like the shading of the old setting sun." Local lamas took the decline as a sign of the fading activity of the Karmapa. On the eighth day of the eighth moon of the lunar year, he was temporarily struck dumb, fell heavily in a faint, and his limbs shook. When his breathing stopped, his meditative expertise enabled him to breathe again, and with a vase breath he experienced extreme joy, his breath and mind united. However, uncontrolled shaking of his body occurred for several days, and afterward it was necessary to lift and carry him about for a month. He then seems to have recovered, and there is no further mention of mobility or speech difficulties: the mobility problem was apparently temporary.

Additionally, despite the omens of approaching death—he mentions three of the "six omens of death" having appeared—the testament states that his practice of his favorite teaching, the "introduction to the three (or four) kāyas," helped to stabilize his condition.[161] Karma Pakshi's testament then makes the point that life is an imperfect interplay between consciousness and breath, hence there is no self-control in the death period (bardo), when there is no breathing. He encourages all future students to understand that, due to the unchanging nature of the mind, realization of the four kāyas and their perfect integration will mean attaining inner and outer control of one's life force.[162]

Assuming that Karma Pakshi was the author—or originator—of his second testament, it was written some time in later 1282 or early

1283. The date given for his death in the *Red Annals* was in the Sheep Year (1283), on the third day of the ninth month. Situ Panchen's account in his *Rosary of Crystal Jewels* of the deathbed scene has Karma Pakshi's relatives asking him to engage in a long-life rite, whereupon he replies that "when Mount Meru is shaking," they should be strong and silent. According to Situ Panchen, Karma Pakshi then spoke in verse about death:

> Even though this beggar's life has passed,
> Signs will occur in the clear sky.
> My bodily remains will become *ringsel* relics—
> Abiding in the afterlife state, my reflexive awareness will be
>   self-illuminating.

> Integrated with the stainless dharmakāya,
> Thus capable of blessing others' consciousness,
> Immeasurable benefit for beings will indeed occur
> Because we all will comprehend the stainless dharmakāya.

> I have not even an atom of fear for death:
> Due to being free of any basis for future transmigration and
>   its process,
> There will be no transmigration within the
>   dharmakāya—*aṃ!*[163]

He asked those present not to touch his body for seven days after death. Several accounts describe the signs that occurred at the time of death or shortly thereafter: two suns appeared in the sky, and there was a "rain of flowers" and unusual sounds. Karma Pakshi's cremation, at his prior request, took place within ten days after his death—it seems he did not favor embalming. Various relics were found afterward in the cremation ashes: Karma Pakshi's heart, tongue, and eyes, as well as ringsel relics with markings associated with tantric practices (rare conch shell designs, deity insignia, and seed syllables of meditation deity mantras). The great man had gone.

Rebirth

The birth of the child who was to become Karma Pakshi's successor occurred on the eighth day of the first month of the Monkey Year (1284)—obviously an improbably short human gestation period following his death just four months earlier, unless the dates given are not reliable. Such a short period is not remarked on in the accounts, nor is there extensive debate about any factual inaccuracy. Given the beliefs associated with reincarnations (*yangsi*) and the transference of consciousness (*powa*), it might seem that Karma Pakshi's remark to the itinerant-potter couple—"loan me a dwelling place"—some months before his death meant that the mother Jomo Yangdren was pregnant at that time or would be shortly thereafter.

So perhaps Karma Pakshi had somewhat miraculously identified Jomo Yangdren's embryo as being his own reincarnation. Karma Pakshi himself is reported to have spoken of twenty-one instances of prior, concurrent, and future incarnations. In a text identifying the twenty-one, there are vignettes given of three "co-incarnations" living at the same time as him: two yogins, one living in the Uighur area and one in the Yarlung Valley, and a hunter in the Nepal-Tibet borderland.[164] It may be that the unborn child of Jomo Yangdren also could be thought of as a co-incarnation, although such an explanation is not explicitly mentioned.

Another puzzle about the timeline derives from the accounts of Karma Pakshi's "transference of consciousness" after death, into the body of a recently deceased child (known as a "drongjuk" practice). The most well-known account of this episode is in *The Blue*

Annals.[165] The transference is first alluded to, with little detail, in the Third Karmapa's *Verse Liberation Story*: when Karmapa Rangjung Dorjé was a child he had spoken of the process to Orgyenpa, and then later in 1324 had included it briefly in his autobiography.[166] *Red Annals* has a more elaborate and gruesome version: that the "revived corpse" of a three-year-old child disturbed its parents so much that mother stabbed its eyes with a needle.[167] Blinded, Karma Pakshi thought it better to be reborn in another body, and left the child's body for the pure land of Tuṣita, from where he eventually took birth as a human.

Ruth Gamble, in her *Reincarnation in Tibetan Buddhism*, presents a discussion of the rebirth process from the Second to the Third Karmapa.[168] She also provides a translation of some of the Third Karmapa's writings on the subject in her *The Third Karmapa Rangjung Dorjé* in the Shambhala Lives of the Masters series.[169] Normally one would not expect an autobiographical account of, in Buddhist terms, the transition period between death and next birth. Yet several of the later Tibetan historians refer to a useful source for them that they name as a *bardoma* text, reputedly about the transition for Karma Pakshi to his rebirth as the child of Tönpa Chöpel and Jomo Yangdren. In the eighteenth century, the great scholar Situ Panchen opened his chapter on Rangjung Dorjé with reference to a bardoma liberation story. As Ruth Gamble has pointed out, there is in one of Rangjung Dorjé's autobiographies a section referred to as "Liberation Story of the In-Between State," which may be the bardoma work or similar to it.[170]

The succession of the nascent Karmapa lineage passed to Rangjung Dorjé when the latter, as a child aged five, born into a family of potters, was acknowledged by Orgyenpa. Humorously, when the black hat entrusted to Orgyenpa as a symbol of succession was placed on the five-year-old's head, it was of course too large, so those present laughed. The child was given the name that

Karma Pakshi most frequently used to refer to himself: Rangjung Dorjé. Eventually the precocious child received Karma Pakshi's dharma instructions and transmission from Karma Pakshi's students Orgyenpa and Nyenré Gendün Büm. The dharma legacy was thus secured for future transmission.

CHAPTER 7

Legacies

AFTER THE DEATH and cremation of Karma Pakshi in late 1283, his family and students were left with several monasteries to maintain, and the lineage of his teachings—oral and written—to protect and conserve. As for the monasteries, the physical structures for preserving religious continuity, it was in Karma Pakshi's teenage years, when Pomdrakpa had told the boy that he had had a vision of him as being Düsum Khyenpa, that the initial connection had been made to the monasteries. Later, after years of education and retreat, as his teacher Pomdrakpa was dying, he encouraged Karma Pakshi:

> You uphold the victory banner of Buddha's doctrine;
> You have enhanced the significance of the practice lineage
>   teaching.[171]

After Pomdrakpa's death, Karma Pakshi eventually had proceeded to reenergize the several monasteries that Düsum Khyenpa had founded, a significant part of his life's work.

Monastic Seats

Having begun locally with the smaller monasteries in Kham, it was in middle age that Karma Pakshi had first gone to Central Tibet and to Tsurpu. The monastery had become dilapidated since Düsum Khyenpa's death, and the monks still residing there had apparently been drinking alcohol. After six years' work of restoration at Tsurpu, Karma Pakshi had traveled to China and Mongolia, establishing and repairing Buddhist buildings and stupas in addition to his preaching, healing, and peace-making efforts. He had returned to Kham, with considerable riches, to commission new statues for the monasteries he was responsible for, and thence went to Tsurpu for further commissions and for the enlargement and improvement of the monastery buildings. Thus the structures built for the Karma Kamtsang lineage had been restored and were well established in the Kham and Ü regions, and Tsurpu was established as the primary seat.

The succession of the abbacy leadership of Tsurpu after Düsum Khyenpa's death in 1193 had gone initially to his students, and later to their associates. Once Karma Pakshi had arrived in 1249, the abbacy position was preserved among Karma Pakshi's familial descendants for almost two hundred years. According to *The Blue Annals*, the responsibility immediately after Karma Pakshi's death went to a maternal nephew, Ön Rinpoche, and after him another nephew, Lama Nénangpa, and so on through the generations, a succession of nephews or their brothers or cousins (except for a brief interlude of six months by a "usurper") up until the fifteenth century.[172] The last abbot with a family connection was Jamyang Döndrup Özer, who held the position for forty-three years. Then Gushri Peljor Döndrub (1427–1489), subsequently known as the First Gyeltsap Rinpoche, was appointed abbot as a teenager by the Sixth Karmapa in about 1440. Thereafter, the abbacy succession seems to have been determined by the recognition of reincarnations.[173]

Reincarnation Lineage and Students

In terms of the continuity of Buddhist practices that the buildings and artifacts were intended to support, Karma Pakshi's principal legacy was ensuring the transmission of lineage through the idea of reincarnation. After his own recognition by Pomdrakpa, in his memoirs he refers half a dozen times to his self-identification with Düsum Khyenpa. For example, in a passage about wisdom and ignorance, he reflects that "the previously deceased person known. as Düsum Khyenpa and the present-day stainless Dharmakāya Rangjung Dorjé, even though these are different names and they lived at different times, earlier and later, they are of one essence in reality." So, for example, as he puts it:

Although there are many drops of water,
When they are merged into a great ocean,
Each one is not individual.[174]

Regarding the continuity and identity beyond his own life, Karma Pakshi seemingly indicated, in oblique terms, the mother (Jomo Yangdren) of his future birth successor, as recounted above. Subsequently, when Orgyenpa had arrived for his three-day visit to Tsurpu, Orgyenpa was entrusted with the "transmission" of spiritual knowledge to be passed on to the unborn child who was eventually to take up the mantle of successor. Orgyenpa then met the boy at age five, whereupon the child was given the name Rangjung Dorjé, the name by which Karma Pakshi often referred to himself in his memoirs.[175] Additionally, the continuity of the transmission to the child was also ensured by Lama Nyenré Gendün Bum, a close student of Karma Pakshi.[176] In the tangka paintings of Karma Pakshi in which other human figures are also portrayed, Nyenré Gendün is often portrayed as Karma Pakshi's close disciple. In a collection of songs ascribed to Karma Pakshi, the colophon of one song explains that it was written for the benefit of Nyenré.[177] It is a song of spiritual advice:

I pray to the jewels of the world,
The Oral Lineage masters of retreat—

Blessed by Lord Mila,
May ordinary and excellent spiritual accomplishments be
    bestowed.

The excellent Buddha and his bodhisattvas went to the
    mountains
And practiced as they wandered in remote areas;
All beings who have been our mothers
Will not achieve such an example of benefit to oneself—
To be surrounded by a mandala of bodhisattvas
Is advice that is vitally useful.

Bestowing blessing on body, speech, and mind
When one is meditating uninterruptedly,
The inconceivable activity of the form dimension—
The precious lama of the lineage,
Head of all buddhas throughout time—
When one meditates on him in indivisible unity,
One has grasped the Kagyü top level:
The heart-essence of the ocean of ḍākinīs
Existing in the wind-mind combination.

In the palace of the fourfold mandala,
When piercing through to the essential point of life energy,
Like a cloud of ḍākinīs in the three places,
The mode of being of awareness and mind—
The identity itself of self-arising wisdom—
Is not influenced by dullness and excitement.

When one has mastered the indivisible,
One has found the three kāyas of a buddha within oneself—
The inconceivable activity of the dharmakāya

In the mandala of the realm of indivisibility.
The virtues accumulated throughout time
Will be completely shared for the great enlightenment,
And I have offered this completely pure prayer.

Nyenré and others who roam remote areas
Should act in such a way to cultivate their practice,
Not subject to the influences of desire or aversion,
Looking to not rely on fluctuations of gathering and
      loosening—
Highly intelligent Tséra Dorjé Drak,
With this sacred dharma, you should master this.

Among the available lists of students of Karma Pakshi—about forty
to fifty different names given across several sources—there are three
named according to their hat color: white, yellow, or red. However,
it was not until Drakpa Sengé (1283–1349) was given a red hat by
the Third Karmapa as a ceremonial recognition of religious status,
that the title Shamarpa (The Red Crown Lama) became well known.

Practice Lineages

As to the practices passed on to the disciples, Karma Pakshi has
become best known for two deity practices, that of the Gyelwa
Gyatso deity sādhana (also known as Red Chenrezik) and the
Mahākāla protector rite. Both those figures feature prominently in
tangka paintings of Karma Pakshi in which he is portrayed as an
idealized historical figure receiving offerings from Möngke Khan.
The origination of the Gyelwa Gyatso practice is ascribed to Padmasambhava. According to Tāranātha's (1575–1634) biography of Padmasambhava, the latter was for a few years at "Bhangala" (Bengal),
where he practiced in retreat for six months with a female consort

described as having the characteristics of the *padma* (lotus) family.[178] *The Blue Annals* has the lineage passing from Padmasambhava to "Vārāhī of Bhangala," so it may be that the initial transmission occurred during the retreat in the forest north of Pandua in Bhangala. A Nyingma tradition has Padmasambhava transmitting the practice to a Siddhirājñī. Thence the tradition passed eventually to Tipupa, Rechungpa (1083–1161), Zangri Repa, Drogön Rechen, Pomdrakpa, and so to Karma Pakshi, who initiated Orgyenpa. The practice continues in modern times as an important part of the Karma Kamtsang's tantra tradition.

In tangka portrayals of the Bernakchen form of Mahākāla, with two arms and wearing a voluminous blue-black cloak, it is often Karma Pakshi who is above the main figure. This positioning indicates his primary role in the transmission of the practice for the Kamtsang lineage. The main protector practices of the earlier Kagyü lineage holders were not of Bernakchen—it is with Karma Pakshi that the Bernakchen tradition became the main protector associated with the lineage. The Bernakchen lineage is said to have come to Karma Pakshi from his father (from a Nyingma lineage), but this protector lineage is also traced from Drogön Rechen to Pomdrakpa to Karma Pakshi. The tangka depictions of the Bernakchen and Rangjung Gyelmo figures riding a mule together also feature Karma Pakshi in prime position above the deities—it may be that he was responsible for introducing this "brother-sister" practice to the Kamtsang lineage.

The practice that Karma Pakshi in his writings most often refers to is that of the "introduction to the three kāyas" (or variously four or five kāyas—Karma Pakshi himself mostly refers to "four kāyas"). He passed on the instruction to Orgyenpa, and the Third Karmapa also wrote on it briefly.[179] Two hundred and fifty years later, the Eighth Karmapa wrote a lengthy work on the subject, available in three or four volumes.[180] A short work written by the Fourteenth Karmapa in the nineteenth century also deals with the subject. Karma Pakshi does not seem to have written directly on the practicalities of the subject, although there is a short, two-folio text ascribed to him: *A Key to Essential Points on Subtle Winds and Mind*.[181] His only literary work referring in detail to the doctrine of the "introduction to the kāyas" is his *Text of the Wish-Fulfilling Ḍākinī*.[182] However, the practice itself does not seem to have become widespread, despite Karma Pakshi's extensive efforts in preaching it in China and Mongolia.

Termas and Karma Pakshi

Two practices that have become widespread and quite well known among converts to Tibetan Buddhism in Europe, the Americas, and Australasia are about Karma Pakshi himself rather than practices passed on or developed by him. Both are known as *terma*s, or "treasures": one is from the seventeenth century and one from the twentieth century, and both are inspired by Karma Pakshi.

The first, probably discovered in 1653, is a terma from the treasure revealer (*tertön*) Yongé Mingyur Dorjé (1628–1708). When he was at Dzodzi Monastery (northeast of Chamdo in East Tibet) practicing a Bernakchen sādhana, a dawn vision of a seated Karma Pakshi appeared in front of him, with Padmasambhava above and surrounded by several deities and protectors. A near-contemporary biographer of Mingyur Dorjé, Tükyi Dorjé, has the story:[183]

In his twenty-fifth year (the Year of the Snake), residing at Dzodzi Monastery, he was doing the practice of Bernakchen. At dawn—in a real experience, not a dream—he saw the siddha Karma Pakshi with Orgyen seated above his head. To his right was Hayagrīva, to his left was Vārāhī, behind him

was Rechungpa, and in front was Bernak with the Mother
Protectress and the smith (Dorjé Lekpa).[184] Karma Pakshi
gave him this advice:

> Kyé ho! The indescribable wisdom of self-knowledge—
> In a mirror of appearance of the environment of
>   desire,
> The basis of delusion arises following the energy of
>   knowledge.
> The habitual tether of clinging to projection as truth
> Is revealed as whatever illusions appear in manifold
>   ways.
> Whatever has arisen, a realm of unreal suffering and
>   happiness,
> Look nakedly at that—rest in naked self-awareness!
> The symbolic lama appearance, the arena of
>   appearance,
> Unattached to whatever has arisen is self-liberation—
> How wonderful, emaho!
> That is the way to see the fundamental mind itself—
> Its appearance is the lama symbol.
> That is the way to meditate on the nature of the mind,
> Then there is the way of training in the arena of
>   behavior on the path.
>
> Kyé ho! At the time of the nonstop multiplicity of
>   appearances,
> Out of confusion, whatever despondency, fixation on
>   dualism, or hopes or fears have manifested,
> Look at them as though they are the direct face of the
>   five poisons.

This aspect of delusion that has arisen, caused by
  emotions,
Is the mind desiring contentment, craving the three
  poisons.
In terms of food, wealth, enjoyments, status, and
  friends,
Be free of activity—devoid of fixations and
  anticipations—
Rest in the expanse of the fortuitous realm beyond
  intellect.
Not clinging to whatever has arisen, a state of self-
  liberation from whatever has arisen,
That is the path of seeing nakedly the awareness of
  mindful non-distraction.
That is the way to train the mind on the path—
Samaya!

Kyé ho! From the flow of naturally occurring
  self-knowledge,
Whatever has manifest, free of the complexity of non-
  desire or desire-fixation,
In a state of simplicity, apparent experiences are
  purified.
The realm of appearance is empty, as empty as the
  expanse of the sky.
In its midst, wisdom resides, inexpressible, beyond
  intellect,
Staying unwavering, unmistaken, nakedly seeing,
And without substance—it manifests multiplicity.
The activity of projecting out and gathering in is the
  coursing of the energy of consciousness—

Whatever activity occurs, its unreality is revealed on
   the path of liberation:
If you realize this point, you will become a buddha in
   one lifetime!
Samaya!

The envisioned Karma Pakshi proceeded to give further instructions to Mingyur Dorjé. Later, the treasure revealer found within
a boulder a scroll of instructions on the practice.[185] The eventual
Karma Pakshi guru yoga, as included in Jamgön Kongtrul's Precious
Terma Treasury collection (nineteenth century), has become known
worldwide among Kagyü practitioners. Since the Sixteenth Karmapa's first missionary tour to Europe and North America (1974–1975),
Karma Kamtsang hierarchs and lamas have strongly advocated the
seventeenth-century sādhana as a principal guru yoga practice for
those who have received the initiation and instructions.[186]

   A modern sādhana including Karma Pakshi as an important
figure of meditation was developed in 1968 by Chögyam Trungpa
(1939–1987) while he was at the Tiger Nest Cave—sacred to Padmasambhava and the Dorjé Trolö practice—in Bhutan. Trungpa
translated the sādhana into English, in collaboration with his traveling companion, the actor Richard Arthure (1940–2018), while they
were still in Bhutan. By the end of the year it was being practiced in
English at the Samyé Ling Tibetan Centre in Scotland. The sādhana
has become known as *The Sādhana of Mahāmudrā*, although the
earliest translation has it as *The Sādhana of the Embodiment of All the
Siddhas*. The Tibetan title, in translation, could be seen more fully
as *Mahāmudrā Ritual That Reverses the Outer, Inner, and Secret Hea-
thens' Mighty Warfare, and Actually Accomplishes the Truth Lineage of the
Ocean of Siddhas*.[187] A 1979 published transcript of two of Trungpa's
oral teachings (both given in 1975) on the creation of the sādhana
gives some detail of his intentions in writing the sādhana.[188] He

was hoping to develop a unity between the Nyingma and Kagyü traditions in his presentation of the dharma to Western students, hence the presence of both Padmasambhava and Karma Pakshi in the visualizations of the practice.

An Early Rimé Influence

Trungpa states in passing, in his oral teaching mentioned above, when discussing Jamgön Kongtrul Lodrö Tayé (1813–1899) and the nineteenth-century Rimé ecumenical movement in East Tibet, that "the initial inspiration for the Rimé school came from Karma Pakshi."[189] Such acknowledgment of Karma Pakshi's influence on ecumenical impulses could be said to go back further in time. In the seventeenth century, before the Rimé movement, the prolific Karma Chakmé (1613–1678) had written in his retreat guide, *Mountain Dharma*, that Karma Pakshi's intention was the unification of both the "new" (Sarma) and "old" (Nyingma) tantra traditions, and his ultimate intention was to unify Dzogchen and Mahāmudrā.[190]

Karma Pakshi had been educated at the important Nyingma monastery at Katok, some seventy years after it had been founded. As recounted earlier, he had a particular connection with the Red Chenrezik and Mahākāla Bernakchen practices, both of which had Nyingma origins, and the two practices subsequently became important to the Kagyü tradition. In his writings, Karma Pakshi would quote or refer as often to Nyingma tantras as he did to Sarma tantras. In his biography, he makes the point that "The Great Perfection (Dzogchen) and the Great Seal (Mahāmudrā) have different names, but their meaning is in essence the same."[191] One can see why later writers came to see him as an early figurehead for an ecumenical movement.

However, Karma Pakshi's writings do not seem to have been as widely read and quoted as one might expect from his prominence as an iconic figure for the Karmapa lineage.[192] Historical writings that recount his life story—in particular those by Pawo Tsuklak Trengwa and Situ Panchen—have used passages long and short from Karma Pakshi's memoirs for their biographical accounts of him. But it would not be reasonable to say that his other writings were hugely influential to later writers. Rather, the most notable aspect of Karma Pakshi's legacy is that he is credited as a figurehead for the catenate reincarnation tradition for Tibetan ecclesiastics. The full institutionalization of the nascent tradition took some further lifetimes to fully develop, yet, once it had developed, the meme of reincarnate ecclesiastics spread far and wide, despite the limitations of communication and travel of the times. It is a tradition that has continued for eight centuries in Tibet and now survives—under the Chinese Communist regime, among the Tibetan diaspora, and among converts worldwide.

Writings

CHAPTER 8

Preincarnations

_____

IT IS A commonly heard remark that Karma Pakshi is well known
for being a "first reincarnation" in the Tibetan Buddhist tradition.
However, the epithet is problematic, even though it serves as a
pointer for general use. As a youth, Karma Pakshi was told he had
a close connection to Düsum Khyenpa, a saintly character of the
twelfth century. Karma Pakshi himself became known as Karmapa,
a title posthumously extended to his predecessor, and thus the
eight-hundred-year lineage of the Karmapa reincarnations began
its development.[193] Karma Pakshi did not refer to Düsum Khyenpa
as Karmapa, yet he referred to himself as Karmapa (Karmāpa) in
his memoirs about fifty times.[194] The epithet "first reincarnation"
is a woolly way of describing his place in history, because of course
in Buddhist terms every human and every creature is considered
to be a "reincarnation," or perhaps better described as a "rebirth."
Indeed, to be more precise, as one of the earliest acknowledged
specified reincarnations of a well-known teacher, Karma Pakshi
was also not the first—the meme had begun in Tibet in the previous
century.[195]

Nevertheless the epithet of "first reincarnation," or "first tulku,"
does serve a purpose in indicating that the extant Karmapa lineage
has very early beginnings in the history of Tibetan tulkus or "living
buddhas." However, there is a tendency to see the incarnation lineage as a thread of saintly lives proceeding in a discreet, singular
fashion. The imagery often used is that of the beads on a rosary—

life after life, along one thread. In fact, both Düsum Khyenpa and
Karma Pakshi, and their successor the Third Karmapa, Rangjung
Dorjé, wrote of earlier lives—preincarnations—that were almost all
different for each of these three earliest Karmapas. Also, they each
referred to (or were reported to refer to) co-incarnations, that is,
"emanations" living at the same period as themselves. In terms of
the future incarnations, each of the first three Karmapas referred to
subsequent incarnations that would not necessarily be Karmapas.
The multiplicity of such "ancillary incarnations" subsided in the
writings of most of the other Karmapas from the fourth (Rolpé
Dorjé, fourteenth century) onward, until in modern times the Fifteenth and Sixteenth Karmapas of the twentieth century wrote of
having several preincarnations who were not Karmapas.

Karma Pakshi, in his memoirs, in three passages in verse and
prose, writes of incarnations in general, and of specific incarnations
of both Düsum Khyenpa and himself, with some elaboration about
his thinking on the subject of reincarnation. These three passages
are presented below.

———

From the memoir section entitled *An Enlightening Account of My
Inconceivable Omens and Miracles*:[196]

In unlimited pure lands in all space,
The Buddha with his bodhisattvas, transcendent victors,
Have caused a continual rainfall
Of innumerable nirmāṇakāya emanations—
Perfected displays of miraculous bodies
In their palaces in innumerable pure lands:
In accord with however trainees have appeared,
The teacher to train them does come.

In this actual mundane world,
Due to the totally perfect intentions
Of the 1002 buddhas,
Düsum Khyenpa Siṃhanāda—
Knower of the Three Times, Lion's Roar—
Will emerge with hundreds of millions
Along the tracks of Protector Maitreya's teaching,
With the name Siṃhanāda.[197]

Therefore, leading as a guide the six types of beings on the
     path,
The teaching will remain for a long time;
And, in the especially sublime pure land,
The spontaneous great palace itself
With the tree of supreme enlightenment,
Is a source from which all that is needed and wanted will come.
It is centrally adorned by a lotus
And the seven main jewels and the secondary seven attributes.

The cakravartin Buddha and his bodhisattvas
With Brahma, Indra, and the lokapāla protectors,
Are on a bejeweled throne of pure perception;
Buddhas and bodhisattvas float like clouds,
Endowed with fivefold wisdoms, their supreme speech,
Inexhaustible, an ornamented cycle of teaching,
Causes a rain of so much holy dharma to fall
In however many languages there are for the six types of
     beings.

The Buddha's three teachings, in four cycles,
Are teachings that exist for a long time

So sentient beings are established on the enlightenment path.
The banner of dharma present in this world,
Düsum Khyenpa, a tenth-level son of the Lord Buddha,
Has arrived, indistinguishable from the perfect Buddha
    Siṃhanāda
Because of his singular essence of the three kāyas:
I revere the one who is omniscient.

In previous generations gone by,
On the large western island of Tantraba,
There had been one called King Tobchen Gyelpo.
He had unbelievable strength
And had subdued a vast area;
The king's son was Yiong Tongna Gawa.
Düsum Khyenpa became his best teacher,
Called Gelong Lekparkur
Endowed with the six clairvoyances.
The king and his sons
Brought all in the kingdom to happiness;
The king and his sons, nurtured by dharma,
All went to Sukhāvatī.

The manifestation of Düsum Khyenpa,
Born in a sensate and living body,
Performed immeasurable benefit for beings—
A nirmāṇakāya master yogin.

At the eastern pure land Conch Mountain,
As he was practicing yogic disciplines and maturing,
Demonstrating naturalness in the midst of the snow
    mountains
And recognized by profound signs,

A yogin of spacious bliss—
After the six kingdoms had been blessed,
Infidels were put in a citadel of virtue.

Gaining control over mind and breath,
Düsum Khyenpa is manifest once again:
Now in this very world,
Blessed by the paṇḍita Nāropa
And preserving the holy history of Düsum Khyenpa,
The yogin Rangjung Dorjé [Karma Pakshi],
With yogin discipline, enacts the benefit of beings.

The seat of vajra immutability, Vajrāsana, is in this world
In which the teaching of Śākyamuni is deteriorating.
Sentient beings are difficult to tame
When they behave in multiple wrong ways.
With golden activity
Manifest from Heruka's effulgence,
Came a king with worldly charisma.

After having demonstrated about the ways of destruction and
     killing,
Manifesting like a miraculous illusion
In one instant, when he showed the way of healing,
He was second in the lineage of miraculous victors,
As though manifested from a deity.

As for the king with his contemporary ministers,
In this divine realm descended from deities;
In the first of early times,
Through the blessing of the buddhas
And the connection of karma from previous practice,

After the secret Vajrayāna yogin
Had been born in this world,
The king with his ministers and entourage
Would be trained over many lifetimes.

Even just seeing or hearing of him
Is like a child meeting its father and mother.
In this northern snowy region,
In the seven holy places of Lhodrak,
A man called Dharma Siddhi,
Through purifying his being through study, reflection, and
    meditation,
Has demonstrated the way to attain a certain degree of
    siddhi.
His activity is accomplished by ḍākas and ḍākinīs;
His fame is spread by the gods above.

The passage continues with Karma Pakshi's fame coming to the notice of "Prince Gobla" (Kubilai Khan), and then the subsequent trip to the Mongolian courts.

————

Secondly, in the second part of his testament, referred to as *The Testament Liberation Account of the Karmāpa*, Karma Pakshi discusses the two testaments left by his teacher Pomdrakpa, and he continues to express the idea that his reincarnations have manifest in response to the conditions of the times:[198]

————

I managed to fulfill the intention of all the Kagyü lamas and precious Pomdrakpa. Look at the scroll text kept at the capital seat of the Kagyü [Tsurpu], and it will become impartially clear. It says,

"Henceforth you ought to practice according to the Buddhist teaching, and you must practice universal activities in the future. If you have not accomplished and not perfected the trio of deeds, spiritual activity, and teaching in the three times, how will you fully accomplish Mahāyāna deeds and spiritual activity?"

Therefore, beforehand, when the first Indrabodhi, foremost of the Kali Yuga era, miraculously radiated light rays in the world—at the time when the yogin Namkha Ö was manifest—the *mantradhārin* Rangjung Dorjé realized the oneness of the natural state and was the first engaged in the breath control of life-force energy (*prāṇāyāma*).[199] Look at the discussion in the liberation account biography and it will be clear.

Thus, in accord with the perceptions of trainee sentient beings, my manifold different births and deaths have happened, and I have shown the necessity of proceeding in various guises not under my own influence but through the influence of others. In accord with the statement that "One is born due to the conditions of all phenomena," although there is no alteration for the unchanging natural state, my various characteristics go forth according to the many conditions.

———

Thirdly, in the main, longer part of the memoir collection, titled *My Biography: A Dissertation on Realizing the Unity of All Time and Timelessness and on Perfecting Great Potentiality*, the author goes into some detail on his thoughts about reincarnation:[200]

———

Therefore, for the one with the renowned name Karmāpa, even though there is an example of one sesame seed settling anywhere in the storehouse, I am not myself reflexively aware and have been uninterruptedly confused in the three lower realms and three higher realms of clinging to the self.[201] It seems just now that I understand slightly the ways of limitless samsara, and even if I explain often that "I was this person, born in this place," who would understand, and who would believe me?

From the beginningless past, influenced by ignorance, even the renowned Karmāpa has followed bad teachers and been incorrectly taught the view, meditation, and action in terms of the various tenets of the heretics. From life to life, I have taken birth as various physical and nonphysical beings in the citadels of the six classes of beings. I have been born in Cha,[202] Indra, and Viṣṇu groups and have been born with good, middling, and lesser capabilities for being good. I do remember the untold actions done. There have been immeasurable, innumerable explanations of being this person and being born in this place, doing this good or bad action. Because there is no witness, who would believe them, and who would consider them valid?[203]

Even for the renowned Karmāpa in the beginningless previous past, the tenets of Buddhism have changed his mind. Under the influence of confused ignorance, I followed the teachers of the three baskets relating to provisional truth. I have endlessly studied, reflected, and meditated, for innumerable, limitless eons in various ascetic trials and hardships: elimination and acquisition, ceasing and accomplishing, protecting and binding, getting rid of and taking, and faith and focus. I gained birth in high, middling, and lesser heavens and as such great worldly people as the brahmin and cakravartin kings. Although I experienced tainted happiness, I remember some particularities and understand them. There is not enough time to explain the various details about "from here, I was born there, and I died there."

However, even if I had spoken, trainees confused by ignorance would not understand the truth, and they would be consumed by doubts and would exaggerate or denigrate. It is like when a person

who cannot speak has a dream, although their mind knows about
it, they cannot tell others about it, and they will not be understood.
Over unquantifiable, beginningless time, for a long time even the
renowned Karmāpa was stalled in terms of the fulsome meaning
of the four meditative stabilities of the Śrāvaka Vehicle. Despite
my uninterrupted meditative absorption on the sixteen instances
of non-referential wisdom, I have not gained the fourfold fruits of
the *śramaṇa* practice of virtue and have strayed toward the divini-
ties of the form realm. Attached to the deep meditation of the four
meditative stabilities, I have been born in finer, middling, or lesser
existences of the seventeen classes in the form realm. Having lived
therein for a long time, I do know several of the existences. Because
I have spoken about and explained to people about the future they
have not yet experienced, they do not understand it with any real
confidence—hordes of confused people have become dizzy about it!

Indeed I, the renowned Karmāpa, influenced by confused ignorance for uncountable previous eons, have been absorbed in the
last stage of the nine stages of samādhi and have been attached to
the four subtle attentions. Because of my fear and anxiety about
being separated from them, I have not realized the wish-fulfilling
"one and a half" nonself state of a *pratyekabuddha*, a level of true
bliss. Having strayed into the fourfold limits of perception of the
formless realms, I was born with the name Tseringpö Lha (Long-
Lived Deity). I lived and wandered everywhere, my mental body
living as a wandering mendicant. I know I do remember several
wanderings. I was born as a formless god: lacking any powerful
experience, although I spoke of and explained a historical account
of the fourfold limits of perception of the formless realm, why would
anyone have faith in it, however much they understood? If they
were buddhas who spontaneously accomplished the three kāyas,
then they would see and understand everything. Below the peak
of existence, despite there not being anywhere not pervaded by a

greater, lesser, or middling extent of ignorance, visionary experiences of the form realm (*rūpakāya*) based on minimal ignorance cause one to think that one has seen a vision. However, one's own mind is unchanging, and whatever happens is an understanding of the dharmakāya.

Lord Indrabodhi and Tilopa—essentially indistinguishable but assigned two names—blessed and gave instruction to Nāropa, Riripa, and Kasoripa.[204] Even though immeasurable buddhas have come and stayed, the meaning of what they have said has not been able to cure the six types of beings stupefied by blind ignorance. It is like this: not aware of the fundamental basis of consciousness and influenced by black-and-white mental factors, sentient beings are fundamentally confused about the varieties of virtuous and unvirtuous conditions. Their accumulation of virtue causes them to take birth in the three upper realms, and the influence of ignorance makes them behave in unvirtuous ways and achieve birth in the three lower realms. Because of the endless suffering, buddhas come and spread throughout the three realms. They remain and are seen by sentient beings, who then are liberated from suffering. The unchanging realization of the wisdom that is self-aware of one's own ignorance permeates all sentient beings.

Even the renowned Karmāpa hitherto is not self-aware of the all-pervasive, fundamental basis of consciousness. My virtue and nonvirtue both have influenced my situation, and from the peak of existence down to the worst of hell realms I have been confused and existing in samsara. I experience non-realization, erroneous realization, and partial realization in an uninterrupted stream. I have erred in the twenty-one views of ego clinging, and as an ignorant person wandering the realm of dharma, I have created each condition for each of the twelve interdependent links. I am not liberated from the three realms, yet in the immeasurable, beginningless confusion of samsara, I now understand slightly and seem to be aware. I calculate that "from here I was born here, and from here I transmigrated there," and it is difficult.

In times gone by, at the end of the last eon (*kṛta yuga*) and in the first period of the present eon (*kali yuga*), the king of Śākya was respected by all. In a time prior to him being a king, glorious Vajradhāra and Indrabodhi, undifferentiable, had disseminated in the human realm the secret mantra Vajrayāna, and because immediately the unrealized persons of the best ability in self-aware wisdom had immediately trained themselves in the lower six vehicles, he understood that the time had come for realization and knowledge. When light rays of saṃbhogakāya and nirmāṇakāya had spread out, pervading and blessing the world, at this time of the beginnings of first conflict in the world, there was a yogin called Namkha Ö Yeshé Dripa Mépa, whose outstanding abilities shone and were visible yet intangible, like a rainbow in the sky or like a light above. It was like drinking rainbow water in summer, impermanent and unstable. The most gifted people saw this and applied a variety of names to it, such as Dharmakāya or Original Indrabodhi. Whoever saw or felt the lights realized the wisdom self-aware of one's own ignorance. For those of lesser and medium abilities, the emanation of the Buddha taught the Tripiṭaka dharma. In Rājagṛiha, Piṇḍola Bhāradvāja and Vrājaka saw this.

At that time, the renowned Karmāpa saw the Śākya family, in whose presence he behaved pleasantly. I recall in my own mind the indescribable echo of the sound of "Namkha Ö Yeshé Ying." When I think about that recollection, it is like showing oneself in a mirror. For the realm of the unchanging nature of one's mind—the five characteristics of its essential nature—once one's previous ignorance becomes self-aware, the mind knows the essential nature, the five wisdoms, like a reflection appearing in a mirror, once the nondual mind realizes connascent wisdom. Up until that point, the unlimited spaciousness of the secret mantra Vajrayāna, in particular the

Mahāmudrātilaka secret mantra title and so forth—all the terminology of inseparable means and knowledge—are assigned the conventional designation "yoga of light." Just by recalling that, like lifting a lamp in darkness, the inherent integrity of all the dharma in the completely stainless tantras, prophecies, and intentions of indistinguishable Vajradhāra and Samantabhadra is borne in mind and one understands the view that first realizes autonomously the wisdom that is self-aware of one's own ignorance. That is a time to understand being self-aware of ignorance and to demarcate the levels.

Therefore, after the secret mantra Vajrayāna first arrived in the human realm and blessed it, several fortunate people, independent of cause and conditions or cause and result, were autonomously aware of the wisdom that is self-aware of one's own ignorance, and confusion dawned as wisdom. The immaculate Dharmakāya Rangjung Dorjé—without obscuration and according to my understanding and recollection—was named as the first Indrabodhi. He had a human body and was not surrounded by an entourage of queen and sons. Although he was assigned the various names Vajradhāra and Samantabhadra by the fortunate ones, from the *Samantabhadra and Vajradhāra Tantra*:

> The teaching of the dharmakāya is recognized in its own
> place.

So, since the immaculate Dharmakāya Rangjung Dorjé was aware of and realized that, he now understands the way it is; he has accomplished it in reality and in name. Although he is not primordially the first, middle, or latter Indrabodhi-Vajradhāra, trainees of various capabilities exaggerate the various different ways of seeing him.

The yogin Rangjung Dorjé remembers the first aspect of realizing the wisdom that is self-aware of one's ignorance of the fundamental consciousness. From then on, even though trainees with various connections—through good karma and prayer and through various previous connections with the six types of beings living in their environments—show many ways of being born, living, and dying throughout the three realms, with my mindfulness there are no causes and conditions for the occurrence of manifesting birth, living, and death. I had not engaged with the helplessly confused ignorance about the lives and deaths of sentient beings. At present I seem to remember slightly and understand. At the time of Vajradhāra and of the four kāyas that magically make emanations, according to Vajradhāra's prophetic intuition, the yogin emanation of Vajradhāra himself was given the name "middle Indrabodhi." Although he lived in accordance with the guise of a saṃbhogakāya Jina with a queen and sons surrounded by a palace and the spontaneous five aspects of pleasure, his trainees of differing capabilities perceived him in various guises and occupations, in agreement with the tantras, text transmission, and instructions of the teaching of the five teachers.

At that time, in that period, after the mantradhārin Rangjung Dorjé had somewhat perfected the skill in the realization and conduct of the four kāyas that are neither melded nor separated, through merely realizing the sameness of one flavor of the multiplicity of all phenomena, without separating this and that, I remember that I had become the manifestation of the saṃbhogakāya Indrabodhi with *vidyādhara* entourage.

Then, in that period, worthy recipients were present who had not had the actual and the symbolic tantra texts, transmissions, and instructions of the spontaneous teaching of the five families [of buddhas]. The spontaneously natural teaching of the dharmakāya *Anuttarayoga* was transmitted to them like a miraculous echo: once it was apparently set down in writing, it was blessed in the natural location of self-arisen Orgyen and was hidden. Because it seemed to stay there, I say that the secret mantra practice was somewhat of a mirage that was not understood in the human realm, and that is the first possible explanation. Out of the three Orgyens that there are, the naturally arising dharmakāya is the Orgyen of the first Indrabodhi; then there is a representation, the moderately blissful saṃbhogakāya, the Orgyen of the intermediate Indrabodhi; and the location of the nirmāṇakāya—material things, vegetation, trees, groves, and sentient beings—is the Orgyen of the period of Śākyamuni. Out of the three Indrabodhis, I am named as the last Indrabodhi.

The manifested male and female vidyādhara siddhas foretold my realization of Samantabhadra-Vajradhāra. The actuality of the secret mantras had been set down in written letters, was taught throughout the world, and appeared naturally everywhere. Nowadays the mantradhārin Rangjung Dorjé has revealed as much as he knows and has realized, and the benefits are that unrealized sentient beings are universally blessed by his introduction teaching, so they have no doubts and do not vacillate.

Thus previous nirmāṇakāya buddhas manifested, their "seven generations." A future time will come and, in general, 1,002 buddhas will last for the length of time known by those who know the past, present, and future. When the buddhas are actually present, they teach the Three Collections (Tripiṭaka) and parts of the three outer tantras. After a complete escape from suffering (parinirvāṇa)—speaking of following prophecies from the three scriptures—the manifestation of undifferentiated Vajradhāra-Indrabodhi has come as illimitable numbers of vidyādhara siddhas. Their inconceivable and infinite actions instantaneously mature and liberate the better, middling and lesser trainees. Likewise, nowadays because the mantradhārin Rangjung Dorjé has understood, however slightly, the spaciousness of realizing the sameness of the one flavor of multiplicity, and because that appears to have become manifest, that is the purpose of teaching completely frankly all those points.

The point of calling it "secret mantra" is that one should not look at cause and condition or cause and result. Regarding composite phenomena, when the unconditioned Buddha unexpectedly and momentarily extended and flexed his arm, all the trainees were each individually introduced to the wisdom that is self-aware of one's own ignorance of the fundamental basic consciousness, and they were blessed. Then for each one confused within the range of experience of self-aware wisdom, wisdom arose; if they could realize the introduction, they knew both the sound and meaning of "secret mantra" and were called "great meditators"—indeed, they are allotted many names. Was it due to that point that previously Rangjung Dorjé remembered the appearance of the past yogin Namkha Ö Yeshé Ying? Until I was given the name Indrabodhi I was only slightly knowledgeable; after that my realization of the self-aware wisdom was continual. From the start up until now, cause and condition and cause and result have not existed, and in the future there will be no hindrance in all tenets, like a sun shining in a cloudless sky. I seem to remember without the slightest haziness being introduced to the unity of nondual self and other, and being blessed.

Thus, in the first era when there was conflict, up until the king who was honored by all the Śākya family, there were 990,000 kings of the Śākya family who were like patrons. After the seven buddhas— the victors with their bodhisattvas—had thought to train the middling and lesser trainees of Vajradhāra, innumerable miraculous manifestations of the seven Buddha teachers, suitable for the era, established in the heavens the trainees with whom they had a connection. At such a time, the bodhisattva Rangjung Dorjé acted to perfect his intention to achieve their teachings at the feet of the seven nirmāṇakāyas, and he established many beings in the higher realms. Those with the best faculties seemed to have a ḍākinī's wish-fulling jewel on their heads. Blessed by the lama, yidam, and ḍākinīs, and by means of the information in the "introduction to the four kāyas" that introduced them to the wisdom that is self-aware of their own ignorance, the unstained dharmakāya benefited sentient beings.

Nowadays, the renowned Karmāpa remembers and speaks about many particulars, without a shadow of a doubt and free of exaggeration. Why speak of them so much? As the nirmāṇakāya Śākyamuni was indeed a manifestation of Vajradhāra, the scriptural teaching of his thoughts is from the root tantra *Mahāmudrātilaka*.[205] King Śuddhodana is Hevajra, an emanation of Vajradhāra; the beautiful goddess mother has been pronounced to be an emanation of a female buddha, Varaprasāda; the son Prince Siddhārtha, Yaśodharā, and so forth are the royal entourage. Vajradhāra male-female consorts, with hosts of ḍākas and ḍākinīs, manifested instantaneously as the king and his entourage. Once the middling and lesser trainees had been established in the three vehicles of teachings, the emanations were validly prophesied to be Indrabodhi and his entourage, in tantras about the body, speech, and mind of a buddha such as the *Rigi ā ra li'i Tantra Rāja*.[206] Therefore, since all doubt has been eliminated about the indivisible three kāyas, after Śākyamuni's *parinirvāṇa* (complete passing beyond suffering), the oral instruction was given according to the endless categorizations for both new and old secret-mantra Vajrayāna, and there was blessing. Thus, in the *Blazing Meteorite of the Fierce Ones Tantra*:

> Hūṃ, in the totally pure mandala
> Stand wrathful buddhas in the ten directions—
> For wrathful training, there are ten fierce ones;
> For the lesser vehicle, the eight supreme ones;
> For peaceful training, there are eight bodhisattvas.
> For achievement in this life,
> There are said to be eight yogins.
> Hūṃ—the basis of unchanging good fortune
> Is to abide in Hūṃ.

Out of ignorance and not realizing the dharma factors of the fundamental source, the six classes of beings are deluded. The five characteristics of the natural, essential, spatial basis of the unchanging innate state exist inherently in HŪṂ. Although there are many such terms as "purified" and "realized," other than knowing solely the stainless dharmakāya, everything arises as the projections of trainees. In order for the lower vehicle *śrāvaka*s to experience the Mahāyāna, the eight great śrāvakas appear. For the appearances of the broad-minded Mahāyāna practitioners, the eight "close son" bodhisattvas manifest and show the gradual completion of the ten levels and five paths. For the sake of taming and liberating fierce and harmful trainees, the hordes of herukas and the ten fierce ones manifest to demonstrate the manner of taming and liberating harmful beings. The essential information of the peerless secret mantra Vajrayāna instantaneously manifests the eight great siddhas in the form of Vajradhāra. Due to teaching for a few months and years the way to achieve siddhi accomplishment, he is able to demonstrate to trainees the various actual signs of accomplishment on a par with the infinite peaceful and wrathful deities. Not only his emanations, but also the emanations no different from the Vajradhāra-Indrabodhi master of the fourteenth level, are uninterrupted at all times and inconceivable. Nowadays the bodhisattva Rangjung Dorjé knows slightly the tantra transmission and is remembering this. Even though I have explained a lot about "It is such and such," not everyone understands or has rid themselves of doubt.

In a previous age, the tenth-level middle Indrabodhi blessed the secret mantra accomplishment teaching of Samantabhadra—the eight-transmissions tradition up to the Anuyoga—as magically manifest words. From the pure vision of King Ja, teaching came like falling rain on Mount Malaya and Śrī Laṅkā. Also at that time, the mantradhārin Rangjung Dorjé had become the grandson of King Ja, named Vajra Śrī. He knew the terminologies up to the Anuyoga transmission and understood them. Although nowadays I speak about people of yesteryear who knew and taught those concepts, as though at nighttime speaking of earlier waking up, it is more like remembering everything immediately on waking up. Because the words and meaning of the ancient secret mantra had been realized and validated, I made a completely perfect analysis of each of the tantra transmissions and instructions and did not mix them up.

In a time gone by, I seemed to be in the lineage of the thirty-seven groups of deities and to be living at the top of an excellent royal palace in the form of Ānandagarbha, a disciple-son of the ema-nated deity Vajrasattva. I understood the full completion (*dzogchen*) infinite space of the primordial wisdom self-aware of the ignorance about all phenomena of samsara and nirvana. When nothing at all was "incomplete," I seemed to have come, as a true emanation of Samantabhadra, to the kingdom of King Prahati, into the mind of his daughter, as a nun. Being inseparable from the divine son Ānandagarbha, she blessed the human realm with her incredible understanding of the Dzogchen tantras such as the *Great Perfection Infinite Space Tantra*.[207]

When the best, middling, and lesser trainees were aware, and when they had perfected and realized that they were buddhas from the very beginning, the Dharmakāya Rangjung Drimé Dorjé had become Toktse Neljor Wangchuk, who understood and was knowl-edgeable about the words and meaning of the Dzogchen infinite *dharmadhātu*. Nowadays, even those who have no experience and no realization have engaged with the tenets for those without beliefs. Some have pure aspirations, some accomplish spontaneously, and some aspire to the four spontaneous accomplishments. The four spontaneous accomplishments stray into four views of clinging to an ego. For those seeking primordial purity—the pure *kriyāyoga* is space—if they analyze each word, with its meaning, of the infinite dharmadhātu Dzogchen, they recognize everywhere the dharmadhātu infinite wisdom, self-aware of ignorance, within the insuperability (*akaniṣṭha*) of the truly intrinsic self-arising wisdom. Being blessed, because I had completed the imperfect and the perfect limitless ocean of teaching without being taught, I was assigned the epithet Dharmakāya Svayambhū Vajra (Dharmakāya Rangjung Dorjé).

Furthermore, in an earlier period of the past, the middle Indrabodhi had written down in letters the prophetic thoughts of Śrī Vajradhāra and the *Means and Knowledge Tantra* and the *Nondual Means and Knowledge Tantra*—including their transmission, esoteric advice, and new mantras—as though they were a magical manifestation. He developed the self-manifesting Gandhola Temple of Orgyen.[208] Those entrusted with the direct instructions of the ḍākinīs, the eight *mahāsiddha*s of the four lineages—such as Lavapā,[209] Nāgārjuna, and Tilopa—thought that the time had come to mature and liberate the trainees with eight forms of esoteric wisdom: an unlimited ocean of wisdom, the conjoined skills and understanding precepts of the intentions of Vajradhāra. They welcomed the tantras, and the practitioners who studied them achieved, uninterrupted, the supreme and ordinary siddhis.

The mantradhārin Rangjung Dorjé, blessed by the yogin Namkha Ö Yeshé, understands the meaning of the fundamental intentions of Vajradhāra. Remembering that now, in analyzing the esoteric treasuries of the Sarma ("new") secret mantras according to their connections in terms of meaning, they are as similar as the times of "daybreak" and "dawn." Through the cycle of the dharmatā four vital points of the "introduction to the four kāyas," I as an ignorant trainee recognized instantaneously the wisdom that is self-aware of my own ignorance, and I was blessed. So, I was assigned the epithet Great Meditator Rangjung Dorjé, although no one spoke about it, nor was it made public.

Thus, later on, because Düsum Khyenpa had been blessed with

the self-arising wisdom of the Indrabodhi emanation, for however
many trainees there were, incredible miraculous manifestations
were visible like reflections in a mirror. Being quintessentially the
same as the Great Brahmin Saraha, he wore, wherever it had not
yet appeared in the world, his shiny black hat emblazoned with
gold, as a symbol of the immutable dharmatā—it was marked with
various symbols of the connascent wisdom of mahāmudrā. From a
song of the renowned Karmāpa,

> The lama is the Great Brahmin;
> His oral instructions are the mahāmudrā.

Furthermore, thinking about the import of that, the Great Perfection (*mahāsandhi*) and the Great Symbol (*mahāmudrā*) are two
terms that have different names yet are quintessentially one. When
one has realized the meaning of the infinite dharmadhātu, then
"completion" and "non-completion" are not boundaries.

Therefore, after the renowned Karmāpa had attained realization of the great transmission of the infinite scriptures, he then
perfected and analyzed each subject without mixing up with
non-understanding, wrong understanding, or bias. After he had
discussed with the ḍākas, ḍākinīs, bodhisattvas, śrāvakas, pratyekabuddhas, and so forth the "limitless ocean of teaching" in accordance with the intentions of the buddhas, then he was in harmony
with all the tenets. He knew and realized that within himself was
the Buddha of the five kāyas.

In times gone by, in the presence of the seven nirmāṇakāya
buddhas, the monk Rangjung Dorjé arranged in three baskets the
twelve branches of the sutras. His actions in totally adhering to
and maintaining the terminology in the lower six vehicles were in
accord with the examples where he remembered the explanation
and analyzed each individually in keeping with the written works

of the six vehicles. He recognized the wisdom that is self-aware
of ignorance: this is the limitless scriptures of the nirmāṇakāya,
concise and collected.

In the past, in Orgyen in the West, when a minor Buddhist king,
Balavat (The Powerful One) ruled, one aspect of Lord Düsum
Khyenpa's emanations appeared as an accomplished practicing
yogin named Abhayakīrti,[210] who was able to demonstrate any miracle. Farther south, over many lifetimes a king had been involved
with beliefs from wrong views and was surrounded by killers. He
wanted to be reborn among his relatives, so he developed a wrong
attitude. He killed sentient beings such as the followers of Maheś-
vara and was continually making offerings of meat and blood. He
made the wish, "May I gain control over the lives of everyone." He
became a charismatic king who said he was delighted to kill *tīrthika*
infidels. While this king was disrupting everything and killing people, an emanation of Düsum Khyenpa, Abhayakīrti, was reborn as
an elephant among a herd of five hundred—one that could compete
for stability on the ground with the elephant of the exalted deity
Indra. The malevolent king was pleased with this elephant and
put on top of him a large throne adorned with cotton and a variety of material, so on many occasions he rode around the palace,
surrounded by his beloved son, queen, concubine, and soldiers
wherever they went on the grounds. They then went to destroy King
Balavat. When they got close to the place where the latter king was
with his ministers, the elephant rolled over, everyone hit the ground,
and the elephants charged. The malevolent king and his entourage
were trampled, and all the grief-stricken soldiers returned to their
own country. Once King Balavat and his entourage understood
that the elephant was an emanation, he welcomed it and gave great
gifts. The large elephant vanished without a trace; when the king
and his court were especially convinced that it was an emanation of
Abhayakīrti, they were transported to the liberated heavenly realms.

The malevolent king was born in a remote area, and because he had experienced Abhayakīrti's extraordinary compassion, he had faith in the religious artifacts of both Buddhists and non-Buddhists and sponsored them. Due to his vast accumulations of ignorance, in a later life he was reborn as someone called Kampo Dza, in a Bön family named Regé Kya. This was because of his previous bad karmic traits. Once he had become a Buddhist monk, he had powers of great virtue, and later, when Lord Düsum Khyenpa was living at Nenang, he gave away all his wealth as a completion of a great accumulation of merit. In a subsequent life, he was born as a king of the Soten, in the borderlands between Sogdia and Kashmir, who had faith in the tenets of both Buddhists and non-Buddhists, did no harm to sentient beings, and acted in highly virtuous ways toward both Buddhists and the tīrthika infidels.

Thus far, written and oral accounts of Lord Düsum Khyenpa and the renowned Karmāpa, undifferentiable in the past, have been collected together. Future trainees connected to them—knowing and understanding the accounts without exaggeration, diminishment, omission, or duplication—should gain realization. A biography of Lord Düsum Khyenpa states in three instances that in future he would "be born among the seven practice places of Lhodrak, for the benefit of one trainee"; that "after recognizing the Yangtze River, one individual will fulfill my intentions"; and that he "should not guide on the path his benefactor Gönpawa for two or three rebirths." Thereafter, for the sake of perfectly accomplishing three such intentions of the Lord Düsum Khyenpa, nowadays the renowned Karmāpa, remembering and being mindful of them, has been born to a noble family of Ü in the dharma-wealthy area of Drilung [a valley of the Yangtze].

CHAPTER 9

Meditations

IN SEVERAL INSTANCES in his memoirs, Karma Pakshi refers emphatically to a teaching on a meditation practice that seems to have been his main interest during his preaching itineraries, the journeys from Central Tibet to Karakorum to Almaliq to Xanadu and back to Tsurpu, lasting more than fifteen years. At times he calls the meditation practice and doctrine "introduction to the three kāyas," but he mostly writes about the subject in terms of "four kāyas," and very occasionally in terms of "five kāyas." Successor Karmapas who wrote on the subject tended to keep to the three kāyas topos—in particular the Third Karmapa Rangjung Dorjé, the Eighth Karmapa Mikyö Dorjé, and the Fourteenth Karmapa Tekchok Dorjé—but Karma Pakshi himself usually referred to four kāyas. It could be said to be his favorite proselytization topic.

As can be seen from the six translation extracts in this chapter, Karma Pakshi largely writes on the subject in theoretical terms. His successor, the Third Karmapa, wrote a short treatise on the subject (about twenty pages) in more practical terms. He presented it as a meditation practice, with preliminaries, the main body of the practice, and an additional physical exercise.[211] The Third Karmapa had received teaching on this subject from Karma Pakshi's close disciple Lama Nyenré Gendün Bum.

The first passage given below, on the subject of introduction to the kāyas, is a segment found toward the conclusion of Karma Pakshi's "First Testament."[212]

An ignorant mind is the disposition of the "vajra family." Thus, a body produced by it has the disposition of the vajra family, the vital essence has the disposition of the vajra family, the subtle channels have the disposition of the vajra family, and the subtle winds have the disposition of the vajra family. Are these five not widespread and existent in all ignorant sentient beings? Because there is nowhere that this does not happen, due to the perpetual cultivation and use of these five, beings have attained accomplishment of the cycle of delusional ignorance. Sentient beings have achieved this perpetually in the three realms. The mark of this is that the continuously returning cycle has arisen.

With inseparable skill and knowledge, from undifferentiable Samantabhadra and "sixth Buddha" Vajradhāra down to the yogin Rangjung Dorjé, in terms of the "introduction to the four kāyas" all phenomena of samsara and nirvana are neither staying nor spreading nor finished—they do not exist at all: the five poisons are realized to be five wisdoms.

When one is aware of the four kāyas—the three of "body, speech, and mind," with "appearances" as the fourth—then the innumerable Sāṃkhya fivefold groupings for one's non-awareness, such as the five *skandha*s, are present as innate wisdom recognizing the five kāyas as the method of perfecting oneself as the five Buddhakāyas. Then, integrated with the five-letter self-arising Jinasāgara, the life-sustaining subtle winds effect perpetual transformation.[213]

With such power, since the Sāṃkhya thirteen calculations or anything else incalculably immeasurable has not influenced the realm of wisdom, and since one has obtained the power naturally, one has gained a multiplicity of siddhis equivalent to those of the Jinasāgara peaceful and wrathful deities. One displays perpetually various signs of accomplishment throughout the three realms. The key point here is that this is not the sphere of activity of anything else whatsoever. It is the particular distinction of the siddha Rangjung Dorjé. The *Samantabhadra and Vajradhāra Tantra* also states that "the so-called subtle winds create all activity."

Now, for the point "When one has gathered together the hosts of tathāgatas, one will attain the holy siddhis." If one is reflexively aware of one's own ignorance of the five temperament dispositions and has attained mastery of both subtle winds and mind—up until one has reached the outer limits of the various accomplishment-signs like those of previous buddhas and siddhas—then provided one is possessed of this essential point, the ability to display everywhere the accomplishment signs is truly valid.

The "introduction to the four kāyas" is the effortless accomplishment by the life-sustaining subtle winds of the infinite activity, which has been gained by a degree of control over the vaselike subtle winds.[214]

I, renowned Karmāpa, encourage all trainees to write down this key point regarding the perpetual arising of the adepts of the three times, and to make evident the signs of accomplishment.

Where will the signs of accomplishment occur, as long as one has not obtained mastery of both subtle winds and mind?

May glorious, blazing good fortune decorate the world!
This is a testament of the renowned Karmāpa.

———

The second and third passages presented here are from Karma Pak-shi's second testament. The second passage discusses meditations in the context of his mortality, after Karma Pakshi had returned to Tsurpu (Central Tibet) in his late sixties or early seventies following his extensive travels in China and Mongolia:[215]

———

After I had gone to the Tsurpu seat of Lord Düsum Khyenpa in Ü–Tsang, once a long time had passed, the outer, inner, and esoteric activity of my actual essence, with the slight veils of emotional habits (the subtle cause of unwise hopes and fears) in combination with various good and bad conditions, emerge as four māras ornaments. Rather like the several temporary appearances to Lord Mila of the hordes of māra and spirit armies, the realized Rangjung Dorjé not only had immutable control over both body and mind, but also a variety of conditional appearances—inner, outer, and betwixt—appeared in multiple fearsome ways as sentient beings of the six realms and as māras. These were omens of a separation of the body and mind. Several unpleasantries such as illness and obstacles occurred fleetingly. Passionate hopes for heavenly existences and the endless fears of being separated—in whatever the length of time and whatever the many circumstances for death—emerged. From the occurrence everywhere of both inner and outer appearances, since I had realized the wisdom regarding the connascent multiple causes and conditions, I mastered the actual essence of all phenomena as the connascent nonduality of all that is dual.

In terms of my inner vision, for a period of forty days I perfected my identity as a pure realm mandala of infinite peaceful and wrathful buddhas extending as far as space. I have taught about the nondual realization-experience of the delusive machinations, experiences, and apparitions regarding the outer world and its inhabitants pervading the three realms—the hordes of the directionless, deluded, and unknowing sentient beings. Yet there still occurred self-manifesting appearances of all sorts, either occasionally in dreams and so forth or in any other kind of experience.

Furthermore, although there were premonitions of the separation of body and mind, I had accomplished the three kāyas spontaneously. After I had been certain that the mere premonitions completed the great play of the inseparable confluence of the four kāyas, regarding previous advice about introducing the four kāyas, there also were for me several developments and simplifications of ideas about the three kāyas.

Are there obscurations that maintain the four kāyas as an idea of habitual imprint? It is apparent that I do not feel that that is so. Consequently, the four kāyas being inherently aware of ignorance, after I had introduced the idea of maintaining the four kāyas stainless dharmakāya as one kāya—any difference not being existent from any origin whatsoever—my introduction is a matter of blessing in the self-arising wisdom. It is an introduction for all the suitable or unsuitable trainee-vessels.

The third passage, also from the second testament:[216]

The completely perfect Buddha Śākyamuni determined all dharmas to be nirvana, and his 100,000 spoken testaments remain. The renowned Rangjung Dorjé of the Śākyamuni tradition had become an excellent trainee to maintain the heritage of the Buddha, teaching followers to practice according to the instructions of the Buddha. Uniquely, it had been necessary to have taught about change by remembering being born, remembering living, and remembering transmigrating. In terms of the present and the future, in order to explain and teach throughout the world his testament and the many types of future activity, the Tokden Rangjung Dorjé has collected together all dharmas of samsara and nirvana and blessed them with his "introduction to the four kāyas." All is beyond inclusion and exclusion for the four kāyas, and there is not even a hair's breadth of non-realization: the wisdom that is reflexively aware of ignorance pervades the worldly realm and will continue uninterruptedly.

First, when a lama master becomes realized and perfects great skill, all future students—their faith being direct perception—do indeed understand this fully. However, with a master without signs and results introducing the four kāyas, for disciples of such a tradition of arrogance and deceit it is like the winnowing of sterile husks. Even though they may have meditated uninterruptedly on an explanation without signs, where will there develop any perfected direct perception regarding the spontaneous three kāyas, the four kāyas—beyond inclusion and exclusion—and the five-kāya buddhahood?

Therefore, because the stainless dharmakāya Rangjung Dorjé has realized the five natural states—the unlimited, infinite space of dharma—as possession of the dharmakāya five wisdoms, and because he has perfected that skill, all future students also will be self-aware of their own ignorance and without hope or anxiety whatsoever about any non-realization concerning his uninterrupted dharmakāya activity. The realized mind is Buddha in the dharmakāya.

With the key information on introducing the four kāyas, to realize speech is to realize the saṃbhogakāya and to perfect that capability. Thus, with the key information on the life-force energy one realizes that throughout the infinite dharmadhātu the five families are primordially the ten male-female consorts. The unity *alikali* (vowels and consonants), self-arisen in the throat-usage cakra, has gained the great wind for speech universal. All the sensory spheres (*āyatana*) of the teeth and mouth, at the present time associated with uttered speech, will, due to the appearance of future trainees, eternally be present as the power of a great amount of self-manifesting relics material and excellent speech—an uninterrupted introduction to maturation and liberation.

With the key information of introducing the profound four kāyas, as there will be no stopping of the endlessly pulsating manifestations of one's own and others' bodies, there is no striving for the kāya of manifesting bodily realization. The spontaneous three kāyas arise, without obstruction, from innumerable trainees. All phenomena of the enumerated eight accumulations of consciousness are realized as the nondual indivisibility of one kāya with four kāyas, and familiarization with this is the perfecting of a great skill. As exemplified by sun and sunlight, all manifold delusions are not included among the singular wisdom space: there is not even a hair's breadth of individual differentiation. In accord with the statement on the stainlessness of delusion and the singular wisdom-space, a sphere of activity of wisdom self-aware of the particular, the inconceivably indescribable, self-manifesting Karmāpa has perfected such a capability. This has not been secret; it has become evident.

Thus, with the essential point of introducing the four kāyas—an introduction that is universal—one is blessed by the self-manifesting wisdom space: do not hope for unfabricated buddhahood among the fabricated. Do not look for any causes and conditions whatsoever. The true nature is not changed by anything at all. When the five characteristics of the natural essence realm are not known at all, one is deluded in the six families of beings associated with the bardo. That is an introduction to the ignorance cycle for sentient beings in samsara. When anyone knows and realizes [the five characteristics], one is introduced to perfecting in oneself the five Buddha kāyas, and one is blessed. For both buddhas and sentient beings, the boundary between awareness and ignorance is nothing at all, not even a boundary between sunshine and shadow.

Dharma action done, there are no pollutant dharma stains. When "Karmā Rangjung" self-manifesting wisdom activity has realized the very essence of all dharma and the potential has been perfected, it will introduce and bless the entirety of a trainee's body, speech, and mind. All who are self-aware and self-realizing from the very beginning, they are buddhas. The key information of this instruction instantly distinguishes oneself from being ignorant and deluded.

This key point, in a mere instant, differentiates a buddha and a sentient being, and "One instantaneously has become a perfect buddha (*sangs rgyas*)."

By means of the key information of the "introduction to the four kāyas," the grasping mind is purified (*sangs*); the field of perception develops (*rgyas*) as the embodiment of infinite peaceful and wrathful Shitro deities. The hordes of thoughts manifest as a realm of knowing the entire ocean of self-arising wisdom and perfecting potential as same-flavor wisdom. This key information of introducing the four kāyas has not appeared previously and will not occur later. At present, the occurrence in this period of the vajra all-pervading, self-arising wisdom is a valid actuality. A trainee's aspirations, caused and conditioned out of ignorance, ought to be known impartially through their hopes. For example, if a king is a father, there is no son of his who does not take the name of Prince. As future trainees are suitable as receptacles and there are no unsuitable ones, this information will not perfect anyone oneself as a five-kāya buddha without being spoken of, so everyone should be engaged in the introduction and listen! Just by listening, shortly thereafter one's ignorance itself becomes self-aware, and one will become a buddha.

Buddha Siṃhanāda came to the world with his continuously miraculous activities, and unfortunately it was necessary for him to depart.[217] His philosophy was communicated by Lama Rechen to Pomdrakpa.[218] Precious Pomdrakpa blessed the apparently self-manifesting Karmāpa, and given that Pomdrakpa left two testimonials, were they not heard at Karma Monastery at the spot where the great sponsor of Karmā Sangyé's monastic seat heard it? Everyone knows this. Because Vajrāsana and the seat of Karmā Sangyé are similar, and because everywhere it is Karmā pervading all the roots of the monasteries, all future students will also gather at Karmā. Do service, meditation, practice, and offering; not long after one will become a buddha in terms of the non-fluctuating four kāyas.

This activity done by Lord Düsum Khyenpa has flourished impartially, and this is the root source for the completion of all his intentions. All the students of renowned Karmāpa should know this. Although the mass of Buddhist dharma is inconceivable, it has not attained the mastery that is in the introduction to the four kayās winds-and-mind. Until one has perfected that skill, one does not achieve mastery over birth and death. It is not that all sentient beings will never be liberated from both birth and death; but, because of the lack of understanding of all sentient beings, they should all know about ever-present obligatory death.

Therefore, the supreme Buddha Samantabhadra-Vajradhāra was born, following the lamas of the siddha lineage, as an ordinary manifestation of Buddha Śākyamuni. Even the perfector of the intention to protect the doctrine, Rangjung Dorjé Karmāpa, is, because dying is obligatory, someone of ordinary birth like other sentient beings. Even though ordinary sentient beings, such as animals, live in a dark house of ignorance and are never separated from death, yet I manifest a way of being born. Despite not staying, I show a way of living; despite not dying, I show a way of dying. So, I show various testaments of my uninterrupted activity enacted in the three times and the various signs of death. Later, I will demonstrate miraculously various details of the future. There is no certainty about the particularities of death for the yogin Rangjung Dorjé, the self-arising Karmāpa—who knows them?

There is the example of a candlelight glowing clearly at the point of death, and this eliminates the wonderings of those wanting to know. It was like this with the refined certainty that occurred to Mahāsiddha Urgyen as a siddha. Because I knew that many fortunate students would come and stay for the duration of a teaching, as they have not been summoned by various bad conditions, there was no fear of sudden conditions. Then, due to their wishes to attain the siddhis of immortality, students should gain self-control in both the mental five-letter self-arising Jinasāgara and the "introduction to the four kāyas"! Do not have belief or confidence in others who are arrogant and deceitful!

Thus, this testament of Karmāpa is victorious over the obstacle of the māra of death. The first testament was about negative conditions arising as an ocean of siddhis and good qualities. Unaware trainees, whoever and wherever they are, should engage with all that has been written and study it all. After meditation and realization, all future trainees should be taught the instructions on the introduction to the three spontaneous kāyas and the non-fluctuating four kāyas. With the wisdom that is self-aware of one's own ignorance, they should be enlightened. If one has not realized the mind's true nature, and if one has not attained control over the life-force breathing, one has not gained control over both life and death. All future trainees and dharma practitioners should be made to know and understand this. The scroll held at the Kagyü main center is one that does not confuse oneself or others. These two testaments are of one source, and everyone should know this. Many people are far away—people in Kham should look in the text where Karmāpa has said he spent these years, and they should be clear about what he said about staying here and there in any country, in such a year, and what he would practice.

May glorious blazing good fortune adorn the world!

With the virtue of addressing several questions with one
    answer,
May I and other beings without exception,
In accordance with the activity of a dharma lord,
Realize the primordial meaning of manifest phenomena.

———

A fourth passage is taken from Karma Pakshi's main autobiographical work, *My Biography: A Dissertation on Realizing the Unity of All
Time and Timelessness and on Perfecting Great Skill.*[219] The passage
extols the virtues of the "introduction to the four kāyas" teaching
and meditation.

———

The renowned Karmāpa, with uninterrupted Buddha-activity
in the past, present, and future, has indeed been born as many
yogins accomplished in yogin-discipline who previously emerged
in India.[220] From now into the future he will come in the style of
a great meditator-yogin. Through his various practices of yogin-
discipline, he exhibited the signs of introducing the four kāyas. He
is also known for many widespread disseminations of secret mantra
prāṇāyāma practices that give rise to this lineage.

Therefore, the skillful tantras and the spiritual knowledge tantras
situated in the Okmin infinite dharmadhātu—an ocean of wisdom
of undivided means and knowledge—are blessed pronouncements
of Hevajra and Vajradhāra, indifferentiable from Indrabodhi and
Vajrapāṇi. The yogin Namkha Ö Yeshé Ying—given the epithet
Indrabodhi—blessed the mantradhārin Rangjung Dorjé with the
introduction to the words and meanings of "introduction to the four
kāyas," the instructions and transmission of the *Tantra of Twenty-
Five-Essences Mahāmudrā.*[221] He matured and liberated innumerable
trainees in an uninterrupted lineage from tantra to final tantra. Now,
therefore, in this present degenerate era of conflicted teachings,
one is not dependent on the causes, conditions, and results of the
nine vehicles. Among the plentiful fabrications, there are no suitable or unsuitable trainees not hoping for an unfabricated Buddha.
This key information of introduction to the wisdom self-aware of

ignorance and the four kāyas blessing did not occur until the great meditator Rangjung Dorjé had arrived. It had not occurred before and will not occur later. Now that it is truly and validly present, the best, middling, and lesser trainees will be self-aware of their ignorance and will go beyond any measure of innumerable realizations.

> Every single instant he has specified,
> Instantaneously he has become a perfect Buddha.[222]

Although the universal sun of introducing the four kāyas has risen, this has not been known by those in the dark.

At this point in time, after renowned Karmāpa had obtained the great transmission in the teachings about the infinite, the series from his *Limitless Ocean of Doctrine* until his *Limitless Ocean of Wisdom* would be in four-line verses.[223] Among the series, those two were requested as a teaching to pervade the world and to be a summation. Many biographical texts have been disseminated. As for the perambulations in the many lengthy or condensed biographical texts of the yogin Rangjung Dorjé, traveling countries and regions, the distances are not comprehensible.

Nowadays, the trainees of the undifferentiable Lord Düsum Khyenpa and Omniscient Rangjung Dorjé fully know and have heard throughout the world these narrative and oral biographies about the three iron-wheel emperors.[224] The tales have been evident in 360 different languages and have not been kept secret: they are a holy witness, a sun rising in a cloudless sky.

Due to the hero Rangjung Dorjé's infinite activity with his immeasurable compassion, the dharma and instructions of renowned Karmāpa, the hordes of his trainee disciples and the artistic representations of body, speech, and mind, traditionally cast and embossed (repoussé) and so on—even the dharma throne, seat, bed, hair, fingernails, and suchlike—will appear continually for the benefit of beings in all times, in the various regions of the world. Even more so than the term "great compassion," according to the saying,

Even each single strand of hair
Will be curative for all sentient beings.

Nowadays, because renowned Karmāpa has perfected his skill in controlling both subtle winds and mind, then on seeing, hearing, or remembering him, or in deep concentration (samādhi), wherever one is, there will occur limitless, truly authentic signs and miraculous blessings. Since this is a combined synopsis of the textual and oral biographies up to the present, trainees ought to know and understand this!

The dharma teachings of the Buddha are said to be virtuous in the beginning, virtuous in the middle, and virtuous at the end. In particular, the orally taught realization of the *Twenty-Five-Essences Mahāmudrā* tantra of noble Vajradhāra—an ocean of wisdom of undivided means and knowledge—perfected my skill in both subtle winds and mind, the introduction to the fourfold kāyas as the singular essence of all phenomena. Then, because five-kāya buddhahood itself was instantaneously perfected, I was in past times undifferentiated from Vajradhāra.

Now, in present times, the three aspects of Indrabodhi—the lamas of the lineage of siddhas—have given the introduction blessing in this lifetime to affiliated trainees by means of inconceivably miraculous manifestations of the non-fluctuating four kāyas. From the great meditator Rangjung Dorjé onward, this has not been secret in the world: it has all become entirely evident, and now is truly valid.

It will arise in the future—
For example, even though today the sun passes,
Tomorrow the sun will reappear.

Therefore,

A buddha will not completely go beyond suffering,
And the dharma will not deteriorate:
The activity of the rūpakāya is uninterrupted.[225]

So it has been said.

The mantradhārin Rangjung Dorjé,
Although he has completed the actions of this life,
When he does not appear in this world,
His affiliates—which appear as superior, medium, or lesser—
Together with the six types of beings in the bardo,

are introduced in their locations to the four-kāya wisdom self-aware
of ignorance and are blessed.

The appropriate body emanates as a nirmāṇakāya,
Speaks the dharma in appropriate speech,
Is nourished by food with appropriate elements,
And demonstrates various samādhis for the appropriate
    personalities,

so his behavior pervades everywhere in accord with all beings'
modes of conduct.

Without transferring from the dharmakāya,
He is the rūpakāya appearance for trainees,

His various aspects manifest anywhere—
Like a mirror image of the moon in water
Manifests anywhere according to causes and conditions.

———

The fifth and sixth passages on meditation come from a shorter
autobiographical work, *My Own Biography: An Introduction to Oral
Teaching on Realizing Connascent Wisdom.* The fifth piece is largely
on the subject of the meditation level of one-flavor realization.[226]

———

OM HŪM. OM SARVA SVASTI SIDDHI HŪM.

When great meditator Rangjung Dorjé has uninterruptedly
turned the wheel of his "introduction to the four kāyas" and the
dharmatā four essential points for present and future trainees in
his "introduction to the four kāyas," multiple signs along the path
of experience and realization will occur. Ultimately, the four kāyas
are unified, and as such they are an inconceivable and wonderful
instruction that culminates in five-kāya true buddhahood.

At first, all are fully established in the fundamental basis, and
such binaries as buddhas and sentient beings, virtue and sin, composite and incomposite, whatever and wherever they are, are primordially insubstantial. Like the examples of a cloudless sky, or
clear water, or absent pollution, they are not demonstrable. The
unchanging nature abides, unaffected in its own nature. Whosoever
is aware of it, that is a sign of buddhahood; being unaware of it is the
sign of a sentient being. Universally, the infinite, limitless dharmadhātu always pervades everywhere and everything is naturally clear.

The very essence of all dharmas is not inanimate. Essentially,
the multifarious discursive thoughts—innately, completely empty—
are unhindered and uncultivated; they occur naturally. Resting

naturally within oneself is either called the "natural state" of the essential nature, or the "fundamental basis." Although it is assigned several names, in absolute terms no one at all can assign a name. Vajra wisdom—naturally occurring self-awareness within its own natural state—thus recognizes the meaning of the "introduction to the four kāyas." So, because the best, middling, and lesser trainees are not mistaken about the points of instruction, the pollutions of various mental activities do not permeate them. If one meditates intensely for a long time, when the wheel of the dharmatā four essential points on subtle winds and mind has been turned, it is not feasible for the four signs not to arise. First there is understanding one flavor, then one-flavor realization, then habituation, and then being familiar with one flavor. For everyone, it is not possible that individual achievement of personal freedom will not fully occur.

As for so-called one-flavor understanding, when the wheel of the essential information on subtle winds and mind is uninterruptedly turned with regard to the singularity of all phenomena self-resting and self-arising, since this is a sign of hearing the dharma teachings on all tenets—Buddhist and non-Buddhist—within samsara and nirvana, expert knowledge flourishes. Since there is not the slightest incomprehension or misunderstanding, various impressions of thinking will occur:

> His great knowledge instantaneously
> Retains full comprehension of all dharmas.[227]

On reflecting that the teaching is indeed this, there will occur a vast understanding in thinking about "the appearances of manifold detailed explanations of tenets are of one flavor" and various spiritual experiences will happen, and yet that is not a pure realization. Regarding the accumulations of knowledge and acts

of knowing, through various analyses one knows that one understands, and through thinking about it there is one flavor. After
skillful knowledge of the cycle of the points on subtle winds and
mind has blossomed, one understands multiple aspects to be of one
flavor.

————

A sixth passage, from the same autobiographical section as the fifth
above, provides some correlations between Karma Pakshi's "four
kāyas" teaching and several tantras.[228]

————

Without the instructions of the Cakrasaṃvara and Hevajra tantras,
even for those taught the instructions of the "introduction to the
four kāyas," multiple freely made-up and imagined mental wishes
will create confusion about self and others, and is pointlessly tiring.
The means-and-knowledge tantras demonstrate many thousands
of conceptualizations as an "introduction to the four kāyas," in
terms of the mental activity in the development and completion
visualizations. Even so, if there is no understanding of the fruition
tantra *Lamp of Reality*,[229] it is as though one has worked the fields
for a year and even though there is much chaff, there is no fruit. If
one has done many mental activity visualizations, it serves to confirm the pronouncement that it is extremely difficult to complete
the actual buddhahood of the five kāyas. Hence, I have taught
universally the instructions on the introduction to the ocean of
innately natural wisdom.

When the reading authorizations and instructions of these tantras are brought together, they are the authorization of the teaching
of the undifferentiable Samantabhadra-Vajradhāra and Vimalamitra.[230] Henceforth, for any people who are not aware and not realized and have been involved continuously with words and concepts,

they are unrealized and unaware about self and others. Therefore, after hearing and knowing a mere echo of pure appearances, the words of anyone bewildered—such as "the tantra has explained the tantra, the spoken authorization has confirmed authorization, the advice has introduced advice"—are not required. With the mantradhārin Rangjung Dorjé, the oral transmission and instruction of the Cakrasaṃvara and Hevajra tantras—the inseparable means-and-knowledge of the "forty secrets" and "twenty-five drops"—both the summary into the five natural states of the vajra family and the more elaborate introduction are truly valid.

One night, in a premonition, because this *Lamp of Reality Tantra* is a tantra that presages the realization of the wisdom self-aware of one's own ignorance, I felt I ought to practice extensively the introduction. I held a breath while in the realm of the natural state abiding in its own place. In the elaborated *Lamp of Reality Tantra*, due to its limitless qualities, the tantra, oral transmission, and instructions are bound into one. When an introduction to the self-manifesting threefold, fourfold, or fivefold kāyas opens an individual to the natural state, one ought to view the apparent occurrences of an earthquake or various magical appearances as the lamp of the fruition tantra *Lamp of Reality* and be clear about it.

Thus, the mantradhārin Rangjung Dorjé's ideas on biographical visions, oral teaching, and tantric oral transmission and advice are not a cause for ignorance and error.

CHAPTER 10

Verse Narrative

Imperial Death Warrant, Exile, and Reconciliation

———

IN HIS RECOUNTING of events in his memoirs, Karma Pakshi presents information on the factual aspects of his history mixed with accounts of visions, prayers, and discussions of doctrinal matters. Regarding historical tales, one section five folios long is in seven-syllable verse, giving a poetic rendition of dramatic events at the court of Kubilai Khan.[231] The passage includes an account of a prayer for long life that Karma Pakshi composed for when he was threatened with execution, followed by reference to his exile and imprisonment, and it ends with his reconciliation with the Kubilai Khan after the Mongolian khanate succession war had ended—when Karma Pakshi was in his sixties.

———

O spontaneous, total perfection of the five kāyas
Abiding in the state of infinite dharmakāya—
To the very nature of self-realized esoteric wisdom
I offer homage.

Future manifestation of Siṃhanāda;
Past Düsum Khyenpa himself;
Current Rangjung Dorjé;

Primordially uncreated, the pure lion's roar
Has thus resounded.

Through realization of the infinite dharmakāya,
I have unconditionally accomplished beings' welfare.

After a forceful and fierce trainee
Cast extremely harsh language,
He cast hot and harsh weapons
Like Yama slicing a human.

When I roared the terrifying sound of "Ha! Ha!"
Holding aloft the banner of the Buddha's teaching.

———

A century after Karma Pakshi's passing, Kachö Wangpo (the Second Shamarpa) included most of these verses in his biography of Karma Pakshi, but he inserted at this point a section of fifteen lines. A translation of all inserted fifteen lines is included here, as they may have belonged to Karma Pakshi's original work.[232]

———

Hordes of fiercely violent ones
Were brandishing lethal weapons:
The apparent enemies stated
We would be immediately pulverized into dust
With a great fearsome ball of flame.[233]

The Ma-Gön protectors of the doctrine
Surrounded the myriads of the army of deities.
Once they had arrived very rapidly

They said, "We shall liberate instantaneously
This enemy of those who harm the doctrine!"

Their roaring, like a thousand dragons, a terrifying HŪṂ
Stabilized this yogin's mind
And totally freed me from physical fear.
The deities of virtuous existence
Have set up the victory banner of the doctrine—*ema!*

———

Continuing with the tale acknowledged to be part of Karma Pak-shi's memoirs,

———

Spontaneous peace—*ta-la-la!*
Ema! How wonderful! I have become an excellent yogin—
I said, "Now, fear is shown!"
And I caused my teaching to spread throughout the world.

Even without plentiful words
Such as "utsuma" and so forth,
Is it possible that apparent existence can be stopped
By their appearance in books, or is that indeed a mistake?

However, the dharma is masterful—
Look here and now at the state of this era:
Leprosy, cancer, insanity,
Epidemics, and multiple bad omens.

According to the legal tradition of the heretics,
The bearded one was said to be an evil spirit.

Although such a tradition is bad,
When applied, what must the executioner do?

Looking properly at this situation,
See the retinues of the protectors and guardians of the
    Buddhist teaching
Enjoying red meat and blood!
See in front of Palden Lhamo
Red *rakta* swirling around!
See the heated and stricken trainees,
Terrified and panicking.

Now, this yogin says,
"I am Rangjung Dorjé,
The totally free vajra king.
I have realized the primordial dharmakāya,
I am superbly adorned with saṃbhogakāya qualities,
And I have attained the stability of the fearless
    nirmāṇakāya.

Because I do not fear for my life,
I am like a powerful lotus king.
I have put the malevolent gods and spirits in their place
By binding them all with oaths."

When I rose 200 *lebar* higher
Above the impure earth,
There was a messenger of the earth-dominating emperor
Called Elagan.

Sentient beings have become sinful,
The bad karma times have been irksome—

Much slander and sarcasm are proclaimed,
So hailstorms fall throughout the region.

The continual flood of violent existence
Washes away humankind and feathered friends,
And dogs, oxen, camels, and herds of sheep,
Along with tents and chariots—
All carried off to an ocean isle.

Kyé ma! Kyé ma! Alas! Compassion for these impure sinners—
The Palden Lhamo armies
Say "Jo! Jo!" to the hateful enemies
Of the samaya-vow-keeping yogin.

All the planetary deities, māras, harmful forces, and
    malevolent spirits
Have said "You are an adept at all activity."
So the entourage of disciples and patrons
Attached to Rangjung Dorjé
All became emboldened.

At that time this yogin said,
"A yogin who realizes the dharmakāya,
Is at all times pure by nature,
He has no fear of the fire and water elements."

"O, enemies with angry minds,
Now behold this miracle!
Through the subjugation of apparent existence,
I have engaged the cycle of both subtle winds and mind—
Wherever I may go, I will be free of enemies."
Thus I said to the aggressive ones.

The final time had arrived;
The slanderous words of the jealous had been spoken,
So the world-emperor became extremely angry,
The executioner was powerless—
Upset with anger, he was agitated with his suffering,
But I, the yogin, was unmoved.

In a self-manifesting deity palace,
All the Kagyü lamas
And a congregation of all the siddhas, ḍākas, and ḍākis,
Along with the twenty-four ḍākinīs, spoke in unison:

"Now, in this impure age,
The sinful are so vicious;
They are extremely difficult to tame—
Pray to the well-qualified lord!

"The siddhi of deathless life will come to you;
Definitely you have prevented inopportune death,
Your glorious body is superbly adorned."
Thus they sang delightedly.

At that time, Rangjung Dorjé,
Realizing the infinite dharmakāya view,
Internalized in his mind hundreds of qualities.
From a collection of mellifluous songs,
He made this auspicious prayer:

"From peerless pure truth,
In the all-good infinite dharmakāya,
I offer homage in taking complete refuge—
Please prevent untimely death.²³⁴

"To the great Vajradhāra, residing
In the supreme place among the great gathering of the peerless,
I offer homage in taking complete refuge—
Please prevent untimely death.

"To the five families, spontaneously and naturally perfect,
In the supreme place of the lotus holders,
I offer homage in taking complete refuge—
Please prevent untimely death.

"To the lamas of the root lineage,
From the supreme place of the directionless four directions,
I offer homage in taking complete refuge—
Please prevent untimely death.

"To the vajra holder (Vajrapāṇi) of the supreme secret
In the palace of Aṭakāvatī,
I offer homage in taking complete refuge—
Please prevent untimely death.

"To good Prince Tailo (Tilopa)
In the Śrīnagar monastery
I offer homage in taking complete refuge—
Please prevent untimely death.

"To Paṇchen Nāro,
Residing in the monastery of the golden mountain,
I offer homage in taking complete refuge—
Please prevent untimely death.

"To the supreme human Marpa Lotsā
In the northern snow-land,

I offer homage in taking complete refuge—
Please prevent untimely death.

"To Milarepa,
Abiding in Tisé (Kailash), the residence of the buddhas,
I offer homage in taking complete refuge—
Please prevent untimely death.

"To Dawa Shönu,
Residing in Gampo, the mount for vultures,
I offer homage in taking complete refuge—
Please prevent untimely death.

"To Düsum Khyenpa, as predicted,
Residing in the supreme region of glaciers,
I offer homage in taking complete refuge—
Please prevent untimely death.

"To the great cotton-clad master yogin
At the Buddha-seat of Karma,
I offer homage in taking complete refuge—
Please prevent untimely death.

"To the lord of the true essence
In the paradise of unpolluted dharmakāya,
I offer homage in taking complete refuge—
Please prevent untimely death.

"To Rangjung Dorjé,
Residing in the paradise of the fully perfected five kāyas,
I offer homage in taking complete refuge—
Please prevent untimely death.

"To the Kagyü lamas,
Manifestations of all buddhas of the ten directions,
I pray with pure higher motivation—
May I obtain the level of vajra deathlessness."

When I prayed thus,
Rainbows filled the three realms.
Impure people became faithful—
They understood in their minds the judgment.
The world ruler was extremely annoyed,
And the executioner committed suicide.

At that time, from the northeast direction,
Palden Lhamo, astride a mule
And with an army of forty-four thousand soldiers,
Set off promptly with great speed.

"Ha! Ha!" she roared with a great laugh—
"This yogin who has samaya—
If even an iota of him is harmed,
Won't I crush you into dust?
I will diminish your status," she said, laughing.

There and then, her activity was invoked,
So the goddess was very angry:
The triple-faced black goddess of tempest
Summoned terrifying messengers,
Creating lightning and wind that filled the three realms.

They threw down from the sky a rain of insanity and
     sickness
As earth, stone, and mountain rocks—

All the tents and wagons were smashed
Like scattered bird feathers.

People cried out "*Kyé ma! Kyé hu!*"
The gods held aloft white victory-banners;
Palden Lhamo strutted and strode;
The malevolent enemies yelled at the deities
And were afflicted by unbearable terror and fainted—
The earth trembled and the mountains shook.

Some people lost their precious lives;
The number of those struck by illness was unimaginable.
For some, their body hair shook and shivered—
They all fully awakened their faith.

Previously, such a miracle
Had not been seen or heard of by anyone;
Nowadays, such perversity
Is inexhaustible for those with sinful karma.

On an island shore,
I benefited beings for three months.
I acted the master, like a son of Vaiśravaṇa;
I sent out an envoy of the Lord of Mantra—
The fragrant and cooling rainfall
Delighted everyone.
This is the liberation tale of Rangjung Dorjé.

Then I went to the court of the king,
Who was not the slightest bit happy.
Furthermore, to invoke faith in those who had no faith,

I demonstrated signs of accomplishment for seven days
In the Avalokiteśvara temple.
The door was sealed with cast-metal nails,
And three men kept guard in shifts,
Acting in turns as watchmen.

At that time, I had an experience of great bliss.
From the twenty-four sacred places,
Single-Faced Lady Lhamo
Had actually arrived, with unobscured countenance,
Everyone saw her in absolute clarity.

With four wisdom ḍākis present
From the cremation ground of Ha Ha La,
After sixteen-year-old, fully developed
Brahmin daughter, Seldenma (Clarity),
A pure and unsullied person,
Had died, her lifeless corpse
Was blessed by the ḍākinīs.
Surrounded by a gaṇacakra assembly,
Ḍākis of the twenty-four places,
From the Malaya cremation ground,
Brought various fruits of supreme smell and taste
And offered them.
The virtuous deity-attendants of the sky
Cast a rain of the hundred excellent flavors.

The Sangchö (Secret Offering) Vajrayoginī
Brought continuously,
From the palace of her vulva,
Various foods and drinks of the lineage king.

Buddhas and bodhisattvas of the ten directions
And all the hosts of yidam deities
Were present, continually clear;
In a palace of the pure-vision deity,
I created realization for dullards.

Then, when seven nights had passed,
I had made the royal ruler of the earth happy—
Taking up my lotus feet to his crown,
He expressed words of joy.
Everyone who had been jealous said,
"*Ema!* Is he not a wondrous great man?"

All the great meditators, holders of the practice lineage—
Do they not maintain the Kagyü seat?
All the ordained sangha together—
Do they not spread the teachings of Śākyamuni?
All the mantrins who have amassed power—
Have they not recited the great protective teaching?
All the furious vīra heroes—
Have they not pacified and tamed?
All the buddhas and their bodhisattvas who have bodhicitta—
Have they not planted the dharma banner?

The valuable advice of the profound aural lineage
Brings out the best in everyone.

For all who have comprehended such,
Through the great merit-accumulation of the thirteen
     syllables,
It is not difficult to traverse the levels and paths.

The great accumulation of virtue, garland of *padmākara*,
Chief of the sons, Delek Nyingpochen,
Of the immaculately glorious Queen Lekminma[235]—
Maintaining the champion's tradition, may the teaching
flourish.

The path of a hundred qualities, blazing good fortune,
Is for any person of the Buddhist doctrine.
In their meritorious attitudes,
Adorned with the ornament of altruism,
May they assuredly have this most beautiful jewel.

CHAPTER 11

Prose Narrative

Dreams of a Buddha Statue and a Horse

———

DURING KARMA PAKSHI'S extensive travels in northern China and Mongolia, begun in 1255, and after he had spent time at the Möngke Khan court in Karakorum, he proceeded farther westward to the area of the capital of the Chagatai Khanate, Almaliq, by the west-flowing Ili River. His memoirs about his stay there do not remark on any enthusiasm in the royal receptivity to his Buddhist teaching—the court was sympathetic to Islam—but the general populace he met in the area, by his own account, seem to have been impressed.

While in the Ili area, he had a significant dream that was to lead to a project to build a huge statue when he had returned to Tsurpu, a project that occupied him in his later years. The statue of a seated Buddha, when completed, become one of the tallest in the thirteenth-century world.

During his return to Tibet from the Ili River area, while traveling through a "huge range of snow mountains" that Karma Pakshi calls Aras—he was possibly crossing the Tian Shan range to get to what he gives as "Kecu" (either Kucha or Turpan) along a northern Silk Route—he dreamed of riding a miraculous horse.

The accounts of these two dreams are in a section of his memoirs entitled *Account of the Erection of Great Deity Ornament of the World*.[236]

———

At a time when I would accomplish enormous benefit and happiness
for sentient beings, the moral virtue of normal sentient beings was
diminishing. Due to the influence of the great obstructiveness of
negative forces (*māra*), the world was agitated, and it was a period
when it had become like the Wildness Park of the warring gods
and demigods.[237]

At this time, when I, Bodhisattva Rangjung Dorjé, was residing
in the Sokpo region called Ila, I thought it fitting that through
the bad actions of many lifetimes I had fallen into such a state and
must live like this. So, I invoked the holy mind of the Buddha,
offered veneration, and donated to sentient beings great gifts of
cloth and so on.

When I had invoked for seven days the continuum of the holy
mind, one night in a dream a single statue of Śākyamuni, about sixty
feet (ten arm spans) high, shone like the sun risen in a cloudless sky.
At that time, a sound from the light, the sunrays radiating everywhere, made me think that it resoundingly proclaimed, "Before too
long, after you have gone to the country of Tibet, erected a statue
of the Buddha this size, and pacified the trickery of the negative
forces, the kingdom will become happy."

I thought, "At a time of such domestic and foreign conflict,
when I have eventually arrived at Tibet, where is this deity statue
to be made?" Again, I had cause to think that the resonant sound
from the light rays said, "Because you are blessed by the Victor, his
bodhisattvas, and the worldly protectors, pray without any doubt
whatsoever, and the statue will be made."

During my return journey to Tibet, in the borderlands of the
Hor people and Sokpo people, on a mountain called Aras in a
huge mountain range, when I had come close to a place said to be
an abode of worldly protectors, in a dream I was alone on the peak
of a black mountain, which pierced the sky. As I was slowly, slowly

falling, a white horse suddenly arrived with birdlike wings, and
I rode on it. The horse appeared to have hooves like human hands,
so it climbed the rock in just a moment. When we got to a pleasant,
open, and wide plain, I spoke without waking from the dream:

> Excellent horse, you are like a golden goose;
> I, an excellent man, am like Prince Siddhārtha—
> I will liberate you from great fear.

As we rested, I thought that, from the light rays radiated everywhere
out of the unified form of the horse and myself, there resonated the
sound of a statement:

"Furthermore, when all the hordes of corporal and noncorpo-
ral spirits appear before you as māras, you will become terrified.
Matured by that, you will become fully victorious." Then I woke
up. It was such a good manifestation that there was no difference
between being asleep or awake.

When I reached the borderlands of China and Hor, it was as if
I had come to Yamāntaka's city, for all the people of the kingdom
were wailing cries of great fear. It was a time when rage, tyranny,
and danger abounded. After Pal Lhamo, surrounded by hordes
upon hordes of powerful spirits gathered like clouds amassing, had
arrived and appeared settled, I prayed as I invoked the continuum
of her holy mind:

> "Unique mother goddess, Palden Lhamo,
> Pray bestow liberation from terror
> And bestow the siddhi of a deathless life span.
> I shall protect the teaching of the teacher,
> And lead the six classes of beings on the path—
> Mother, the time has come, *samaya*!"

Then I thought that this resounded:

> "Have no fear, yogin, have no fear,
> I shall liberate you from great fear."

The Great Brahmin (Saraha) and nine four-faced deities radiated like shooting stars in all directions, and when they passed by, the power of their great magical display overwhelmed me and pacified all fear.

Then I sent a formal letter to Tibet in which I proclaimed that a ten-fathom-high great deity statue called Ornament of the World should be built. I also stated that I would come and ordered that the proclamation be heard everywhere.

————

Karma Pakshi proceeded further to Kecu, which could refer to either Kucha or Turpan. He stayed there eight months, working on his Limitless Ocean series. His last meeting with Möngke Khan, before Möngke's demise in 1259, and the fateful re-encounter with Kubilai Khan and subsequent torture and imprisonment were yet to come. It may be that Karma Pakshi felt the vision, depicted above, of Palden Lhamo and the message of "fearlessness" had been something of a preparation for the difficulties that came later, when Palden Lhamo again inspired him.

————

CHAPTER 12

Conversations with Mañjuśrī

IN HIS MEMOIRS, Karma Pakshi refers to a visionary encounter with Mañjuśrī, a Buddhist deity associated with knowledge, learning, and wisdom:

> When I, Karma Pakshi, had been banished to the banks of the lake by the town of Ke'u Je'u in China and then summoned back, there occurred the blessing of Ārya Mañjuśrī, along with many miracles, and we actually met. During this period, I wrote about valid cognition and debate in the *Twenty-One Questions and Answers*. Due to the blessing of the Mañjuśrī wisdom-being and the complete glory of his great knowledge, I perfected the naturally arising wisdom that has no lack whatsoever of knowledge or realization about all phenomena of samsara and nirvana. I was spoken of as Omniscient Rangjung Dorjé.[238]

Karma Pakshi also refers elsewhere in his memoirs—translated in the third section of the *Preincarnations* section beginning on page 137—to his having "erred in the twenty-one views of ego clinging," which would seem to be relevant to the questions-and-answers discussion with the Mañjuśrī vision, as can be seen below.

In Karma Pakshi's writings there is a lengthy volume—more than one hundred folios—entitled *On Meeting Ārya Mañjuśrī: A Limitless Ocean of Questions and Answers*, part of his Limitless Ocean series.[239]

The text is primarily concerned with, as he puts it, "twenty-one points of view about the self," and is arranged as a series of questions and answers. In fact, the text consists of twenty-four questions and answers.[240] Below are translations of just the questions from the discussions Karma Pakshi had with Mañjuśrī, given with some context where it is deemed useful.

———

[1] Determining the reasoning and scriptural authority on the twenty-one views of ego clinging, an infinite realization clarifying the darkness of ignorance is a limitless ocean of questions and answers.

From the *Limitless Ocean of the Teaching of the Five Teachers*, with reasoning and scriptural authority—on such topics as the introduction and conclusion, the measure, the name, the basis, the examples, the inferences, the established principles, the influences, and so forth—the twenty-one views on ego clinging and the wisdom of self-arising mahāmudrā are totally realized.[241] Out of such limitless totality, all the yānas of the limitless ocean of reasoning are established. After distinguishing all the inner and outer yānas, all arguments are eliminated. Due to its elucidatory mastery of the questions and answers and subsidiary points, this thesis is vindicated in its explanation.

Grasping at a self is said to arise from one's own being or to be itself a cause. If the interconnecting conditions for "self" (inherent) and conditions for "other" (external), and the causes and conditions of both, mutually delimited, are assembled as arising from a singular condition, then, through dependence on a basis of the logical and illogical, knowing and understanding the doctrine (expounding that they solely arise due to karma) should provide an answer. The main accounting of the doctrinal commentaries on the immeasurable self-arising wisdom, the infinite realization of mahāmudrā, is explained in five points and should be understood.

When discussing scripture and reasoning, is there one ultimate essence? If there is not a sole quintessence, then if a cause for a singular essence of everything is not feasible, the occurrence of a variety of tenets and vehicles occurring is not feasible. Why is that?

[2] Reasoning in the Buddhist scriptures is introduced with a question about assessing the nature of the reasoning of the pure and impure scriptures and their logic.

[3] The instance of a question about the paths of accumulation, preparation, and vision in the mantra tradition.

[4] Regarding meditating on immediate mahāmudrā, is there the absolute and the relative?

[5 and 6] A question about what is the nature of the basic fundamental state.

[7] A question about what is the root of all phenomena: When one realizes that body, speech, and mind are the root of all phenomena in samsara and nirvana, the Buddha's three kāyas are perfected in oneself. Since it is said that not realizing this is the cause and result of samsara, those are its three roots. The source of all appearances is the physical, the source of all sound is speech, the source of all memory and reasoning is the mind, and the source of those three is the enlightened mind. One ought to be certain that that is the actual dharmatā.

[The seventh topic ends with the following:] When one realizes
that the trio of body, speech, mind is the root of samsara, that is
the kāya of a buddha. Due to that, one realizes the mahāmudrā
that all phenomena of samsara and nirvana are the limitless,
infinite realization mahāmudrā. When one has become familiar
with this, because it is perfected in the Buddha himself, who has
perfected completely the five kāyas of immeasurable mahāmudrā.
That was the seventh question, on the immeasurable mahāmudrā.

[8] The questions are: Is "mahāmudrā," as it is called, emptiness?
Is it or is it not meditating on the empty essence of all material
phenomena?

[This eighth topic concludes with a quotation ascribed to Saraha:]

> All phenomena of apparent existence
> Are primordially and intrinsically blissful—
> Realizing in oneself the five kāyas of the Buddha
> Is not a term of emptiness.

So the eighth question was about the immeasurable wisdom that
realizes mahāmudrā.

[9] An instance of asking, "As for the self-arising wisdom of mahāmudrā, is the singular basis for the essential nature of materiality
the erroneous views and the accumulations of nonvirtuous kleśas,
or is it the mahāmudrā of all realizations? If one is not realized,
is this the samsara of the three realms?"

[10] When one asks, "When realizing the connascent wisdom as
the natural state of materiality, do tenets of the non-Buddhists
permeate or not permeate mahāmudrā? Does mahāmudrā per-

meate or not permeate the tenets of non-Buddhists? As for the natural basis, its basic state is unchangeable and is a realization—will this not become a non-Buddhist idea of permanence?"

[11] From a question about when one is meditating on the mahāmudrā quiddity of all phenomena: Does one realize or not realize the divisions and boundaries of the nine vehicles taught by the five teachers? Is all the doctrine taught by the Buddha either good or bad, and does it have or not have divisions and boundaries? When there is categorization, is it necessary or not necessary to do all three practices of studying, reflecting, and meditating?

[12] From a question about when one has meditated on and realized mahāmudrā: Are the tenets of both the insider Buddhist and the outsider non-Buddhists realized or not realized as co-emergent wisdom? Even though one has realized mahāmudrā, is it necessary or not necessary to know all the tenets?

[13] From a question about the period of engaging in and meditating on and realizing instantaneous mahāmudrā: Is empowerment, initiation, necessary or not necessary? If one is initiated, does one realize mahāmudrā, or if one is not initiated, does one not realize mahāmudrā? After realization, is one developing buddhahood?

[14] When one realizes mahāmudrā, then as for the nine stages of the vehicles of the insider Buddhists, the 360 wrong views of the outsider non-Buddhists, the classifications of the mistakes made by the six types of unrealized beings, and the completely perfected five kāyas of a buddha, are they—as extensive as the dharmadhātu—the entire mahāmudrā? Or is the list incomplete?

When one realizes mahāmudrā, is that the realization of all doctrines?

[15] As explained within the Mantrayāna, four "weights" are spoken of, and they do exist. It seems that you Tibetans do not understand the meaning. What are the reasons? When in images drawn of great, medium, or lesser lamas a physical likeness of Mañjuśrī has been portrayed in their entourage, the so-called weight of the lama's cleverness is consequently not accurate. What is the reason? It is because there is no one more wise than Mañjuśrī. In terms of the so-called weight of the mudrā of a great meditator, with the premise of a Mahākaruṇā created in the entourage around a lama, it follows that the so-called weight of the mudrā of a great meditator is not accurate. What is the reason? It is because in the particular terms of meditating on marvelous *mahākaruṇā* compassion, no one is superior to Ārya Avalokiteśvara...What are the reasons? Is the best lama the dharmakāya Vajradhāra? Is the middling lama the two form kāyas or not? Is the lesser lama merely the polluted and unpolluted, or is he not?

[16] A question about whether or not in the sutras taught by the completely perfect Buddha there are—in the past or in the future— good or bad, greater or lesser attainments of buddhahood.

[17] In the three realms all sentient beings have not gone beyond the ego and clinging to a self, and that seems to permeate everywhere. A question about whether buddhas, bodhisattvas, pratyekabuddhas, and śrāvakas have a sense of ego and clinging to a self.

[18] A question about what is the root of samsara and nirvana

and another about how is it that the root of both buddhas and sentient beings is said to be the mind.

[19] The natural state of basic materiality has not been extant at all for a buddha nor for any sentient beings and is everywhere assigned the name samsara or nirvana. Regarding the means to realize the essence right now, realizing it is based on what kind of causes and secondary conditions there are—a question of what are the contrary conditions that make one not realize the unique essence of the duality of appearances and mind?

[20] A question about how someone with middling faculties travels the Buddhist path, and what are the means by which they realize the natural mahāmudrā.

[21] A question about what is the mind-training in the nine vehicles for people of lesser faculties, and what are the means of comprehending the twenty-one views of ego clinging.

[22] A question about whether or not there are times for meditating and realizing mahāmudrā.

[23] A question of whether—despite not having realized mahāmudrā—at the point of death can one become a buddha through the "transference" meditation.

[The commentary on this question includes a quotation from Marpa Lotsāwa:]

> The buddha of meditation is *tummo* inner heat;
> The buddha of non-meditation is transference.

[24] A question about the lineage of the nine vehicles of teaching
by the five teachers with their instructions, subsumed within the
three baskets of scriptures: What is the meaning of explaining
the levels of the five excellences? The five excellences are the
excellent teacher, the excellent teaching, the excellent place, the
excellent entourage, and the excellent time.

Following the twenty-four questions with their commentary
responses, in more than a hundred folios, there are a couple of
folios of conclusion. Part of the conclusion includes a number of
titles of Karma Pakshi's other written works.

Through the logic of the actual quoted and rational reasons, all
phenomena of apparent samsara and nirvana have been delineated: a limitless ocean of questions and answers about the
infinite realization that clears away dark ignorance is completed.

My root text, *Limitless Ocean of the Doctrine*, consists of 149
sentences, both mother and son, from which comes a large text in
sections.[242] *Limitless Ocean of the Excellence* is like a commentary to
them. Coming out of the Mahāyoga yāna is the *Limitless Ocean of
the Esoteric*, and emanating from the basket of bodhisattva sutras
is the *Limitless Ocean of the True Bodhisattva*. Teaching mainly on
the Śrāvaka and Pratyekabuddha yānas is the *Limitless Ocean
of Discipline*. Analysis of each idea of the tenets is the *Limitless
Ocean of Assertions*. Drawing out the very essence of everything
is the *Limitless Ocean of Instructions*. Proceeding from that is the
Limitless Ocean of Profound Doctrine. Establishing the scriptures
and reasoning regarding the twenty-one views of holding on to a
self, and the infinite realization that clears away the darkness of
ignorance, is the *Limitless Ocean of Questions and Answers*. Because

all of these, one after another, are maintained, there ought to be the understanding of the nature of all dharma.[243]

———

Similar lists of Karma Pakshi's titles, possibly conceived of as a series, are also found in several of his other works, each giving the *Limitless Ocean of the Doctrine* as the root, and with slight variations for each ensuing list. Yet overall the lists are remarkably consistent. It would seem that after writing the *Limitless Ocean of the Doctrine*, the author had mapped out a whole series of Limitless Ocean works. The germination of this seminal work, as described in his memoirs, was that he was inspired by a vision of a huge mandala of Cakrasaṃvara deities hovering like a mist over China, a vision he had during his stay for eight months in the Kecu area (either Kucha or Turpan), on a northern Silk Route. Hearing the speech of the skyborne deities as dharma, he was inspired to write a work on the nine vehicles of the dharma, followed by a more elaborate version ("mother and son"), before setting off to return to Tibet: this work was the *Limitless Ocean of the Doctrine*.[244]

The journey back to Tibet was interrupted by the Mongolian civil war that followed Möngke Khan's demise. Arrested, imprisoned, and "exiled," Karma Pakshi took the opportunity to write the *Questions and Answers*, with its list of the Limitless Ocean works. It may have been that much of Karma Pakshi's Limitless Ocean series was written in China, by a large lake, during his period of exile.

———

CHAPTER 13

Reflections on Tantra

In some passages of his biographical writings, Karma Pakshi weaves in references or allusions to several tantras that seem to have been important to him. In a separate work, dedicated to a discussion of the tantras, he refers to more than five hundred different tantra titles.[245]

The first passage of the two presented in this section is from the beginning of the first of Karma Pakshi's testaments, written toward the end of his life.[246]

ŌM SARVA SVASTI SIDDHI HŪM

The renowned Karmāpa instructed great meditator-yogins of all types. When signs of accomplishment were displayed everywhere and there were no causes to ascribe to them, I was assigned many epithets such as "great meditator-yogin," "level of a hermit" and "siddha." Yet I produce an incalculable number of foolish medita-tions—it is assigning the name "lion" to a dog or a wolf. The Buddha lets us all know that wearisome, pointless suffering has flummoxed myself and others—we must not act like evil spirits!

In former times, in the locations of India such as Khachö and Orgyen, there were eight great mahāsiddha meditator-yogins, the Oral Lineage such as Tilo and Nāro, fifty-five male and female sid-dhas, eighty-four siddhas, and so forth, both excellent and ordinary.

Numerous people attained the best, middling, and lesser accomplishments. These innumerable, illimitable adepts—for as long as the thousand and two buddhas have not finished exhibiting the best, middling, and lesser signs of accomplishment—have been displaying, by whatever means, a variety of signs of accomplishment, not secret and hidden, that are manifest proof.

Lord Virūpa displayed multiple signs of accomplishment, such as forcing the sun to be stationary and reversing the Ganga River upward. Also, Lord Lavapā demonstrated unwavering constancy and stability to the extent that his canopy was like a timber house against a rock, and so forth. There are no best, middling, and lesser accomplishment-signs that have not been displayed or not established by great meditator-yogins. When asserting that great meditator-yogin hermits have constantly demonstrated a variety of accomplishment signs, it is necessary to establish that. If one supposes that great meditators, adepts, yogins, or hermits have existed continuously in Tibet at all times, being unrivaled and indisputable they would display unending supreme and ordinary signs of accomplishment. Their wisdom, reflexively aware of ignorance, would be uninterruptedly active, like the middle of a river, to mature and liberate. Wishing to attain the accomplishment of a great meditator-yogin, some people reach the ultimate end of all such hermits, other people do not. Has the establishment of accomplishment signs occurred or not?

Therefore, on reflection about an explanation for the lack of accomplishment signs in northern snowy Tibet, even though they seem to fill the world like the winnowing of fruitless chaff, why is it that here not even one person anywhere has heard about signs of accomplishment? All great meditator-yogins ought to know the signs!

Thus, for Lord Mila up to the renowned mantradhārin Rangjung Karmāpa, regarding the singular, unique continuum of the realm of wisdom, the fivefold characteristics of the quintessential, immutable, fundamental natural state of reality for all sentient beings are—due to their personal ignorance of their own nature—mistaken by everyone for the five poisons. The way in which the enumerated five groups of five (twenty-five) or the cycle of unquantifiable, immeasurable ignorance are mistaken is in the enumeration in the *Tantra of Eighty Characteristics of the Secret of Undifferentiated Samantabhadra and Vajradhāra* and is in the workings of delusion in the *Tantra of Twenty-Five Bindus of Mahāmudrā* and is spoken of in the *Tantra of Inseparable Means and Knowledge*.

———

The passage continues with a discussion of one of the five categories mentioned above, the "vajra family," which is included in first piece of the Meditations section of these translations.

The second passage is taken from the longest text of the collection of Karma Pakshi's memoirs, which begins by mentioning several tantras.[247]

———

From the collected works of Mahāsiddha Karma Pakshi, *My Biography: A Dissertation on Realizing the Unity of All Time and Timelessness and on Perfecting Great Skill*.

ŌM SARVA SVASTI SIDDHI HŪM

The renowned Karmapa, with regard to advice for his future disciples on the topic of instructions on time, takes this view: as for beginningless time—time's duality of "before" and "after," the threefold times, and "time of completion" (abiding in Okmin)—the infinite, borderless and centerless dharmadhātu is comprised in a trio of "outer tantras": *Inseparable Means and Knowledge Ocean of Wisdom*, the *Hevajra Tantra*, and the *Vajradhāra Tantra*.

In the Golden Age (*kṛta yuga*), all is included in the teaching transmission and instructions of the Anuttara and Mahāyoga skills tantras, the spiritual knowledge tantras, and the inseparable means and knowledge tantras. The tantras such as the *Forty Secret Characteristics Tantra* (extrapolated from the *Secret Charnel Ground Cuckoo's Enjoyment Tantra*) and the *Tantra of the Twenty-Five Bindus of Mahāmudrā* (extrapolated from the *Vajra-Essence Ornament Tantra* and so forth) are conjoined into the one tantra, *Inseparable Means and Knowledge*. From it, there are the modes of the vajra mind class of all sentient beings, the modes of being of the vajra body class, the modes of being of the vajra subtle channels, the modes of being of the vajra bodhicitta "drops" class, and the modes of being of the vajra subtle energies class.

With regard to these five, in their immutable, fundamental basis nature, when one knows of these five markers of the natural essence expanse, if one does not cognize the signs of five Buddha wisdoms, one lives in common with all beings. Together with the six classes of beings and those of the intermediate state (all endowed with the characteristics of the fundamental universal source), one has examined while not being self-aware.

Hence, if the essential point of the "introduction to the four kāyas" is defined in terms of categorizing into two tantras, there is the *Wisdom Expanse Tantra*[248] about not being personally self-aware; and, if one is mistaken about the inherent state within one's actual nature, there is the *Tantra of Mistaken Ignorance*.[249] The Buddha said, "This cycle of mistaken ignorance is incessant and is not productive." Consider this statement.[250]

CHAPTER 14

Musings on Consecration

———

TEMPLES, STUPAS, and statues seem to have been a particularly important part of Karma Pakshi's missionary activity, both in the commissioning and creation of new works and in their repair and conservation. He undertook such work in East and Central Tibet and in West China. The reparations in Tibet itself were largely to restore and enlarge the buildings that had become dilapidated since their foundation by Düsum Khyenpa half a century previously. The projects in China were at times new builds (for example the Trulnang Trulpay Lhakhang, built in 101 days in Gha, Minyak) and in other instances were repairs. The repairs may have been to structures dilapidated by dint of the passage of time, or else to those harmed by invading military forces, or due to the Daoist rivalries with Buddhists. After his sojourn in Karakorum, Karma Pakshi used his plentiful funds, provided by Möngke Khan, for such works in China and Tibet.

In part of his memoirs, Karma Pakshi writes at some length on the great statue Ornament of the World he had commissioned to be built at Tsurpu in Central Tibet. The statue was as tall as a six-story building, and in the memoir he gives indications of his thinking on the value and consequences of creating and consecrating religious works of art, especially statues.[251] He also writes of the blessing such consecrated works bestow to mountains and valleys, to the natural environment.

The passage opens with Karma Pakshi's journey on one of the

203

so-called Silk Routes near Kecu, as he traveled homeward toward Tibet. The account then leaps forward in time to his last years in Tsurpu, adding a discussion of the benefits of consecration.

———

As I led my horse by its bridle to the country of Tibet, I received blessings from the Victor and his bodhisattvas.[252] Hordes of physical and nonphysical spirits, everywhere in the sky, sang praise for me, and the beings who saw, heard, or remembered this were ripened automatically. I was endowed with the activity that liberates.

The local gods and demons of the visible world, such as the ocean of oath-bound ones, had taken absolute control of the wealth of the Hor, Chinese, Minyak, and Tibetans. The great deity statue Ornament of the World, blessed by buddhas, manifested like a magical illusion through the powers of the fierce ones and the miracles of the dharma protectors. After the statue was erected, a brightness issued from the top of the throne as an omen of hindrances instigated and conflict caused by powerful deities and demons who delight in evil and hold heterodox views. For two days, earthquakes occurred for several seconds at a time and caused a pillar to lose its structural integrity. Monastery artists were killed there, and when the magic of negative forces entered the hearts of the whole school of artists, made up of Buddhists and non-Buddhists, a great series of conflicts began.

When the negative forces set their magic in the hearts of several workers belonging to the group involved with offering food to the monks, a nephew of Lord Düsum Khyenpa established those workers on the path to enlightenment. Yet the whole region abounded with conflict and numerous calamities.

After I, the mantradhārin Rangjung Dorjé, had become aware of and understood those magical tricks of the negative forces, I manifested clearly and firmly a form of Hayagrīva Vajrarākṣasa with his consort, within a mandala of Lord Yakṣa Vajrarākṣasa, to feed the negative forces throughout the world for seven days. When I dispersed great magical light rays from my overpowering meditation, the army of negative forces were then overpowered so that all the mountains and valleys of the upper and lower parts—in particular the earth, stones, trees, and forests of the upper valley of Tsurpu— were blessed as a mandala of Vajrarākṣasa and remained stable as far as the outer borders.

In particular, as light rays from Hayagrīva Vajrarākṣasa firmly set on a rock right in front of the monastery, even though I was looking from a distance, I could see Hayagrīva Vajrarākṣasa, his secret consort, and the wisdom ḍākinī. The trio of the master and his attendants, together with a mountain of fire, were clearly stable and emanated blessings. Once the great statue Ornament of the World had been erected, the negative forces were tamed and stopped. It was a period of total conquest over negative forces.

Then, within a mandala of "vajra-like meditation"[253]—completely victorious over the three realms—the king of meditation, revealer of the intrinsic characteristics of the natural essence of all phenomena, bestowed blessing to consecrate the vast world with widespread peace. In particular, 108 pulsating light rays from the consecrated and immutable great statue blessed all the rocks and mountains of Tsurpu in the upper valley as a mandala of the three bodies of the Victor, and the consecrating meditation light-rays radiated everywhere. Indeed, all the rocks were consecrated by the immutable vajra-like meditation. The meditation rays were particularly directed into the one rock, Soring Zamka, so people who respected and were interested in it could wipe away their bad faults.[254]

In relation to a religious artifact's effectiveness and usefulness, consider the quote in the *Tantra of Extensive Samantabhadra*:[255]

Truly, with the yoga of realization,
For seven or twenty-one eons
A consecration will not be destroyed.

It says that when anyone understands the quintessential reality of all phenomena,[256] exhales the "great breath," and has perfected the great skill, if through the power obtained in realizing the one flavor in all manifold phenomena they consecrate any artifact drawn or sculpted from earth, wood, or stone in the whole country, at best the yogin has blessed such artifacts to not be destroyed for as long as twenty-one eons. Or, more moderately, the consecration blessing prevails uninterruptedly and is not destroyed for seven eons, or at least for three eons.

Even though the true nature of all phenomena is nonexistent, as illustrated by the example of space, just like space it is not blank:

In such space there is no attachment;
There is powerful attachment in all sentient beings.

The meaning of this is considered to be as follows: an artifact that is endowed with the spontaneous consecration of the three bodies (kāyas) engages the minds of sentient beings. If any person or other being has come into the presence of artifacts consecrated with the essence of all phenomena, their mind is at ease and they do not seek in their hearts to be separated from such artifacts, because a stable mind is happy, clear, and nondiscursive:

It engages the minds of sentient beings;
It captivates the minds of sentient beings.

This is the point spoken of in the text. Further, considering both consecrated artifacts endowed with such qualities and the quintessential, spontaneous wisdom of yogin great meditators, the qualities of a consecration are inseparable from the concomitant wisdom. Therefore, erecting the great deity statue Ornament of the World and consecrating it raises the nutrient essence of the soil of the Ü–Tsang area. For three years there will be good fortune and bountiful harvests everywhere.

What aspects are there that ignorant people know of or are not aware of? If they have not fully overcome the disruptions of the aforementioned māras, whether in the smaller Ü–Tsang province or even in the wider world, the trickery of māras and much warfare will take place. Because the might of the majestic master of all supreme secrets, the glorious Vajrarākṣasa, with his perfect skill in meditation had fed and pacified the armies of māras that quarreled in the indigenous and foreign regions, spontaneous calming activity occurred and will continue to occur in these regions. Because it is known this will happen, the great deity statue's influence will perpetually become more widespread and even better.

People of diverse languages venerate the statue, even from a great distance away, and many embrace and worship it. Many omens will occur, such as the trembling and shaking of the statue in visions, a visible radiance due to light rays, and the impression that it communicates verbally. The visions of average and lesser sentient beings give them joy, and they offer respect, prostrations, and gifts. Just by merely having venerated and stayed near it, the sufferings of sentient beings and physical maladies from evil spirits are alleviated.

When the mind is naturally at rest, it has no desire to go anywhere. In order for many signs of experience of this desirable state to arise, one ought to see the great statue Ornament of the World, hear about it, prostrate to it, and make offerings. Because one will experience infinite worldly and supramundane qualities and accomplishments, good fortune and truly excellent harvests will occur in the local regions. Also, armies of enemies will be pacified, epidemic disease will end, and the attainment of supreme and ordinary accomplishments, as well as an ocean of infinite qualities of a buddha, will continually arise.

If the above statements are not false but are true, the Buddha and his bodhisattvas will naturally accomplish their activities, such as continuing to be present in samsara.

If people have not touched a deity artifact and its surrounding deities yet have continually worshipped and praised them, then the wisdom-protector brothers and sisters will be established in their own abodes, and the group of eight deities and spirits—in particular Vajrasadhu (the uncle and his nephews endowed with swiftness) with the Tenma of Tibet and Khams, female worldly protectors, the Nyentang deity, Karnak Dorjé Gyelpo, and so forth, plus the nāgas and earth lords—will perpetually accomplish, by the strength of their important samaya vows, their activity as wealth protectors, sponsors, great deity *dharmapālas*, and the doctrine protectors, each according to their own vows. For the sake of having the four special Buddha-activities spontaneously performed and having the doctrine present for a long time, this is extremely important, and one ought to know that it is so very important.

As for the ray of light that struck the Zamka rock, because this was a consecration that had entered the rock as a blessing of *tattvatā* (the quintessential truth of reality), the blessing will be more extensive for a longer time than the blessings and activities of many lamas and geshés. Seeing, hearing of, or remembering this will cleanse one of sins, and one will be blessed.

When this mirage-like Hayagrīva Vajrarākṣasa on the rock, which is indeed the actual glorious Hayagrīva Vajrarākṣasa, had touched a side of the rock with the enlightening activity of the forceful light rays of his samādhi meditation, this was subduing obstructive forces and it tamed the māras. So, in this region the hordes of obstructive forces do not stay and māras do not influence the knowledge-holder adepts. Thus the adepts have the blessing to stop and overwhelm the hordes of māras.

People afflicted by sickness, disease-causing spirits, leprosy, madness, depression, and suffering have paid homage in front of the rock deity, made offerings, and invoked his holy spirit.[257] They have prayed to Vajrarākṣasa, and, provided they were not affected by doubt, it is certain that they will be freed from suffering, sickness, and harm.

Therefore, amongst all the mountains and valleys of Tsurpu, the consecration of quintessential truth endures and has blessed the Buddhist teachings. If confused people harbor doubts and lack faith prior to coming before a deity, where will blessings and accomplishments come from? In terms of faith and blessing, if anyone has relied on faith, devotion, and conviction toward an artifact endowed with consecration blessing, there is no doubt that, instantaneously, the good qualities and accomplishments have affected their disposition.

As for the light rays that went into the Zamka rock, one should bathe the image and then drink the ablution water. Then, if one circumambulates devotedly for about a week, this purifies the five heinous sins, the ten nonvirtues, the four main transgressions, the eight wrong views, and so forth. One will have a variety of good dreams, signifying the purification of karma stains, and pure appearances will arise. One ought to understand that there will be an easement of body and mind, with an experience of the alleviation of multiple sufferings.

If the large sacred statue Ornament of the World, as tall as it is, were no more than the bits and pieces of its materials of manufacture, then it would be inconceivable that it spreads the Buddha's teaching and makes sentient beings happy. Nevertheless, that is what it does. Furthermore, in order to construct the main statue and the five types of victors in a way that benefits the Buddha's teaching and brings happiness to many sentient beings, the copper and brass raw materials were blessed and consecrated.[258] Even though such blessings enhanced and increased the nutrients of the soil in the whole region, dull-witted and doubting sentient beings still do not understand the distinction between truth and falsehood. In the upper and lower parts of the central regions, light rays of the five types of victors consecrated and blessed the rocks, thus enhancing the nutrients in the soil and blessing the harvests of corn and barley. In particular, this valley of Tsurpu at present has been blessed with stores of grain and resources due to the fruition of the dharma.

Because the fruition and the signs have been witnessed, the main statue and the five Victor family statues were erected as a support for the timelessly perpetual manifestation of the excellent supra-mundane and mundane siddhis. Accomplishments in great or small measure will occur. Experiences of misfortune or of goodness will be according to whether the requests made by people of the area are based on incorrect views or on pure perception. The various misfortunes and the variety of boons will be made evident according to whatever prayer request was made and whatever veneration is being done.

Yet, regarding the erection of the main statue and the five types of victors, hordes of māras entered the minds of the non-Buddhist and Buddhist people, and a variety of difficulties occurred. After those māras had been subjugated and overwhelmed in the mandala of the glorious Vajrarākṣasa Padmabala, indubitably he made them servant emissaries who everywhere pacified, enriched, or forcefully overpowered. Consequently the hordes of worldly spirits and māras built the great artifact. During the creation of this huge task of virtue, despite being made servant oath-bonded emissaries at the feet of the consecrated artifact, they participated in various conflicts in all the foreign and interior regions. They caused statue craftsmen to die, the patron and priest to disagree, and a benefactor and his entourage to die. Due to the sicknesses they instigated, the artifacts were not finished. Even when they were largely completed, various conflicts were happening between foreigners and locals as far away as the outer borders.

The fact that māras and evil spirits, with their continual negative activity, had entered into people's hearts, were disrupting the Buddha's dharma, and would find various ways of counteracting religious activity, denotes the name Māra. As the Buddha often said, Māra always harms that which is valuable, even a precious dharma object; hence, various difficulties were happening in the construction of the deity artifact. It is Māra's aim to diminish happiness, but the people did not understand.

Because the mantradhārin Rangjung Dorjé, many lives ago, was completely victorious over the Māra warrior and fully subjugated the four māras,

> The army of obstructive negative forces will not affect
> The excellent artifact and the five types of victors.
> When they have become the glory of all the world,
> Beings who see, hear of, or remember them
> Are blessed and consecrated
> To totally conquer the warrior (Māra).
> Due to ultimate wisdom,
> For the excellent artifact that spontaneously manifests the
>   three kāyas,
> The advancement and protection of all beings—
> Its perpetual special activity—will occur.

Infinite victors, peaceful deities, and wrathful deities predicted the great deity Ornament of the World and will continue to bless it. Always and forever the Buddha has stayed in the world and without bias has brought together crowds of sentient beings and been a support to purify their sins. Good fortune and excellent harvests occur, and the whole country is happy and flourishes. Those who see, hear, remember, rejoice, make offerings, prostrate, and so forth have attained the accomplishment of the supreme and ordinary accomplishments. This is an immaculate account of the construction and the endurance of the great deity Ornament of the World, which swiftly bestows blessing from the Buddha to a worldly person.

For whoever writes, keeps, sees, or hears of this teaching, it is no different from meeting the Buddha himself. May an excellent blaze of glorious good fortune appear in the world!

> By the root virtue of composing this,
> May I and sentient beings equal to the sky,
> Having realized the meaning of the teacher's dharmakāya,
> Be imbued with the blessing of the dharmakāya!

The pearl garland biography of the precious Lama is finished.

CHAPTER 15

Song for a Disciple

THE BUDDHAS such as Vajradhāra and so forth
Have come in sequence for the benefit for beings:
If we pray to the nirmāṇakāyas,
Blessing will be granted to spread the practice lineage.

This yogin in control of his winds and mind,
Sings a melody of analogies:

The master of snows, the white lion,
Being never away from the white snowy peaks,
Outshines the wild animals.

Masters in the sky, both sun and moon,
Inseparable from the blue sky,
Outshine the various planets and stars.

The royal eagle, master of the rocks,
Being inseparable from the peaks of snowy rocks,
Outshines the various mountain birds.

Thus far through analogies—
The yogin who is not significant
Seeks to sing a bit more.

Blessed by the lineage of the adepts,
Being inseparable from the essential aural lineage,
One outshines the logicians.

While joyfully practicing in remote mountains,
Being inseparable from fresh, deep meditation
One outshines the gossipers.

The yogin who understands the nonconceptual,
Being inseparable from the truth that is beyond compare,
Outshines the grammarians.

The yogin who has unified the two accumulations,
Being inseparable from the single, actual unity,
Outshines those who know only their own interests.

The ultimate dharma, mahāmudrā,
Being inseparable from the realm of equanimity,
Outshines the various lower vehicles.

The stainless dharmakāya yogin
Has sung a song of overwhelming activity—
May sentient beings quickly achieve buddhahood!

"The Lama of Tsurpu's Overwhelming Activity," sung for Drakpa Zhonu.[259]

CHAPTER 16

Deathbed Song

In Situ Panchen's *A Rosary of Crystal Jewels* collection of biographies for the Kagyü sect, the authors have included in the section about Karma Pakshi a short poem or song by Karma Pakshi, presented in the passage about his approaching death in 1283 (Water Sheep Year).[260] The verse is set in seven-meter lines. Translated below is the introductory passage and the song. The date ascribed to the song is the day that Karma Pakshi died.

Beginning in third month of the Sheep Year, sounds and lights and earth vibrations repeatedly occurred, and a constant rain of flowers fell. Karma Pakshi was asked, "Is this a good or a bad sign?"

He replied, "Do you know that this is like the arising of a sign of a bodhisattva being born or dying?" The sangha group had a great discussion about it. He said, "You all ask a stream of questions, and have asked them with considerable nervousness. I have repaired the ruins of Lord Düsum Khyenpa's monastery abodes, so the spread of the Buddhist teaching will continue for a long time as a result of the scriptural teaching of the prior Oral Lineage. I have done what needs to be done for these seats. I have completed the intentions of the Lord Düsum Khyenpa. Like the regular worldly activity of the sun going down every night yet next day it returns, similarly after a short while, despite my not having been present, due to my activity I will emanate as a tulku appropriate for my trainees. As someone skilled in all knowledge, I will come quickly, as though descending from the sky."

On the third day of the ninth month of the Water Sheep Year, the mahāsiddha became weaker than before, even though he did not have any type of illness. When they thought his physical strength was diminishing, his attendants offered religious services in front of him, so he said, "In the midst of the shaking of Mount Meru, meditate on being a silent, independent rod," and then he said,

> Although I will have passed from this beggar's life,
> Signs will occur in the clear sky—
> My bodily remains will be corpse relics,
> My self-awareness resting in the afterlife state,
>   self-illuminating,
> Equivalent to the stainless dharmakāya.
> And because it is able to bless the stream of being of others
> Immeasurable benefit for beings will indeed happen.
> Because we realize the stainless dharmakāya,
> There is not even a mere scrap of fear of death;
> Because I am free of the basis for future transmigration and
>   its process,
> There will be no transmigration in the dharmakāya—
> *Aṃ!*

CHAPTER 17

An Esoteric Great Treasury

THE MOST COMPREHENSIVE Tibetan biography of Karma Pakshi was included in Situ Panchen and Belo Tséwang Künchab's *A Rosary of Crystal Jewels*, written in the latter part of the eighteenth century. Within the Karma Pakshi section, the second longest in that series of biographies for the Kagyü sect, the authors refer to "ordinary and extraordinary" biographies of Karma Pakshi and include a lengthy quotation from an *Esoteric Great Treasury* biography, "written by the mahāsiddha himself."[261] In seven-meter verse, the quotation from the *Great Treasury* is the longest direct quotation the authors used for their biography of Karma Pakshi. The quoted work itself does not seem to have survived separately, so we rely on the eighteenth-century record of this section of it. The long quote is inserted in the *Crystal Jewels* biography in the passage where Karma Pakshi is back in Tsurpu in his late seventies (in the years 1281–1282), but there is no direct reference as to when *Great Treasury* might have been written.

It is inconceivable how I, the mantradhārin Rangjung Dorjé,
In countless lives
Up to my previous lifetime,
Through the connection of the student and master
With various aspects of the holy doctrine—
The many scriptures and lineages—
Did train disciples.

Supports for sacred body, speech, and mind,
Such as the protector temple and so forth, were amazing—
With a multitude of supports, the benefit of beings
Happens immeasurably:
The collected virtue of previous lifetimes
Ineffably benefits beings.

In this very world
I have now been born—
It is not a birth due to pointless mistakes made.
With the learning of many lifetimes,
With realization and the strength of prayer,
Through the power of an ocean of wisdom,
I was born of a Mahāyāna family—
I extol the greatness of the buddhas.

The activity of maturing and liberating sentient beings of the
    six types,
Developed through both teaching scriptures and realization—
I was born in a virtue-laden area,
A location for expanding the Buddha's teaching.

First, the doctrine of the nirmāṇakāya:
In terms of master and student,
I engaged with the Buddhist teaching,
And perfected the discipline of having the four mental
    stabilities.

Renowned as an authentic leader,
The excellent Mahāyāna doctrine of a nirmāṇakāya
With mastery of bodhicitta,
A universal benefactor of beings, an excellent bodhisattva,

Is renowned for especially superior altruism and love:
A treasury of esoteric scripture and realization.

The treasury of the esoteric introduction to the three kāyas,
Which is blessed by the lineage of Nāropa,
Is to expel a great breath and perfect the great energy,
So the various signs of accomplishment rain down.

Renowned as an especially gifted siddha,
Because I have perfected the power of the unobstructed
     nirmāṇakāya
By the means of bringing together both subtle energies and
     mind,
Physical and formless beings
Are inspired without any bias:
I am well renowned as a great master.

Every material thing and every enjoyment
Of the whole kingdom
Has been controlled without exertion
For offering to the noble and for giving to sentient beings:
I am well renowned for great resources.

In the mandala of introduction to the three kāyas,
Through forcefully bringing together subtle energy and mind
Come the marvelous fierce ones
Such as Vajrarākṣa and so forth:
All the hordes of deities
Will look to me.

With my deeds and behavior so ferociously fierce,
The wisdom sister-brother protectors

And the nine male and nine female haughty demons—
The gods and spirits who live in this world—
Are overcome by my stance, gazes, and samādhi
And dispatched as messengers:
I have protected the teaching and benefited beings;
I am known for my amazing powers.

Innumerable eons ago,
I was empowered with the yidam deity
Jinasāgara Avalokiteśvara;
In the retreat of Sharchok Pungri,
Apparent existence was revealed as Jinasāgara,
The world was totally blessed:
I am reputed to be equal to Avalokiteśvara.

The mantradhārin Rangjung Dorjé
Is born now in this very place,
An inconceivable mode of emanation.
Regarding the tenets of the Buddhists and non-Buddhists
And the accumulation of knowledge and what is to be
    known,
Even by just seeing or hearing of them,
I have acquired the Blissful One's great oral instructions
In the unlimited pure lands of the ten directions,
The dharma spoken by the victors:
By means of the bringing together of both subtle winds and
    mind,
Visionary and aural experiences occur:
I am renowned as being a learned one with no dullness.

Practicing occasional retreat
Like multitudes of *śrāvakas* and brahmins have done,

At times moving about, around the kingdom,
Like lightning appears in a gap in a clouded sky,
At times I act to mature and liberate the six realms of beings
In accord with the activity of the victors.

To the lord of all the rulers of the world,
The iron *cakravartin* emperor,
I gave excellent empowerment
Like a lord of the lord of men.

When the greatest general on earth
Asked me, the master, for empowerment,
I was like a general of generals:
In one person's language for all the countries,
In a temple of body, speech, and mind,
Unparalleled, the hordes of special nobility
As the basis, and with their offerings inconceivable,
My behavior was the equivalent exemplar
Of that of a *dharmarāja* free of suffering:
Activity interrupting the flow of karma,
Like a vehicle that truly delivers the miraculous.

Nowadays, in this lifetime,
A multitude of monastery sites and seats,
Thrones, implements, footprints, and suchlike
Pervade the region and are plentiful.

Through my activity of introduction to the three kāyas,
An inconceivable benefit for beings matured and liberated;
The cycle of dharma in nine vehicles—
The inconceivably profound instructions—
As far as the far-flung boundaries,

Has matured and liberated, an uninterrupted benefit to beings.
The best, middling, and lesser trainees
Are guided—with connection, over obstacle, with logic—
On the liberation path.

Unlimited numbers of students have been matured and
     liberated:
I perform uninterrupted benefit for beings
Like a nirmāṇakāya arrived in the world,
A guide for beings in limitless numbers.

In whatever areas I was in,
I gave blessing to suchlike as stupas,
And because the hosts of ḍākas and ḍākinīs,
The hosts of vow-keepers and nāga deities,
Have been bound by an obedience oath,
Pilgrimage places are blessed,
And because the precept protectors have protected the
     teaching
In the blessed pilgrimage places,
The maturation and liberation benefit of beings is
     uninterrupted.

The cast images, paintings, and likenesses
Of the bodhisattva Rangjung Dorjé—
For whosoever sees them,
Pays respect, and makes offerings,
Gradually the maturing and liberation benefit for beings will
     happen.

The old, the frail, and the sick—
I have paid attention to various respectful sentient beings;

I have taught many:
Thus six realms of beings are guided on the path.

I, the yogin Rangjung Dorjé,
Through understanding the eight secret bodies
Of Hevajra, the ocean of wisdom,
Although unborn, I show the manner of birth;
Although not staying, I show the way of staying;
Although not going and coming, I go and I come;
Although deathless, I demonstrate the way of dying.

Nowadays, in this lifetime,
I perform miraculous emanations,
I am apparent, seen as a person with form—
For the hosts of formless beings,
What have I done to mature and liberate, who knows?

I have written a little on the manifestation attributes
In this very lifetime
Of mantradhārin Rangjung Dorjé:
This destructible illusory form of both body and mind.

At this very time,
I demonstrate pure visions both in the sky and on the earth
To the superior, middling, and lesser trainees.
I reveal various ways of understanding and realizing:
For the superior, the actual reality of dharmakāya is shown;
For the middling ones, the bliss of the saṃbhogakāya;
For the lesser ones, the nirmāṇakāya negates clinging to materiality.

In the boundary between this life and the next,
The mantradhārin Rangjung Dorjé,

His inconceivable activity of maturing and liberating,
Everywhere reveals hordes of deities
In pure visions of the eight secret wisdom forms,
Such as Indrabhūti and so forth.
With the eight secret wisdom forms, the hosts of yogins,
Free of tiredness and weariness, should practice meditation.

When the breath has left and there is completion of great energy,
For the bodily forms as numerous as the trainees,
There is no doubt that the benefit of beings will occur:
One should practice meditation with such an attitude.

Benefit for beings with oneself not yet matured
Is like the blind leading the blind;
When the introduction to the three kāyas is fully mastered,
That is indeed the buddhahood of the five kāyas,
Similar to the sun arising.
How is this point realized and made familiar?
It clears away the dark ignorance of the six types of beings,
So there is no clearing away to do—how marvelous! *Emaho!*

The mantradhārin Rangjung Dorjé,
Throughout many previous lifetimes,
Has excelled in realization
Of the dharma wheel of the nine vehicles—
They all are compressed into an essence:
The supremely esoteric Vajrayāna.

The indivisible skill and knowledge,
Ocean of buddhahood, Hevajra,
Endowed with the key point of introduction to the three kāyas—
The meaning of that has been supreme.

Through unlimited numbers of introductions
To the three, four, five kāyas,
One realizes the basis, the path, the fruition.

In a mandala of connascent male *yab* and female *yum*,
For the six types of beings and those in the bardo
I perform instantaneous maturation and liberation.

I am the yogin Rangjung Dorjé.
From here, when I have become no longer apparent,
The stainless dharmakāya, with no meditation and no
     postmeditation,
I will have personally achieved as a natural state:
The limitless ocean of wisdom
Timelessly endures perpetually.

Having perfected the play of the blissful saṃbhogakāya,
The plethora of activities and of appearances
Of every sentient being of the six types,
In a mandala of the secret eight forms,
Is spontaneously revealed in its essential nature.

Since I have achieved the power of the unobstructed
     nirmāṇakāya,
For the six types of beings along with those in the bardo,
Unobstructed nirmāṇakāyas fall like rain.
For every being without exception,
Their basic natural state, essential nature,
Essential characteristics, and so forth
Are perfected as the inseparable four kāyas brought
     together.

Through manifold miraculous manifestations,
With obstructed and unobstructed connections,
The great activity of maturing and liberating
Has the characteristics of esoteric power
And is conjoined with universal knowledge and wisdom,
Transmitted to those having the characteristics of the three
    aptitudes.
The five poisons and the five vajra families:
Five brought together, a transcendent bestowal of fourfold
    empowerment.

The mantradhārin Rangjung Dorjé
Timelessly occurs everywhere.
Quoted from the tantra scripture on *mamo* existence:
"I have come, even in previous times;
I will come again in future times;
I am here now."

Because I have perfected the skill of being familiar with
The scriptural teaching activity
Of esoteric wisdom's eight forms
And from now on maintain it,
Eventually, similar to the occurrence of various ways of
    maturing and liberating,
Scriptural teaching for three types of people
And tantra scripture instruction
Of the hordes of the ḍākinī mandala will be achieved
For all who have become trainees.

Even in an actual dream of the bardo afterlife,
The oral teaching on empowerment and blessing—

Threefold body, speech, and mind and the fourth,
    appearance—
Will introduce the three or four kāyas.

In this excellent lineage,
Innumerable mantradhārin yogins will appear—
The oral instructions of the tantra scriptures
Will universally spread, without doubt.

This excellent, vital introduction to the three kāyas—
Those having the good fortune to see, hear, or remember it
Not long hence will be matured and liberated.
Even when this beggar is under the ground, dead,
Signs will occur up in the sky—
Though my bodily remains will be a corpse,
I will be wonderfully born as a human:
May fortunate people know this!

Notes

1. See David P. Jackson, *Patron and Painter: Situ Panchen and the Revival of the Encampment Style* (New York: Rubin Museum of Art, 2009). See also online at Himalayan Art Resources, "Teacher: Karmapa, Karma Pakshi Main Page," last modified January 2020, www.himalayanart.org/search/set.cfm?setID=1003.

2. See Yeshe Gyamtso, trans., *Chariots of the Fortunate: The Life of the First Yongey Mingyur Dorje* (Woodstock, NY: KTD Publications, 2006), 22–25, 114–15. For the Tibetan, see Thugs kyi rdo rje and Zur mang bstan sprul, "Gter chen rin po che mi 'gyur rdo rje'i rnam par thar pa skal ldan 'dren pa'i shing rta," in *The Lives of Two Lamas of Nan-Chen* (Bir: Kandro Tibetan Khampa Industrial Society, 1973), 34–37 (BDRC W00KG09218).

3. See Charles E. Manson, "Introduction to the Life of Karma Pakshi (1204/6–1283)," *Bulletin of Tibetology* 45, no. 1 (2009): 25–52. Details of several premodern and modern accounts of Karma Pakshi's life are on pages 50–51.

4. Karmapa Ogyen Trinley, in a recorded lecture in early 2021, identified the birth location's current name as Wangbuding Chun (*dbang po stod grong tsho*). See Karmapa, "Arya Kshema Spring Dharma Teaching, 2021, Day 4," February 19, 2021, YouTube video, https://youtube/5TedCP3WTpk, at about 56:30 minutes, with English interpretation by Khenpo David Karma Choephel. The recording in Tibetan can be found at Karmapa, "Bde byed ma'i spyid chos nyin bzhi pa," February 19, 2021, https://youtube/ywHGr5iTRW4, also at 56:30 minutes.

5. For a chapter on the early beginnings of the trülku reincarnation tradition, see Leonard W. J. van der Kuijp, "The Dalai Lamas and the Origins of Reincarnate Lamas," in *The Dalai Lamas: A Visual History*, ed. Martin Brauen (Chicago: Serindia Publications, 2005).

6. *bstan pa'i me ro smad nas bslangs pa*. See Nyang nyi ma 'od zer, *Chos 'byung*

me tog snying po sbrang rtsi'i bcud (Lhasa: Bod ljongs mi dbang dpe skrun khang, 1988), 449 (BDRC W7972).

7. In his autobiographical writings, Karma Pakshi gives his birthplace as *'Bri klung dam pa chos kyi phyug pa'i yul*, see Karma Pakshi, *The Autobiographical Writings of the Second Karma-pa Karma-Pakśi and Spyi Lan Riṅ Mo: A Defence of the Bka'-brgyud-pa Teachings Addressed to G'yag-sde Paṇ-chen*. Gangtok: Gonpo Tseten, 1978, 89. Henceforth abbreviated as KPRN. See also BDRC W27319, or for an *dbu can* version BDRC W3PD1288, vol. 3, 162.

   The same term is used for this location in the 1363 *Red Annals*. Tshal pa kun dga' rdo rje, *Deb ther dmar po* (Beijing: Mi rigs dpe skrun khang, 1981), 87. Scan available at BDRC W1KG5760.

8. Mother: Sing bza' mang kyi; father: Rgya dbang 'tshur tsha sprang thar.

9. Lha dga' and Klu dga'; see Padma dkar po, "Gdan sa chen po ra lung gi khyad par 'phags pa cung zad brjod pa ngo mtshar gyi gter," in *Collected Works (Gsuṅ-'bum) of Kun-mkhyen Padma-dkar-po* (Darjeeling: Kargyud Sungrab Nyamso Khang, 1973), vol. 4, ff. 12b–13a (BDRC W10736, 4:198–99).

10. See Roberto Vitali, "Glimpses of the History of the rGya Clan with Reference to Nyang stod, lHo Mon and Nearby Lands (7th–13th Century)," in *The Spider and the Piglet: Proceedings of the First International Seminar on Bhutan Studies*, ed. Karma Ura and Sonam Kinga (Thimpu: Centre for Bhutan Studies, 2004), 6–20.

11. The *Grub chen karmā pakshi'i rnam thar bzhugs so*, published (by photomechanical process) by Gonpo Tseten in 1978 as *The Autobiographical Writings of the Second Karma-pa Karma-Pakśi and Spyi Lan Riṅ Mo: A Defence of the Bka'-brgyud-pa Teachings Addressed to G'yag-sde Paṇ-chen*. E. Gene Smith wrote the short preface. The reproduced manuscript is in cursive *dbu med* script and has six illustrations of meditator figures. Some pages in the reproduction have a black background with white writing: in conversation, Ponlop Rinpoche has recalled seeing the manuscript as a child, at Rumtek Monastery in Sikkim, and that the "white writing" was, in the original, silver ink on a black background. Scans of the publication are available at BDRC W27319, abbreviated as KPRN below. All seven sections of the memoirs found in the manuscript also feature, in *dbu can* script, in BDRC W3PD1288, vol. 3. There are no illustrations in the latter edition.

12. See Situ-Paṇchen Chos-kyi-'byuṅ-gnas and 'Be-lo Tshe-dbaṅ-kun-khyab.
    History of the Karma Bka-'brgyud-pa [sic] *sect: being the text of Sgrub brgyud
    Karma Kaṃ tshang brgyud pa rin po che'i rnam par thar pa rab 'byams nor bu
    zla ba chu śel gyi phreṅ ba* (New Delhi: D. Gyaltsan and Kesang Legshay,
    1972), 1:81–82 (BDRC W23435). Henceforth referred to as ZBCS.

13. ZBCS, 2: 443–44 (W23435). My thanks to Tashi Tsering (Amnye Machen,
    Dharamsala) for initially drawing my attention to this section of ZBCS.
    Other echoes of previous connections are present in Karma Pakshi's auto-
    biographical accounts, in terms of six previous incarnations that he men-
    tions therein, and also are elaborated on as twenty-seven preincarnations
    in a biography by his immediate successor, the Third Karmapa, Rangjung
    Dorjé. In a work by the latter's student, Yeshé Gyeltsen (from a recently
    available illuminated manuscript), seventeen preincarnations are iden-
    tified, the text claiming that Karma Pakshi spoke of them himself. The
    text also gives four contemporaneous "co-incarnations" and three future
    "post-incarnations." For photograph scans of the latter manuscript, see
    Ye shes rgyal mtshan, "Rin po che kar ma pa rang byung rdo rje'i rnam
    thar bzhugs pa'i dbu phyogs lags soha," in *Bka' brgyud rnam thar rin chen
    gser gyi phreng ba* (n.p.: n.d.), scans 509–45 (BDRC W3CN674). The
    manuscript is also photographically reproduced in 'Brug thar and Karma
    Bde legs, *Bod kyi snga rabs dam pa rnams kyi gsungs chos phyag bris ma rin
    chen gser phreng* (Lanzhou: Gan su'u rig gnas dpe skrun khang, 2015), vol.
    17, 1–38. At some time scans of the latter set (40 volumes) may appear at
    BDRC W3CN5697. At W1KG13822, Ye shes rgyal mtshan, *Rje grub thob
    chen po karma pakshi'i rnam par thar pa*, there are photograph scans of a
    more recent handwritten copy, 21 folios.

14. His name transliterated is Gtsug tor skyabs. See 'Gos lo tsA ba gzhon
    du dpal, *Deb ther sngon po* [*The Blue Annals*], trans. George N. Roerich
    and Gendün Chöpel (Delhi: Motilal Banarsidass Publishers, 2007), 519.

15. KPRN, 89, or W3PD1288, 3:163.

16. KPRN, 89, or W3PD1288, 3:163.

17. See *Karma pa rang byung rdo rje'i gsung 'bum* (Xining: Mtshur phu mkhan
    po lo yag bkra shis, 2006) (BDRC W30541). The author gives an account
    of the first meeting between Pomdrakpa and Chödzin in both the Pom-
    drakpa life story in vol. 4, 249–51, and in the Karma Pakshi life story in
    vol. 4, 258–260. Karmapa Rangjung Dorjé refers to the location of the
    meeting as "Se ko" and "Sel ko." Karma Pakshi in his KPRN, 91–92

has "Sel go." Situ Panchen (ZBCS, 1:83–84, W23435) has "Sil ko" and "Sel ko."

18. *pha bu phrad pa ltar*. Dpa' bo gtsug lag phreng ba, *Dam pa'i chos kyi 'khor lo bsgyur ba rnams kyi byung ba gsal bar byed pa mkhas pa'i dga' ston* (Beijing: Mi rigs dpe skrun khang, 1986), 2:877. Scans available at BDRC W7499. Henceforth referred to as KPGT.

Also see xylograph print scan at W28792, 2:22.

19. KPRN, 89–92, or W3PD1288, 3:162–66.

20. KPRN, 85, or W3PD1288, 3:158–59. The quotation has not been found in Düsum Khyenpa's *oeuvre*.

21. See BDRC W3CN8399 (three volumes of manuscripts reproduced in color). In volume two, the poem title, taken from its colophon, is *Rin po che'i blo 'das chos sku'i dbyangs so*. "Grub chen pakshir yongs su grags pa'i rdo rje'i mgur," in *Bod yul dmangs khrod kyi rtsa chen dpe rnying phyogs bsgrigs* (Chengdu: Si khron mi rigs dpe skrun khang, 2015), 2:736–37 (W3CN8399). It is notable that in the collection of forty-eight songs therein ascribed to Karma Pakshi, Saraha (or "the Great Brahmin") is mentioned about a dozen times. Likewise there are about a dozen references to Saraha in Karma Pakshi's memoirs. The song also features in W3PD1288, 95:395–96.

22. Śavari was a principal disciple of Saraha. His name in Tibetan is usually given as Ri khrod dbang phyug.

23. The poem, with no title or colophon, is from "Grub chen pakshir yongs su grags pa'i rdo rje'i mgur," in *Bod yul dmangs khrod kyi rtsa chen dpe rnying phyogs bsgrigs*, 2:727–28 (W3CN8399). The poem also features in W3PD1288, 95:390–91.

24. KPRN, 90, or W3PD1288, 3:163.

25. *sku bzhi ngo sprod kyi don la gnad bzhi chos nyid kyi 'khor lo rgyun chad med par bskor ba*.

26. See Martina Draszczyk, "Direct Introductions into the Three Embodiments: Supreme Key-Instructions of the Dwags po Bka' brgyud Tradition," *Revue d'Etudes Tibétaines* 45 (Avril 2018): 145–77. David Higgins and Martina Draszczyk have written several articles and chapters on the Eighth Karmapa's writings on the subject of "recognizing the three kāyas" (*sku gsum ngo sprod*). Karma Pakshi himself used the term *sku bzhi ngo sprod* (four kāyas) almost every time when discussing the subject, rather than *sku gsum* or *sku lnga* (five kāyas). Apart from his memoirs, the only text

ascribed to him wherein he uses the terms extensively is the "Mkha' 'gro
yid bzhin nor bu'i gzhung." See W3PD1288, 10:191–274.

27. For translations of selected material by Karma Pakshi on the "recognizing
the four kāyas" teaching, see the second part of this work, "Writings," in
the Meditations chapter.

28. The location names (*gnam rag* hermitage, by *sel go* monastery, in *ko bo*
area) are as taken from KPRN, 91–92; W3PD1288, 3:165, has *sel go*. Situ
Panchen gives *gnam brag, sel ko, ko bo*.

29. Mkha' spyod dbang po, "Chos kyi rje dpal ldan karma pa chen po'i rnam
par thar pa bsam yas lha'i rnga chen," in *Karma pa sku phreng rim byon gyi
gsung 'bum phyogs bsgrigs* (Lhasa: Dpal brtsegs bod yig dpe rnying zhib
'jug khang, 2013), 3:262–67 (W3PD1288).

30. 'Jam dbyangs rgyal mtshan, *Gsang chen bstan pa'i chu 'go rgyal ba Kah
thog pa'i lo rgyus mdor bsdus rjod pa 'chi med lha'i rnga sgra ngo mtshar rna
ba'i dga' ston* (Chengdu: Si khron mi rigs spe skrun khang, 1996), 37–38
(BDRC W20396).

31. 'Jam dbyangs rgyal mtshan, *Kah thog pa'i lo rgyus mdor bsdus*, 36–37.

32. *Eight Classes of Magical Net*, Tibetan: *Sgyu 'phrul sde brgyad*. *Sūtra of All
Intentions*, Tibetan: *Mdo dgongs pa 'dus* pa. "Space Class of Dorjé Zampa,"
Tibetan: *Klong sde rdo rje zam pa*. The "So, Zur, Nub traditions" are those
originating from So Yeshé Wangchuk, Zurchen Shakya Jungné, and Nub-
chen Sangyé Yeshé.

33. Karma Pakshi, *Bstan pa rgya mtsho mtha' yas kyi bshad pa phun sum tshogs
pa rgya mtsho mtha' yas*, in W3PD1288, 9:159–473.

34. KPRN, 86, or W3PD1288, 3:159.

35. *Karma pakshis . . . nyid kyi mdzad chos rnams kyang phyag rdzogs zung 'jug
mdzad*. Karma Chags med, "'Phags pa thugs rje chen po'i dmar khrid
phyag rdzogs zung 'jug thos pa don ldan 'gro don rgya mtsho lung gi
gter mdzod ces bya ba bzhugs so," in *Mkhas grub karma chags med kyi gsung
'bum* (Nang chen dzong, Gnas mdo gsang sngags chos 'phel gling gi dpe
rnying nyams gso khang, 2010). See BDRC W1KG8321, 54:11.

36. ZBCS, W23435. Another xylograph print edition can be seen at BDRC
W26630, volumes 11 and 12.

37. For tables of the accounts used, see Manson, "Introduction to the Life
of Karma Pakshi," 50–51.

38. Since 2003, this area has been within a UNESCO natural World Heritage Site, named The Three Parallel Rivers of Yunnan Protected Areas,

where there are steep gorges as deep as nine thousand feet. The area contains "one of the richest rich temperate regions of the world in terms of biodiversity." See "Three Parallel Rivers of Yunnan Protected Areas," UNESCO, accessed April 29, 2020, https://whc.unesco.org/en/list/1083.

The peak of Meili Xueshan has not yet been climbed by mountaineers (as of 2021).

39. KPRN, 91, or W3PD1288, 3:164.

40. The Tibetan term for "non-meditation" is *sgom med*, which refers to one of the four yogas of the advanced mahāmudrā practice. For a sixteenth-century commentary on the four yogas in mahāmudrā practice and theory, see Dakpo Tashi Namgyal, *Moonbeams of Mahāmudrā*, trans. Elizabeth M. Callahan (Boulder: Shambhala, 2019), 430–45.

41. The episode is in both Mkha' spyod dbang po, "Chos kyi rje dpal ldan karma pa chen po'i rnam thar pa bsam yas lha'i rnga chen," in *The Collected Writings (gsuṅ 'bum) of the Second Źwa-dmar Mkha'-spyod-dbaṅ-po* (Gangtok: Gonpo Tseten, 1987), 2:15 (BDRC W23928), and in Situ Panchen, ZBCS, W23435, 1:85, or W26630, 11:179.

42. Any such statement ascribed to Milarepa has not been located.

43. Mkha' spyod dbang po, "Chos kyi rje dpal ldan karma pa chen po'i rnam par thar pa bsam yas lha'i rnga chen," in *Karma pa sku phreng rim byon gyi gsung 'bum phyogs bsgrigs* (Lhasa: Dpal brtsegs bod yig dpe rnying zhib 'jug khang, 2013), 3:264 (W3PD1288).

44. KPRN, 92–93, or W3PD1288, 3:166.

45. *The Blue Annals*, 484–85; Karma Nges don bstan rgyas, "Chos rje karma pa sku 'phreng rim byon gyi rnam thar mdor bsdus dpag bsam khri shing," in *The Collected Works of Sman-sdoṅ mtshams-pa rin-po-che karma-ṅes-don-bstan-rgyas* (Bir: D. Tsondu Senghe, 1976), 2:57–58 (BDRC W10982).

46. Karma Nges don bstan rgyas, "Chos rje karma pa sku 'phreng rim byon gyi rnam thar mdor bsdus dpag bsam khri shing," in *The Collected Works of Sman-sdoṅ mtshams-pa rin-po-che karma-ṅes-don-bstan-rgyas* (Bir: D. Tsondu Senghe, 1976), 2:57–58 (W10982).

47. KPRN, 41, or W3PD1288, 3:110.

48. KPRN, 93, or W3PD1288, 3:167.

49. KPRN, 94, or W3PD1288, 3:167–68.

50. ZBCS, BDRC W23435, 1:87, or W26630, 11:181.

51. See Ye shes rgyal mtshan, "Rin po che kar ma pa rang byung rdo rje'i rnam thar bzhugs pa'i dbu phyogs lags soha," in *Bka' brgyud rnam thar rin chen*

gser gyi phreng ba (n.p.: n.d.), ff. 280b–281a, (W3CN674, scans 524–25) or Ye shes rgyal mtshan, *Rje grub thob chen po karma pakshi'i rnam par thar pa* (n.p.: n.d.), ff. 9b–10a (W1KG13822, scans 20–21). That Nyakdre was a preincarnation of Karma Pakshi is also attested in *The Blue Annals*, 565, with the claim Karma Pakshi confirmed this. Such a confirmation of preincarnation is not present in Karma Pakshi's memoirs, so perhaps the author of *The Blue Annals* had access to the Yeshé Gyeltsen text.

52. KPRN, 94–95, or W3PD1288, 3:168–69.

53. See "Grub chen pakshir yongs su grags pa'i rdo rje'i mgur," in *Bod yul dmangs khrod kyi rtsa chen dpe rnying phyogs bsgrigs*, 2:734–35 (W3CN8399). The song description taken from its colophon is *Rin po che karmā pa'i rnam thar skyong ba'i mgur lags so*. The song also features in W3PD1288, 93:394–95.

54. *Sangs rgyas kyi zhing khams lta ba.*

55. *lha srin sde brgyad.*

56. See "Grub chen pakshir yongs su grags pa'i rdo rje'i mgur," in *Bod yul dmangs khrod kyi rtsa chen dpe rnying phyogs bsgrigs*, 2:738–39 (W3CN8399). The song title taken from the colophon is *Karmā pa'i dgongs pa don kyi dbyangs so*. The song also features in W3PD1288, 93:397–98.

57. The "eastern mountain," in Tibetan *shar phyogs gangs ri*, could be a reference to Shar Pungri.

58. De Klerk has noted that in the recording of Lama Norlha there are microtones and constant ornamentation, so his notation is "a highly simplified version" (email message to author, June 17, 2018).

59. The area is now part of a protected UNESCO heritage area, see note 38.

60. See "Grub chen pakshir yongs su grags pa'i rdo rje'i mgur," in *Bod yul dmangs khrod kyi rtsa chen dpe rnying phyogs bsgrigs*, 2:682–84 (W3CN8399). The song title taken from the colophon is *Bla ma karmā pa'i nge shes dpa' brtan seng ge lta bu'i mgur lags so*. The song also features in W3PD1288, 93:354–55.

61. *The Blue Annals*, 519–20. Rin chen dpal bzang, twentieth century, follows *The Blue Annals* almost verbatim. See his *Mtshur phu dgon gyi dkar chag kung sal me long* (Beijing: Mi rigs dpe skrun khang, 1995), 549 (BDRC W20850).

62. Rta tshag Tshe dbang rgyal, *Dam pa'i chos kyi byung ba'i legs bshad lho rong chos 'byung ngam rta tshag chos 'byung zhes rtsom pa'i yul ming du chags pa'i ngo mtshar zhing dkon pa'i dpe khyad par can* (Lhasa: Bod ljong Bod yig dpe rnying dpe skrun khang, 1994), 236. The work is commonly known

as *Lho rong chos 'byung*. For online scans, see BDRC W27302. Christopher Atwood (University of Pennsylvania), in kindly checking the chapters in this work where Mongols feature, has commented on the use of the spelling "Pakshi" in English that perhaps it would better be spelled "Baqshi" in keeping with its Uyghur-Mongolian origins. The widely known spelling is "Pakshi," so that spelling has been kept here. The memoirs manuscripts relied on here have "Pagshi" in the body of the texts (just six instances), but the titles mostly have "Pakshi" (for five titles, two have "Pagshi").

63. The preincarnations manuscript, made more widely available since 2010, can be seen at BDRC W1KG13822, the title being *Rje grub thob chen po karma pakshi'i rnam par thar pa bzhugs*. The songs manuscript is within an anthology of songs (*mgur*) reproduced in 2015, which can be seen at BDRC W3CN8399, 2:675–748. The title page of the Karma Pakshi section of the manuscript is *Grub chen pakshir yongs su grags pa'i rdo rje'i mgur / bka' brgyud rin po che'i 'gur mtsho las / grub pa'i dbang phyug dpal karmā pa dharmā ghu ru zhems [zhal chems] / grub chen pakshir yongs su grags pa'i rdo rje'i gur rnams bzhugs sohā*.

64. *Karma pa rang byung rdo rje'i gsung 'bum*, 4:264 (W30541).

65. There may have been a structure, or the building materials from the ruins of a structure, available to Düsum Khyenpa when he developed the site. The freestanding pillar currently in the courtyard in Tsurpu Monastery has an inscription on it recording some of the rights and duties of a noble family during the reign of Emperor Relpachen in the ninth century. The inscription also has reference to a Lcang bu temple. On the subject of the pillar's inscription, see the writings by Guiseppe Tucci, *The Tombs of the Tibetan Kings* (Rome: IsMEO, 1950), 16–19, 87–90, and Hugh E. Richardson, *A Corpus of Early Tibetan Inscriptions* (London: Royal Asiatic Society, 1985), 92–105.The pillar may well have been moved to its current location from elsewhere..Düsum Khyenpa and Karma Pakshi do not make any mention of the stele in their writings, so it may have been moved after their lifetimes, unless it was already in place when they developed the buildings of Tsurpu and they both saw fit not to remark on the object.

66. ZBCS, 1:96 (W23435), or in W26630, 11:190. Also in book form at BDRC W4CZ295072, 1:238.

67. See "Grub chen pakshir yongs su grags pa'i rdo rje'i mgur," in *Bod yul dmangs khrod kyi rtsa chen dpe rnying phyogs bsgrigs*, 2:700–1 (W3CN8399).

The song's title is taken from its colophon, *Bla ma mtshur phu pa'i pho brang rdo rje lta bu'i mgur lags so*. The song also features in W3PD1288, 93:368–69.

68. Shangri-La was a fictional utopian place invented by the British author James Hilton in his 1933 novel *Lost Horizon*. In 2001 Zhongdian County was reassigned the name Shangri-La (Xianggelila) to promote tourism.

69. KPRN, 98, or W3PD1288, 3:172–73.

70. KPRN, 98, or W3PD1288, 3:173.

71. KPRN, 98–99, or W3PD1288, 3:173.

72. See "Grub chen pakshir yongs su grags pa'i rdo rje'i mgur," in *Bod yul dmangs khrod kyi rtsa chen dpe rnying phyogs bsgrigs*, 2:694–95 (W3CN8399). The song also features in W3PD1288, 93:363–64.

73. KPGT, 2:1416 (W7499). For scanned xylograph prints, see BDRC W28792, 2:593.

74. See Hugh Richardson, "The Karma-pa Sect: A Historical Note," in *High Peaks, Pure Earth* (London: Serindia, 1998), 340, where he posits the location of the meeting "somewhere in the neighbourhood of Tachienlu" (Chinese name for Kanding). R. A. Stein, *Tibetan Civilization*, tr. John E. Stapleton Driver (London: Faber and Faber, 1972), 77, states that Karma Pakshi and Kubilai met "in Amdo in 1255."

75. KPRN, 99, or W3PD1288, 3:173.

76. KPRN, 12, or W3PD1288, 3:73–74.

77. Aficionados of Paddington Bear stories will be familiar with the "hard stare."

78. KPRN, 14, or W3PD1288, 3:75.

79. David Karma Choephel and Michele Martin, trans., *The First Karmapa: The Life and Teachings of Dusum Khyenpa* (Woodstock, NY: KTD Publications, 2012), 86–87. The story also features on pages 7, 192, and 223.

80. KPRN, 87–88 and 100–101, or W3PD1288, 3:160–61 and 175.

81. Translation in Peter Jackson and David Morgan, *The Mission of Friar William of Rubruck: His Journey to the Court of the Great Khan Möngke, 1253–1255* (London: Hakluyt Society, 1990), 236. In Latin the quotation is: *Sed sicut Deus dedit manui diversos digitos, ita dedit hominibus diversas vias.*

82. See John Andrew Boyle, "The Seasonal Residences of the Great Khan Ögedei," in *The Mongol World Empire: 1206–1370* (London: Variorum Reprints, 1977), 145–51.

83. Paul Demiéville, "La Situation Religieuse en Chine au Temps de Marco Polo," in *Oriente Poliano* (Rome: IsMEO), 193.

84. KPRN, 101, or W3PD1288, 3:175.
85. KPRN, 16, or W3PD1288, 3:77–78.
86. KPRN, 101–2, or W3PD1288, 3:175–76.
87. For translations of several of Karma Pakshi's writings on meditation, see the Writings section of this work, in the Meditations chapter.
88. Bettine Birge has posited that the later Mongol courts' interest in Tibetan lamas with their magical rituals may have been influenced by considerations of fertility and long-life health. See her *Marriage and the Law in the Age of Khubilai Khan: Cases from the Yuan Dianzhang* (Cambridge, MA: Harvard University Press, 2017). However, several scholars have seen the Mongol courts' interest in Tibetan Buddhism as being linked to the fearsome protectors of Tibetan Buddhism. Prayers and rituals addressed to protectors may have been perceived as giving advantage in warfare. As for the "entertainment" value of magical feats by Tibetan lamas, claims have been made (unfortunately, widespread on the Internet) that Marco Polo's reference to Tibetan *bakhshi* lamas magically transporting cups of drinks at Kubilai Khan's banquets means that Polo had seen Karma Pakshi at Kubilai's court. As Richardson pointed out in 1958 (*The Karma-pa Sect: A Historical Note*, 342), Marco Polo arrived at the Mongol court in 1275; Karma Pakshi had already left China (he was back in Central Tibet before 1272).
89. See translation in Jackson and Morgan, *Mission of Friar William*, 236–39. The Latin of the quotation is "Vobis dedit Deus Scripturas, et vos christiani non custoditis eas."
90. N. Ts. Münküyev translated a short piece from Chinese of a section of the *Yüan-tien-chuang* (i.e., *Yuan dianzhang*), at chapter 57, which gives information on an imperial edict issued on August 22nd, 1257, at "Tien-chih-êrh." A portion of the translation reads, "An imperial edict proclaimed by emperor Möngke. What shall that be, if not to sentence to *an-ta-hsi* (*aldasi*) whatever people if they are only men who slaughter secretly living beings on the quiet, on the first and eighth days of the first decade, and fifteenth and twenty-third days, these four days of each moon, beginning from this year *ting-ssŭ*?" See N. Ts. Münküyev, "A New Mongolian P'ai-Tzŭ from Simferopol," *Acta Orientalia Academiae Scientarium Hungaricae* 31, no. 2 (1977): 213. F. W. Cleaves also translated this passage; see Francis Woodman Cleaves, "The Sino-Mongolian Inscription of 1240," *Harvard Journal of Asiatic Studies* 23 (1960–61): 72.

91. Jackson and Morgan, *Mission of Friar William*, 236.

92. KPRN, 17–18, or W3PD1288, 3:79–80.

93. For references on multiple languages, see KPRN, 103–4 and 110, or W3PD1288, 3:177–78, 185–86.

94. The nonvirtues and virtues of the Buddhist moral code are generally seen in terms of the activities of body, speech, and mind: in body to not kill, steal, or engage in sexual misconduct; in speech to not lie, slander, use harsh words, or gossip; and in mind to avoid craving, hatred, or wrongful views. Aspiring to virtue can mean the reverse of the ten nonvirtues—i.e., to save life, be generous, be restrained in sexual conduct, and so forth—or it can refer to such virtues as generosity, discipline, patience, and so forth.

95. See "Grub chen pakshir yongs su grags pa'i rdo rje'i mgur," in *Bod yul dmangs khrod kyi rtsa chen dpe rnying phyogs bsgrigs*, 2:685–86 (3CN8399). The song also features in W3PD1288, 93:356–57.

96. References in Karma Pakshi's memoirs to his being in the area occur at KPRN, 22, 107, 127, or W3PD1288, 3:87, 182, 204.

97. KPRN, 22, or W3PD1288, 3:87.

98. This may be an oblique reference to the *Suvarna haṃsa jātaka* tale, about a beneficial golden goose, but the parallel is not obvious.

99. KPRN, 24, or W3PD1288, 3:89.

100. Hugh Richardson saw the statue in 1950 before its destruction during the Cultural Revolution, when Tsurpu was bombarded by cannons in 1966. Richardson estimated the height at sixty feet (see Hugh Richardson, "Memories of Tshurphu," in *High Peaks, Pure Earth* [London: Serindia, 1998], 731). Proportionally, the distance from knee to knee is likely to have been about thirty-five feet. The famous Kamakura Daibutsu statue in Japan, a bronze, seated Buddha created in the same era (1252), is forty-four feet high (thirty feet wide from knee to knee) and has been estimated to weigh about one hundred tons. It is a cast statue, whereas Ornament of the World (Karma Pakshi's name for it) may have been beaten metal, which would help explain the "leaning" of the top, which Karma Pakshi corrected. Richardson refers to the Ornament of the World as a brass statue, but he may have been mistaken. It would seem that Ornament of the World was one of the largest metal statues in the world during the medieval times in Asia and Europe.

101. For a very useful overview of Karma Pakshi's written works, see Matthew T. Kapstein, "The Doctrine of Eternal Heaven," in *Mahāmudrā and the*

Bka'-gryud tradition (Andiast, Switzerland: International Institute for Tibetan and Buddhist Studies, 2011), 304–12. The website Translating the Karmapas' Works (accessed April 16, 2022, www.translating-karmapas .org/karmapas/karma-pakshi/) lists titles of eight volumes of Karma Pakshi's works, derived from a 108-volume collection of the Karmapas' works published in 2013 (W3PD1288, vols. 3–10).

102. If a "dre" (*bre*) of silver is equivalent to 8 "sang" (*srang*) of silver, and as a sang of silver is about 1.3 ounces in weight, that means a dre of silver is 10.4 ounces. Thus a tentative estimate for the amount of silver donated to Karma Pakshi would be 650 pounds in weight, which if correct would require a few horses to carry. If Karma Pakshi was loosely referring to dre in the context of the silver ingots (*süke*) of Möngke's period, the süke each weighed approximately 7.3 ounces, which would mean 1,000 süke was about 456 pounds. An admittedly unreliable estimate of price parity would give the 650 pounds of silver from the Yuan period as being the modern equivalent of $1.4 million, or 456 pounds as $982,000.

103. *yon mchod.* KPRN, 19, or W3PD1288, 3:81.

104. Later Tibetan historical accounts describe the seal as "golden." Richardson's *Memories of Tshurphu* article (see *High Peaks, Pure Earth*, 732) has it that he had seen at the Tsurpu monastery in 1950 a golden seal that was inscribed in *hor yig* and had a dragon for its handle. He believed (writing in 1982) the seal to be in storage at Rumtek Monastery (near Gangtok, Sikkim). If by *hor yig* Richardson meant the script now known as "Pagpa," this script had not been invented before Möngke's death. However, he may have meant a Mongolian script. It may be of interest that a late twentieth-century oral account has it that, apparently, a golden robe given to Karma Pakshi by a Mongol emperor (whether Möngke or Kubilai is not clear), was sold by Topga Tulku (now deceased) to the German collector Gerd-Wolfgang Essen. It seems that since 1998 the item has been in the Museum der Kulturen, Basel. As yet it has not been possible to confirm the account, so it is rather doubtful. For a photograph of what may be the alleged item, see https://www.himalayanart.org/items/3314195 (accessed August 23, 2021).

105. KPRN, 107–8, or W3PD1288, 3:183.

106. See "Grub chen pakshir yongs su grags pa'i rdo rje'i mgur," in *Bod yul dmangs khrod kyi rtsa chen dpe rnying phyogs bsgrigs*, 2:717–19 (W3CN8399).

The song's colophon describes it as *Bla ma karmā pa'i grub gnas 'gran zla med pa'i 'gur lags so.* The song also features in W3PD12888, 93:382–84.

107. A mountain about 60 kilometers on a map due northwest of Tsurpu (height 7048 meters, latitude 29.90390°N and longitude 90.02500°E).

108. This may be a reference to a collection of forty-nine sutras of advice in the Kangyur, known in Sanskrit as Ratnakūṭa (Heap of Precious Jewels), although the single sutra *Kāśyapaparivarta* was also known as the Ratnakūṭa.

109. *'ja' sa drag po,* KPRN, 104, or W3PD1288, 3:179.

110. KPRN, 3, or W3PD1288, 3:52.

111. See Birge, *Marriage and the Law.*

112. *The Blue Annals,* 517. In Tibetan (xylograph prints reproduction), 'Gos Lo tsā ba gzhon nu dpal, *Deb ther sngon po* (New Delhi: International Academy of Indian Culture, 1974), 451 (W7494).

113. KPRN, 3 or W3PD1288, 3:53. Two hundred *li* is approximately equivalent to sixty miles.

114. KPRN, 4 or W3PD1288, 3:54.

115. "Subtle energies" is used here for *rlung sems gnyis.*

116. In another section of his memoirs, Karma Pakshi mentions that two Shangpa lineage people—Lotön and Drakseng—interceded on his behalf with the emperor. KPRN, 104, or W3PD1288, 3:179.

117. The inspiration for Coleridge's poem occurred at the end of the eighteenth century but the poem was not published until 1816. British Library photographs of the manuscript are online at https://www.bl.uk/col lection-items/manuscript-of-s-t-coleridges-kubla-khan.

118. The Shangdu site was abandoned in the fifteenth century. In 2012 the site was designated a UNESCO World Heritage site (https://whc.unesco .org/en/decisions/4792/).

119. The Hexigten area was designated a UNESCO Global Geopark in 2015.

120. *'Phags pa 'jam dpal dang mjal nas zhus ste zhu len rgya mtsho mtha' yas,* in W3PD1288, 5:1–274.

121. KPRN, 105, or W3PD1288, 3:179. The epithet is given as *kun mkhyen rang byung rdo rje.*

122. KPRN, 130, or W3PD1288, 3:207–8.

123. The temple is not identified beyond being an Avalokiteśvara temple.

124. KPRN, 8–9, or W3PD1288, 3:59.

125. See "Grub chen pakshir yongs su grags pa'i rdo rje'i mgur," in *Bod yul dmangs khrod kyi rtsa chen dpe rnying phyogs bsgrigs*, 2:741–42 (W3CN8399). The song description taken from the colophon is *Bla ma karmā pa'i 'khor ba zhan pa rang ldog gi mgur lags so*. The song also features in W3PD1288, 93:399–400.

126. The term is *rgyud ldan*, which may refer to the lama's knowledge of the medical tantras or to a medicinal substance. A Medicine Buddha (Bhaiṣa-jyaguru) painting in the Hermitage Museum, St. Petersburg (inventory number XX-2332), brought from Khara-Khoto, has in the lower left cor-ner a minor figure of a bearded cleric with a black and gold hat, possibly depicting Karma Pakshi. The painting is estimated to date to the mid-thirteenth century: it may be the earliest extant artistic representation of Karma Pakshi and appears to make a connection between him and Medicine Buddha in that region.

127. Rin chen dpal bzang, *Kun gsal me long*, 361 (W20850). Chögyam Trungpa's 1968 terma, *The Sādhana of Mahāmudrā*, uses the same verse among the introductory prayers to the empowerment section of the praxis.

128. Namkhai Norbu, *Byang 'brog gi lam yig: A Journey into the Culture of Tibetan Nomads* (Arcidosso: Shang-Shung Edizioni, 1983), 69–73 (BDRC W00KG03605). Two translation editions (Italian and English) of the Tibetan original were published in the 1990s.

129. Namkhai Norbu, *Chos rgyal nam mkha'i nor bu'i gsung 'bum bzhugs so* (Xining: Mtsho sngon mi rigs dpe skrun khang, 2015), 2:322 (BDRC W3CN5660).

130. See ZBCS, 1:119 (W23435), or W26630, 11:213.

131. KPGT, 2:899.

132. Karma Pakshi's immediate successor, Karmapa Rangjung Dorjé, refers in a poem to the height of the statue as being seven spans, thus more like forty-two feet high. See Rang byung rdo rje, "Mtshur phu'i bstod pa," in *Karma pa rang byung rdo rje'i gsung 'bum*, 5:38 (W30541).

133. Kipling, *Five Nations* (London: Methuen and Co., 1903), 77–8.

134. Incidentally, for a Western comparison, the standing Statue of Liberty at New York is 112 feet from foot to crown and weighs 225 tons. With Victorian-era technology, it took about nine years to create in Paris. Were the Statue of Liberty to be sitting cross-legged like a buddha, the statue would be approximately the same height as Ornament of the World was.

The Angel of the North sculpture in England, late twentieth century, is sixty-six feet high, weighs one hundred tons, and took five years to make in Hartlepool. Seated, Angel of the North would be approximately thirty-five feet high.

135. The "replacement," the large main buddha statue currently at Tsurpu, was created out of beaten metal. This author saw it—and heard it loudly— being made in 1994. Once installed, the replacement has been estimated by a visiting tourist to be 43 feet high in total, including the base.

136. KPGT, 2:902 (W7499).

137. *Grub chen karma pakshi'i bka' 'bum las/ lha chen po 'dzam gling rgyan bzhengs pa'i rnam thar bzhugs sohā.* KPRN, 21–36, or W3PD1288, 3:85–102.

138. KPRN, 27, 31–32, or W3PD1288, 3:92, 97–99.

139. See *Bod yul dmangs khrod kyi rtsa chen dpe rnying phyogs bsgrigs,* 2:730–31. The song description taken from the colophon is *Rin po che'i dam can mkha' 'gro'i tshogs la thugs dam bskul ba'i gsol 'debs rdo rje'i tshigs rkang lnga pa lags so.* The song also features in W3PD1288, 93:391–92.

140. See translation section in part 2, in the Musings on Consecration chapter. Incidentally, the creator of the Angel of the North sculpture (1998), Sir Antony Gormley, is quoted by Gateshead Council publicity in 2018 as saying about his sculpture, "The angel has three functions—firstly a historic one to remind us that below this site coal miners worked in the dark for two hundred years, secondly to grasp hold of the future, expressing our transition from the industrial to the information age, and lastly to be a focus for our hopes and fears—a sculpture is an evolving thing." (https://www.gateshead.gov.uk/article/5303/The-history-of-the-Angel -of-the-North, accessed August 8, 2021). The article credits the sculpture with being "the catalyst for the cultural regeneration" in the area, not entirely dissimilar from Karma Pakshi's claims for the statue at Tsurpu.

141. KPRN, 32, or W3PD1288, 3:98.

142. KPRN, 35, or W3PD1288, 3:101.

143. KPRN, 107, or W3PD1288, 3:181–82.

144. KPRN, 130, or W3PD1288, 3:208.

145. See *Bod yul dmangs khrod kyi rtsa chen dpe rnying phyogs bsgrigs,* 2:696–97 (W3CN8399). The song description taken from the colophon is *Bla ma mtshur phu pa'i gsol 'debs/ sku lnga yongs su rdzogs pa zhes bgyi ba/ sgom chen dar ma seng ge'i don du stod lung mtshur phu'i gtsug lag khang du gsungs pa'o.* The song also features in W3PD1288, 93:365–66.

146. Tshal pa kun dga' rdo rje, *Deb ther dmar po [Red Annals],* 93 (W1KG5760). This remark also features in KPGT, 2:906 (W7499).

147. For the travels of Orgyenpa, see Brenda Li, "A Critical Study of the Life of the 13th-Century Tibetan Monk U rgyan pa Rin chen dpal Based on His Biographies" (PhD diss., University of Oxford, 2011). On page 271 of the thesis, Li remarks that Orgyenpa had met Pakpa at the Chumik convocation in 1277.

148. The title of the song (*mgur dgos med bcu gsum*) is mentioned in the biography by Orgyenpa's disciple, Sönam Özer (Bsod nam 'od zer), *Grub chen u rgyan pa'i rnam thar* (Lhasa: Bod ljongs bod yig dpe rnying dpe skrun khang, 1997), 264 (BDRC W22148). The words of the song are not given (see also Li's thesis mentioned in the note immediately above, page 91).

149. In the 1970s, Michael V. Aris and Topga Rinpoche made a draft translation of a short text on the Vajra Crown, *Dbu zhwa mthong grol rin po che'i bshad pa tshogs gnyis gru gzings bzhugs so*. A typescript of the translation is in the Aris Collection, Bodleian Libraries, Oxford: shelfmark reference MS. Or. Aris 18 (ff. 115–28) in the Weston Library. The Vajra Crown is considered to be a sacred object, given the epithet "the precious liberation-on-sight crown" and used as part of a sacred rite for five centuries until the twentieth century. For a xylograph print, see scans 37-62 at BDRC W1KG26281, vol. 121. The author is Topga Rinpoche (Grags pa yongs 'dus).

The Karmapa lineage later became renowned for both a gold-embossed black hat and the bejeweled black Vajra Crown. The latter was given to the Fifth Karmapa by Emperor Yong-le (r. 1402–1424); any portrait of a pre-Fifth Karmapa wearing the Vajra Crown is anachronistic.

150. KPRN, 85, or W3PD1288, 3:158–59.

151. Rang byung rdo rje, "Dpal o rgyan pa'i rnam par thar pa bzhugs so," in *Karma pa rang byung rdo rje'i gsung 'bum*, 4:342 (W30541).

152. *dge bsnyen rdo rje rgyal po u rgyan pa'i phrin las bsgrub cig*. Bsod nam 'od zer, *Grub chen u rgyan pa'i rnam thar*, 200 (W22148).

153. See ZBCS, 1:146 (W23435), or W26630, 11:240.

154. KPRN, 40–55. See also W3PD1288, 3:109–25.

155. KPRN, 42, or W3PD1288, 3:111. In Tibetan, the stupa is known as *dpal ldan 'bras spungs kyi mchod rten*. The name refers to the stupa that used to exist at Amarāvatī, the capital of the state of Andhra Pradesh in South India. The latter stupa is reputed to be the site where Buddha first revealed the *Kālacakra Tantra*. Several of the carved decorations from the stupa environs are on exhibition in Room 33a of the British Museum (the carvings collection is known as the Amaravati Marbles or the Elliot Marbles).

The stupa itself, now destroyed, was of the large "domed" shape, rather than being the more vertical shape often seen in Tibetan and Himalayan regions.

156. KPRN, 43, or W3PD1288, 3:112.

157. KPRN, 44, or W3PD1288, 3:113.

158. KPRN, 45, or W3PD1288, 3:114–15.

159. A close approximation of these two lines occurs in Tsangnyön's account of Milarepa's *Mgur 'bum*, (Rus pa'i rgyan can, *Rnal 'byor gyi dbang phyug chen po mi la ras pa'i rnam mgur* (Xining, Mtsho sngon mi rigs dpe skrun khang, 1999), 458 (BDRC W21762). See also Christopher Stagg's translation, Tsangnyön Heruka, *The Hundred Thousand Songs of Milarepa* (Boulder: Shambhala, 2017), 315. With thanks to Kristin Blancke for finding the quote (email correspondence, April 24, 2021). The lines are part of a song about fearlessness in the face of eighteen demons that appeared to Milarepa. Blancke also points out that the two lines occur in the Bodleian Library's *Dpal bzhed pa'i rdo rje'i rnam thar* (MS. Tibet.a.11 (R), title derived from the colophon), at folio 126b. KPRN, 45, has the quotation as *glo bur tshe la 'jigs 'jigs nas// ngas rlung sems gnyis la rten 'brel bsgrigs//*. Tsangnyön and the Bodleian manuscript have *nga blo bur tshe la 'jigs 'jigs nas/ lam rtsa dang rlung la rten 'brel bsgrigs/*.

160. One of the "trülkhor" exercises that several Western retreatants may be familiar with in conjunction with the "naro chödruk" retreat practices, is ascribed to Karma Pakshi and is named the So Dunma. See Blo bzang dam chos nyi ma, *Yab chos rtsa rlung 'khrul 'khor gyi lus sbyong thar pa'i lam chen* (Chengdu: Si khron mi rigs dpe skrun khang, 2013), 67–73 (BDRC W2KG1673), where the So Dunma is given as one of the four primary "tummo trülkhor" practices.

161. The phrase "six omens of death" may refer to specific physical indicators of approaching death, such as one's complexion, muscle tone, vision and speech capability, bodily waste functions, and breathing. An extensive analysis of the categories of "signs of death," written in the fourteenth century, features in the work known as *The Tibetan Book of the Dead*, a terma revealed by Karma Lingpa (1326–1386). See Gyurme Dorje's translation, *The Tibetan Book of the Dead* (New York: Penguin Books, 2005), 155–81.

162. KPRN, 47, or W3PD1288, 3:116–17.

163. ZBCS, 1:157 (W23435), or W26630, 11:251.

164. The twenty-one incarnations are given in a manuscript text made more

widely available in 2010 (when found by this author in a kitchen of a lama's dwelling near Dergé). The authorship is ascribed to Yeshé Gyeltsen of the late thirteenth or early fourteenth century. The Karma Pakshi incarnations text is part of a collection of hagiographies, 329 folia, titled *Bka' brgyud rnam thar rin chen gser gyi 'phreng ba gzhan pa'i dbu phyogs lags soha*, among which there is the Karma Pakshi text (19 folios): *Rin po che kar ma pa rang byung rdo rje'i rnam thar bzhugs pa'i dbu phyogs lags soha*. Photograph scans are at BDRC W3CN674, scans 509–45, folios 272–91. At W1KG13822, Ye shes rgyal mtshan, *Rje grub thob chen po karma pakshi'i rnam par thar pa*, there are photograph scans of a more recently copied handwritten version (twenty-one folios), kindly made available to this author by the Seventeenth Karmapa Ogyen Trinley Dorje in 2010.

165. *The Blue Annals*, 487–88. For the Tibetan, see scans of xylograph prints at BDRC W7494, 424–25.

166. Rang byung rdo rje, "Thams cad mkhyen pa rin po che rang byung rdo rje rnam par thar pa tshigs su bcad pa bzhugs pa'i dbu phyogs lags so," in *Karma pa rang byung rdo rje'i gsung 'bum*, W30541, 4:377.

167. *Deb ther dmar po*, 95 (W1KG5760).

168. Ruth Gamble, *Reincarnation in Tibetan Buddhism: The Third Karmapa and the Invention of a Tradition* (New York: Oxford University Press, 2018), 23–48, 78–81, 135–57.

169. Ruth Gamble, *The Third Karmapa, Rangjung Dorje* (Boulder: Shambhala, 2020), 139–51.

170. Gamble has included a complete translation of the *Liberation Story of the In-Between State* in Appendix 3 of her 2013 thesis, "The View from Nowhere: The Travels of the Third Karmapa, Rang byung rdo rje, in Stories and Songs" (PhD diss., Australian National University, 2013), 320–29. Another useful discussion of the transition between lifetimes is by Berounský in two journal articles in 2010 and 2011. See Daniel Berounský, "Entering Dead Bodies and the Miraculous Power of the Kings: The Landmark of Karma Pakshi's Reincarnation in Tibet," in *Mongolo-Tibetica Pragensia: Ethnolinguistics, Sociolinguistics, Religion and Culture* 3, no. 2 (2010): 7–33; and 4, no. 2 (2011): 7–29.

171. KPRN, 41, or W3PD1288, 3:109–10.

172. *The Blue Annals*, 519–20. For the Tibetan, see scans of xylograph prints at BDRC W7494, 453–54.

173. Rin chen dpal bzang, *Kun gsal me long*, 549–50 (W20850).

174. KPRN, 66, or W3PD1288, 3:137.

175. In an introduction to and explanation of the Karma Pakshi initiation (based on the Mingyur Dorjé terma) given by Seventeenth Karmapa Ogyen Trinley Dorje in Berlin (June 8, 2014), the Karmapa stated that Rangjung Dorjé was the "secret name" of Karma Pakshi. See video at https://kagyuoffice.org/the-gyalwang-karmapa-gives-a-karma-pakshi -empowerment/, accessed January 2, 2022, at 6:15 minutes (English translation at 7:54). Immediately earlier in the recording, he states that the name "Karma pa" was a secret name of Düsum Khyenpa.

176. Lama Nyenré Gendün Bum appears in several tangka paintings of Karma Pakshi. Details on him are scarce, and he is usually only mentioned in the context of the transmission of the tantra practices maintained in the Karmapa lineage. His protégé, the Third Karmapa, Rangjung Dorjé, referred to him once as a *grub chen*, a *mahāsiddha*, although the usual epithet is Lama. He was born in Kham, by the Dza River (which farther south becomes known as the Mekong).

177. See *Bod yul dmangs khrod kyi rtsa chen dpe rnying phyogs bsgrigs*, 2:708–11 (W3CN8399). The colophon is *Bla ma karmā pas gnyan ras kyi don du mdzad pa'o*. The song also features in W3PD1288, 93:375–76.

178. See Tāranātha, *A Biography of the Great Master Padmasambhava*, trans. Cristiana De Falco (Arcidosso, Italy: Shang Shung Publications, 2012), 6. In Tibetan, see Tāranātha, "Slob dpon chen po padma 'byung gnas kyi rnam par thar pa gsal bar byed pa'i yi ge yid ches gsum ldan zhes bya ba bzhugs so: 'Di la slob dpon padma'i rnam thar rgya gar lugs zhes bya'o," in *Five Historical Works of Tāranātha* (Tezu, Arunachal Pradesh: Tibetan Nyingmapa Monastery, 1974), 509 (W1KG10418).

179. Rang byung rdo rje, "Sku gsum ngo sprod," in *Karma pa rang byung rdo rje'i gsung 'bum*, 11:1–20 (BDRC W30541).

180. Mi bkyod rdo rje, *Sku gsum ngo sprod kyi rnam par bshad pa mdo rgyud bstan pa mtha' dag gi e waṃ phyag rgya* (Lhasa: Karma Deleg, 2004), vols. 21, 22 (BDRC W8039). A book version in three volumes was published by Vajra Vidya (Sarnath, India) in 2013 and can be found online at W4CZ295067. A scanned reproduction of manuscript volumes, published in four volumes, can be seen at BDRC W23660 (Gangtok: Gonpo Tseten, 1978).

181. See Karma Pakshi, "Rlung sems gnad kyi lde'u mig bzhugs so," in W3PD1288, 3:399–402. The work also features in *Karma pa rang byung rdo rje'i gsung 'bum*, 7, 264–68 (W30541).

182. See Karma Pakshi, "Mkha' 'gro yid bzhin nor bu'i gzhung," in W3PD1288, 10:191–274.

183. For a Tibetan manuscript reproduction, see Thugs kyi rdo rje et al., *The Lives of Two Lamas of Naṅ-Chen* (Bir, India: Kandro Khampa Tibetan Industrial Society, 1973), 34–37 (W00KG09218). For a translation by Yeshe Gyamtso (Peter O'Hearn), see Je Tukyi Dorje and Surmang Tendzin Rinpoche, *Chariot of the Fortunate* (Woodstock, NY: KTD Publications, 2006), 22–25, with the Tibetan equivalent in *dbu can* script at pp. 114–15.

184. In the brief account of this scenario, preserved in the eventual sādhana attributed to Mingyur Dorjé that is used nowadays, there is slightly less information about the mandala of figures around the central guru. However, in the sādhana there is the addition that a woman standing to one side looked at Mingyur Dorjé and pointed to the deities, whereupon the central figure, Karma Pakshi, spoke. See Mi 'gyur rdo rje drag po nus ldan rtsal, "Rje karma pakshi zhal gzigs ma'i las byang bzhugs so," in *Rin chen gter mdzod chen mo*, ed. Kong sprul Blo gros mtha' yas (New Delhi: Shechen Publications, 2007–08), vol. 11, 816 (BDRC W1KG14).

185. The discovery of a text actually *inside* a boulder is perhaps not as uncommon as might be expected. The author of this volume was present in 1993 at the Lotus Lake (Tso Pema) at Rewalsar in North India when Terchen Karma Rinpoche discovered a terma inside a boulder that had cracked open during a retreat. Folios and symbolic objects were contained inside the boulder. A copy of Terchen Karma's interpretation of the terma text is in the British Library, London: *Bka' zab rdzogs chen po: rgyud rnams kun gyi gnad bsdus pa: ma 'ongs bsgyur du bsgrod pa'i thabs: sngon 'gro thos grol chen po dang : sdig chen dang rig gcer mthong pa: thod rgal snang bzhi mthar phyin bzhugs* (502 folios), shelfmark reference 19999.aa.71.

186. Another principal guru yoga of the Karmapa tradition is the "Four-Session Guru Yoga" ("Tunshi Lamay Neljor"), centered on the Eighth Karmapa, Mikyö Dorjé (1507–1554). See Karma pa Mi bskyod rdo rje, "Dpal karma pa chen po la brten pa'i thun bzhi'i bla ma'i rnal 'byor," in *Gdams ngag mdzod*, ed. Kong sprul Blo gros mtha' yas (Paro, Bhutan: Lama Ngodrup and Sherab Drimey, 1979–81), vol. 9, 277–86 (BDRC W20877). A short guru yoga centered on the Sixteenth Karmapa, Rangjung Rigpe Dorjé (1924–1981), is "A Rainfall of Amrita Nourishing the Sprouts of the Four-Kāya Guru Yoga." See Karma pa Rang byung rig pa'i rdo rje, "Bla ma'i rnal 'byor sku bzhi'i myu gu skyed byed bdud rtsi'i char rgyun," in *Rgyal*

dbang karma pa bcu drug pa rang byung rig pa'i rdo rje'i bka' 'bum, ed. Jo sras Bkra shis tshe ring (Dharamsala: Tsurphu Labrang and Amnye Machen Institute, 2016), vol. 3, 177–78 (BDRC W8LS18007).

187. Chögyam Trungpa, *Phyi nang gsang ba'i kla klo'i gyul chen po bzlog cing don rgyud kyi grub thob rgya mtsho mngon du sgrub pa'i cho ga phyag rgya chen po zhes bya ba bzhugs so* (Halifax, Nova Scotia: Nalanda Translation Committee, 1988). The calligraphy is by Lama Ugyen Shenpen (1941–1994). The 1988 edition is an accurate transcription of a photocopy of the earliest available version, created in 1968, which apparently was written by a local Bhutanese scribe while Trungpa was still at the cave. The 1968 manuscript version has no corrections or insertions: it would seem that the original manuscript written by Trungpa as he composed the piece is now lost. The English title given for the 1988 edition is *The Sādhana of Mahāmudrā Which Quells the Mighty Warring of the Three Lords of Materialism and Brings Realization of the Ocean of Siddhas of the Practice Lineage*.

188. Chögyam Trungpa, *The Sadhana of Mahamudra Sourcebook* (Boulder, CO: Vajradhatu Publications, 1979).

189. Trungpa, *Sadhana of Mahamudra Sourcebook*, 12.

190. Karma chags med, "Ri chos mtshams kyi zhal gdams las/ bla med gsar rnying yi dam ḍākki spyi'i yang gsang bla na med pa'i sgrub pa bde chen rab 'bar," in *Mkhas grub karma chags med kyi gsung 'bum* (Nang chen rdzong: Gnas mdo gsang sngags chos 'phel gling gi dpe rnying nyams gso khang, 2010), vol. 32, 387 (W1KG8321). See also in volume 54 of the author's collection, "Thugs rje chen po'i dmar khrid phyag rdzogs zung 'jug thos pa don ldan 'gro don rgya mtsho lung gi gter mdzod," 54:11. For a translation of the latter, see B. Alan Wallace, *A Spacious Path to Freedom* (Ithaca, NY: Snow Lion Publications, 1998), 23.

191. KPRN, 86, or W3PD1288, 3:159. Karma Pakshi's memoir has *rdzogs pa chen po dang phyag rgya chen po gnyis ming la tha dad yod na yang don la ngo bo gcig pa'i phyir/*.

192. Matthew Kapstein remarks that the degree of impact of Karma Pakshi's writings on later Tibetan writers in the Nyingma and Kagyü traditions is not clear. See Barbara Nimri Aziz and Matthew Kapstein, eds., "Religious Syncretism in 13th Century Tibet," in *Soundings in Tibetan Civilization* (New Delhi: Manohar Publications, 1985), 370; Matthew Kapstein, *The Tibetan Assimilation of Buddhism* (Oxford: Oxford University Press, 2000), 105. Kapstein, in "The Doctrine of Eternal Heaven" (304–12, Appendix 3),

gives an analysis of the writings of Karma Pakshi that were available to him at the time (2011).

193. Perhaps a more considered opinion would be that the continuity of the Karmapa epithet did not become fully established until the time of the Fourth Karmapa (1340–1383).

194. Düsum Khyenpa was not referred to as Karmapa in the contemporaneous biographies of him, as noted by Peter Kersten in his 2019 thesis, "Biographies of the First Karma-pa Dus-gsum-mkhyen-pa: Critical Text Edition and Translation of Two Biographical Works; and an Overview of the Dus-gsum-mkhyen-pa Collection" (PhD diss., Université Paris Sciences et Lettres, 2019), 19. Karma Pakshi refers only to himself as Karmapa; the Third Karmapa, Rangjung Dorjé, does not refer to Düsum Khyenpa as Karmapa. The variant spellings of the title Karmapa, in order of frequency in Karma Pakshi's memoirs are as follows: *karmā pa* (50 instances), *karmma pa* (2), *karma pa* (1). The name Karma Pakshi, in his memoirs, also has variant spellings.

195. See Leonard W. J. van der Kuijp, "The Dalai Lamas and the Origins of Reincarnate Lamas," in *The Dalai Lamas: A Visual History*, ed. Martin Brauen (Chicago: Serindia Publications, 2005), 15–31. Also see José Ignacio Cabezón, "On Tulku Lineages," *Revue d'Etudes Tibétaines*, no. 38 (February 2017), 1–28.

196. KPRN, 9–12, or W3PD1288, 3:69–73.

197. Siṃhanāda is the name expected to be assigned to the sixth Buddha of the current "fortunate eon"; Śākyamuni, the Buddha for the current period of the eon, is known as the fourth Buddha; Maitreya is to be the fifth.

198. KPRN, 41–42, or W3PD1288, 3:110–11.

199. Indrabodhi is also known as Indrabhūti, and the first Indrabodhi also is identified with King Ja. Namkha Ö is claimed as a prior incarnation of Karma Pakshi in the latter's main autobiographical text within his memoirs (*Nyid kyi rnam thar dus gsum dus med bcig tu rtogs shing rtsal chen po rdzogs pa'i gleng gzhi*, KPRN, 73). Therein what seems to be a fuller name is given as Namkha Ö Yeshé Dripa Mépa, unless the *sgrib pa med pa* is descriptive ("unobscured") rather than part of the name.

200. KPRN, 69–89, or W3PD1288, 3:140–62.

201. The sesame seed would seem to be an allusion to the example given, in Buddhist discussions of consciousness, of a single sweet-smelling sesame seed perfuming the whole storehouse.

202. Tibetan *phywa*, a term associated with luck and good fortune, and hence divination practices.

203. A text which came to this author's notice in 2010 (in two manuscript versions, one at Pelpung Monastery (Sichuan) and the other at Gyuto Monastery (Himachel Pradesh), both in the same year), has twenty-one instances of Karma Pakshi incarnations: seventeen preincarnations, four co-incarnations (including Karma Pakshi), and four post-incarnations. The author (Ye shes rgyal mtshan) states within the text that it is a report derived from Karma Pakshi's spoken statement. See photograph scans at W1KG13822 and at W3CN674 ff. 272–91 (scans 509–45). Photographs of the latter illuminated manuscript have been published in China: 'Brug thar and Karma Bde legs, *Bod kyi snga rabs dam pa rnams kyi gsungs chos phyag bris ma rin chen gser phreng* (Lanzhou: Gan su'u rig gnas dpe skrun khang, 2015), 17: 1–38. Scans of the latter may become available at BDRC W3CN5697.

204. Riripa and Kasoripa were two "vajra brothers" to Nāropa (eleventh century), who were both helpful in encouraging Marpa the Translator (1012–97) in his search, during his third visit to India, to find Nāropa. See Tsang Nyön Heruka, *The Life of Marpa: Seeing Accomplishes All*, trans. Nālandā Translation Committee (Boston: Shambhala, 1995), 81. See also Cécile Ducher, *Building a Tradition: The Lives of Mar-pa the Translator* (Munich: Indus Verlag, 2017), 198, 283.

205. The *Mahāmudrātilaka Tantra* is of the Hevajra cycle. Trungpa Rinpoche quoted from it (in his *The Tantric Path of Indestructible Wakefulness*, ed. Judith L. Lief (Boston: Shambhala, 2013), 524), where the tantra gives a gloss on the term *mahāmudrā* (*chak gya chenpo*): "*Chak* means the wisdom of emptiness / *Gya* means liberation from the dharmas of samsara / *Chenpo* means union / Therefore, it is known as *chaggya chenpo*." For the tantra, see in the Kangyur collection of Buddhist scriptures, e.g., the *Dpe sdur ma* edition (Beijing: Krung go'i bod rig pa'i dpe skrun khang, 2006–9), 80:208–84 (BDRC W1PD96682).

206. See Kangyur, e.g., *Dpe sdur ma* edition, 80:533–48 (W1PD96682) for this tantra, translated by Shākya Yeshé (d.1072), who was credited with teaching Marpa Sanskrit. The Sanskrit title is given as *Rigyāralitantrarājanāma*.

207. KPRN, 83: *rdzogs pa chen po klong chen rab 'byams la sogs pa rdzogs chen po'i rgyud.* A "Klong chen rab 'byams kyi rgyud" features in the *Snga 'gyur rgyud 'bum phyogs bsgrigs* collection (Beijing: Mi rigs dpe skrun khang,

2009), 32:412–665, scans of which are available at BDRC W1KG14783, but this may not be the tantra referred to.

208. This may refer to the Gandhola Temple, in Northwest India (Himachal Pradesh). The temple currently bearing that name is said to have been founded by Padmasambhava. The Kulu Vase in the British Museum was found in the nineteenth century in a cave near the monastery (item 1880.22). The water pot, with Buddhist decoration, is dated to the first century C.E.

209. Also known as Kaṃbala (Kaṃbalapāda).

210. Tibetan: 'Jigs med grags pa.

211. See "Sku gsum ngo sprod," in *Karma pa rang byung rdo rje'i gsung 'bum*, 11:1–20 (W30541). See also W3PD1288, 21:109–28.

212. KPRN, 38–40, or W3PD1288, 3:107–9.

213. The "five-letter" Jinasāgara (Gyelwa Gyatso or Red Avalokiteśvara) seems to refer to the practice of the five-deity Jinasāgara lineage, alluding perhaps to five seed-syllables rather than a five-letter mantra.

214. I.e. the *bum can* (Sanskrit, *kumbhaka*) breath-holding technique.

215. KPRN, 43–45, or W3PD1288, 3:112–14.

216. KPRN, 48–55, or W3PD1288, 3:118–25.

217. Buddha Siṃhanāda, Lion's Roar Buddha, here refers to the First Karmapa, Düsum Khyenpa (1110–1193).

218. Sangye Rechen Paldrak (1148–1218), disciple of the First Karmapa and teacher to Pomdrakpa (1170–?), the Second Karmapa's teacher. A tangka painting with Sangye Rechen and Pomdrakpa as the main figures, surrounded by lineage figures, is held in the Rubin Museum (New York); see "Teacher (Lama)—Sangye Rechen," Himalayan Art Resources, www.himalayanart.org/items/1019, accessed January 2021.

219. KPRN, 57–118, or W3PD1288, 3:127–94. The extract presented here is from KPRN 108–112, or W3PD1288, 3:183–8.

220. Seventeen of Karma Pakshi's preincarnations are delineated in the manuscripts Ye shes rgyal mtshan, *Rje grub thob chen po karma pakshi'i rnam par thar pa* (W1KG13822), and Ye shes rgyal mtshan, "Rin po che kar ma pa rang byung rdo rje'i rnam thar bzhugs pa'i dbu phyogs lags soha," in *Bka' brgyud rnam thar rin chen gser gyi phreng ba*, W3CN674, scans 509–45. The former manuscript features in an unpublished paper: Charles Manson, "Manifold Manifestations: Karma Pakshi's Various Lifetimes as Recounted in a Newly Available Manuscript (2010)," Aca-

demia.edu, accessed January 20, 2021, www.academia.edu/44826426/ Manifold_Manifestations_Charles_Manson.

221. KPRN, 109: *Phyag rgya chen po thig le nyi shu rtsa lnga'i rgyud*; or see W3PD1288, 3:184.

222. This quotation seems to be from the *Mañjuśrī-Nāma-Saṃgīti*, the verse sometimes enumerated as number 141: "The fivefold factors, in all times, / Every instant specified, / Instantaneously a perfect Buddha, / Bearer of the true nature of all the buddhas.

223. *Bstan pa rgya mtsho mtha' yas* appears in several titles of Karma Pakshi's works (see WK3PD1288 volumes 5, 7, 9). None of them are wholly in verse. Several of the titles of his works include the "limitless ocean" trope. *Ye shes rgya mtsho mtha' yas* may well be another part of Karma Pakshi's corpus of writings.

224. The three *cakravartin* rulers referred to presumably includes Möngke Khan and Kubilai Khan. The third may be their younger brother Ariq-Böke. Karma Pakshi had known, taught and initiated Ariq-Böke.

225. The quotation seems to be an adaptation derived from the *Suvarṇaprabhāsa Sūtra*, popularly known in English as *The Golden Light Sutra*.

226. KPRN, 119–22 or W3PD1288, 3:195–99.

227. A quotation from the *Mañjuśrī-Nāma-Saṃgīti* (verse 117).

228. KPRN, 132–34, or W3PD1288, 3:210–12. The latter version has a fairly large number of typographical errors for this particular text.

229. *De kho na nyid kyi sgron ma'i rgyud*, in volume 80 of *Dpe bsdur ma* edition of the Kangyur collection of Buddhist scriptures, (Toh 423), W1PD96682, 80:416–33.

230. Vimalamitra, born in Western India, was an eighth-century Dzogchen adept invited to the Tibetan imperial court by Trisong Detsen (742–c. 800).

231. KPRN, 1–9, or W3PD1288, 3:51–60.

232. Mkha' spyod dbang po, "Chos kyi rje dpal ldan karma pa chen po'i rnam par thar pa bsam yas lha'i rnga chen," in *The Collected Writings (Gsuṅ'bum) of the Second Żwa-dmar mkha'-spyod-dbaṅ-po* (Gangtok: Gonpo Tseten, 1978), 2:62–63 (BDRC W23928), or W3PD1288, 3:312–13.

233. The huge ball of fire may be a reference to gunpowder cannons, used in some thirteenth-century warfare in Asia.

234. Note that Sharmapa Kachö Wangpo's account of the "untimely death" prayer gives only this first verse (W3PD1288, 3:315–16), whereas in Karma

Pakshi's memoir there are another fourteen verses (W3PD1288, 3:55–56) of the prayer. After the prayer verses, both sources then resume with the narrative.

235. This name could refer to Lakṣmīṅkarā, sister to King Indrabhūti. She became a *mahāsiddhī*.

236. "Lha chen po 'dzam gling rgyan bzhengs pa'i rnam thar bzhugs so," in KPRN, 21–36, or W3PD1288, 3:85–102. The passage on two dreams is found at KPRN 22–25, or W3PD1288 3:87–90.

237. Wildness Park (*Rtsub 'gyur gyi tshal chen po*) seems to be a reference to one of four "parks" surrounding Indra's palace in the Heaven of the Thirty-Three, whose inhabitants are prone to fighting with demigods.

238. KPRN, 104–5, or W3PD1288, 3:179.

239. See W3PD1288, 5:1–274.

240. A sixteenth-century historian, Pawo Tsuklak Trengwa, has in his *Feast for Scholars* the number of questions as twenty-five. See KPGT, 2:895 (W7499).

241. *Limitless Ocean of the Teaching of the Five Teachers* is one of the earlier works in Karma Pakshi's Limitless Ocean series. See BDRC W3PD1288, 8:1–278.

242. In several of his works, Karma Pakshi gives similar outlines of the sequence of the Limitless Ocean series.

243. See W3PD1288, 5:1–274.

244. KPRN, 25, or W3PD1288, 3:90–91.

245. *Bstan pa rgya mtsho mtha' yas kyi bshad pa phun sum tshogs pa rgya mtsho mtha' yas*, about 150 folios. See W3PD1288, 9:159–473.

246. KPRN, 36–38, or W3PD1288, 3:104–7. In all the memoir texts of the KPRN manuscript, in total forty-two tantras are mentioned.

247. KPRN, 57–59, or W3PD1288, 3: 127–30. In the KPRN manuscript edition of the text, the opening text on the reverse side of the title page folio has two illustrations to either side of the text: one of Zangri Repa, a student of Rechungpa and teacher to Drogön Rechen, and one of Pakmodrupa (1110–1170), both wearing elaborate "meditator crowns." See W27319, 58, for the illustrations.

248. *Ye shes dbyings kyi rgyud*, not identified.

249. *Ma rig 'khrul pa'i rgyud*, not identified. A manuscript collection of some of Karma Pakshi's works has a *Ma rig 'khrul pa'i rtsa rgyud bzhugs pa'i dbu phyogs lags so*, two folios: *Karma pakśi gsung 'bum* (n.p.: n.d.), vol. 2, scans 275–78 (BDRC W00KG03996); the manuscript is also reproduced

at BDRC W22467, pages 267–70. A printed version can be found in
W3PD1288, 9:533–38.

250. The line quoted appears in several Buddhist wisdom scriptures (*Prajñā-pāramitā*).

251. KPRN, 25–36, or W3PD1288, 3:91–102.

252. "The Victor" (Jina; *rgyal ba*) is an epithet of the Buddha, referring to his being victorious over the travails of samsara. Bodhisattvas are referred to as his "sons" in the Tibetan.

253. *Vajropama samādhi.*

254. As Karma Pakshi explains further on in this passage, people who witnessed the vision at the time received blessing and later visitors could receive blessing by pouring water over the rock and then imbibing the water.

255. *Kun bzang yangs pa'i rgyud*, not identified.

256. *Chos thams cad kyi de kho na nyid.* KPRN, 28, or W3PD1288, 3:93. "Quiddity of all phenomena," in the philosophical sense, would express it well. Karma Pakshi uses the phrase several times in his memoirs, usually in the context of a passage referring to his "introduction to the three kāyas" teaching.

257. In Tibetan, *thugs dam gyi rgyud*, see KPRN 32, line 1. The editor for W3PD1288 3:98 line 2 seems to have read the short form of *thugs dam* as being *thams cad*.

258. In addition to the huge statue, there were five Jina (Buddha) statues at Tsurpu, as recounted by Rin chen dpal bzang, *Mtshur phu dgon gyi dkar chag kun gsal me long*, 53. The remark comes in his account of Karma Pakshi's life, although he does not specifically mention whether the five statues were created during Karma Pakshi's lifetime.

259. See *Bod yul dmangs khrod kyi rtsa chen dpe rnying phyogs bsgrigs*, 2:707–8 (W3CN8399). The song description taken from the colophon is *Bla ma mtshur phu pa'i spyod pa zil gnon gyi mgur grags pa gzhon nu la gsungs pa lags so.* The song also features in W3PD1288, 93:374–75.

260. See ZBCS, 1:156–57 (W23435), or Si tu chos kyi 'byung gnas, *Bka' brgyud gser phreng rnam thar zla ba chu shel gyi phreng ba* (Sarnath: Vajra Vidya Institute, 2004), 1:304–5 (W4CZ295072).

261. See ZBCS, 1:138–143 (W23435), or Si tu chos kyi 'byung gnas, *Bka' brgyud gser phreng rnam thar zla ba chu shel gyi phreng ba*, 1:285–90 (W4CZ295072).

Bibliography

Primary Sources (Tibetan)

Bka' 'gyur (dpe sdur ma). Beijing: Krung go'i bod rig pa'i dpe skrun khang, 2006–9. BDRC W1PD96682.

Blo bzang dam chos nyi ma. *Yab chos rtsa rlung 'khrul 'khor gyi lus sbyong thar pa'i lam chen.* Chengdu: Si khron mi rigs dpe skrun khang, 2013. BDRC W2KG1673.

'Brug thar and Karma Bde legs. *Bod kyi snga rabs dam pa rnams kyi gsungs chos phyag bris ma rin chen gser phreng.* Lanzhou: Kan su'u rig gnas dpe skrun khang, 2015. BDRC W3CN5697.

Bsod nams 'od zer. *Grub chen u rgyan pa'i rnam thar.* Lhasa: Bod ljongs bod yig dpe rnying dpe skrun khang, 1997. BDRC W22148.

Chögyam Trungpa. *Phyi nang gsang ba'i kla klo'i g.yul chen po bzlog zhing don rgyud kyi grub thob rgya mtsho mngon du sgrub pa'i cho ga phyag rgya chen po zhes bya ba bzhugs so.* Halifax, Nova Scotia: Nālandā Translation Committee, 1988.

Dpa' bo gtsug lag phreng ba. *Dam pa'i chos kyi 'khor lo bsgyur ba rnams kyi byung ba gsal bar byed pa mkhas pa'i dga' ston.* Beijing: Mi rigs dpe skrun khang, 1986. BDRC W7499.

Dpal bzhed pa'i rdo rje'i rnam thar. Bodleian Libraries, MS. Tibet.a.11 (R).

'Gos lo tsā ba gzhon du dpal. *Deb ther sngon po* [*The Blue Annals*]. Translated by George N. Roerich and Gendün Chöpel. Delhi: Motilal Banarsidass Publishers, 2007.

———. *Deb ther sngon po.* New Delhi: International Academy of Indian Culture, 1974. BDRC W7494.

Grags pa yongs 'dus. "Dbu zhwa mthong grol rin po che'i bshad pa tshogs gnyis gru gzings bzhugs so." In *Mkhas dbang raghu wīra dang lokesha tsandra rnam gnyis kyis nyar tshags byas pa'i dpe tshogs,* vol. 121, 37–62. BDRC W1KG26281.

'Jam dbyangs rgyal mtshan. *Gsang chen bstan pa'i chu 'go rgyal ba kah thog pa'i lo rgyus mdor bsdus rjod pa 'chi med lha'i rnga sgra ngo mtshar rna ba'i dga' ston.* Chengdu: Si khron mi rigs spe skrun khang, 1996. BDRC W20396.

Karma Chags med. "'Phags pa thugs rje chen po'i dmar khrid phyag rdzogs zung 'jug thos pa don ldan 'gro don rgya mtsho lung gi gter mdzod ces bya ba bzhugs so." In *Mkhas grub karma chags med kyi gsung 'bum,* vol. 54, 1–30. Nang chen rdzong: Gnas mdo gsang sngags chos 'phel gling gi dpe rnying nyams gso khang, 2010. BDRC W1KG8321.

———. "Ri chos mtshams kyi zhal gdams las/bla med gsar rnying yi dam ḍākki spyi'i yang gsang bla na med pa'i sgrub pa bde chen rab 'bar." In *Mkhas grub karma chags med kyi gsung 'bum,* vol. 32, 374–87. Nang chen rdzong: Gnas mdo gsang sngags chos 'phel gling gi dpe rnying nyams gso khang, 2010. BDRC W1KG8321.

———. "Thugs rje chen po'i dmar khrid phyag rdzogs zung 'jug thos pa don ldan 'gro don rgya mtsho lung gi gter mdzod." In *Mkhas grub karma chags med kyi gsung 'bum,* vol. 34, 1–30. Nang chen rdzong: Gnas mdo gsang sngags chos 'phel gling gi dpe rnying nyams gso khang, 2010. BDRC W1KG8321.

Karma Nges don bstan rgyas. "Chos rje karma pa sku 'phreng rim byon gyi rnam thar mdor bsdus dpag bsam khri shing." In *The Collected Works of Sman-sdoṅ mtshams-pa rin-po-che karma-ṅes-don-bstan-rgyas.* Bir: D. Tsondu Senghe, 1976. BDRC W10982.

Karma pa Mi bskyod rdo rje. "Dpal Karma pa chen po la brten pa'i thun bzhi'i bla ma'i rnal 'byor dmigs khrid dang bcas pa." In *Gdams ngag mdzod,* edited by Kong sprul Blo gros mtha' yas, vol. 9, 277–86. Paro, Bhutan: Lama Ngodrup and Sherab Drime, 1979–81. BDRC W20877.

Karma pa Rang byung rig pa'i rdo rje. "Bla ma'i rnal 'byor sku bzhi'i myu gu skyed byed bdud rtsi'i char rgyun." In *Rgyal dbang karma pa bcu drug pa rang byung rig pa'i rdo rje'i bka' 'bum,* edited by Jo sras Bkra shis tshe ring, vol. 3, 177–78. Dharamsala: Tsurphu Labrang and Amnye Machen Institute, 2016. BDRC W8LS18007.

Karma Pakshi. *The Autobiographical Writings of the Second Karma-pa Karma-Pakśi and Spyi lan riṅ mo: A Defence of the Bka'-brgyud-pa Teachings Addressed to G'yag-sde Paṇ-chen.* Gangtok: Gonpo Tseten, 1978. BDRC W27319.

———. "Bstan pa rgya mtsho mtha' yas kyi bshad pa phun sum tshogs pa rgya mtsho mtha' yas." In *Karma pa sku phreng rim byon gyi gsung 'bum phyogs bsgrigs,* vol. 9, 159–473. Lhasa: Dpal brtsegs bod yig dpe rnying zhib 'jug khang, 2013. BDRC W3PD1288.

———. "Ma rig 'khrul pa'i rtsa rgyud." In *Karma pa sku phreng rim byon gyi gsung* 'bum phyogs bsgrigs, vol. 9, 533–38. Lhasa: Dpal brtsegs bod yig dpe rnying zhib 'jug khang, 2013. BDRC W3PD1288.

———. "Mkha' 'gro yid bzhin nor bu'i gzhung." In *Karma pa sku phreng rim byon gyi gsung 'bum phyogs bsgrigs*, vol. 10, 191–274. Lhasa: Dpal brtsegs bod yig dpe rnying zhib 'jug khang, 2013. BDRC W3PD1288.

———. "Rlung sems gnad kyi lde'u mig bzhugs so." In *Karma pa sku phreng rim byon gyi gsung 'bum phyogs bsgrigs*, vol. 3, 399–402. Lhasa: Dpal brtsegs bod yig dpe rnying zhib 'jug khang, 2013. BDRC W3PD1288.

———. "Ston pa lnga yi bstan pa rgya mtsho mtha' yas las lung chen a nu yo ga las 'phros pa theg pa kun gyi spyi lung." In *Karma pa sku phreng rim byon gyi gsung 'bum phyogs bsgrigs*, vol. 8, 1–278. Lhasa: Dpal brtsegs bod yig dpe rnying zhib 'jug khang, 2013. BDRC W3PD1288.

———. "Grub chen Pakshir yongs su grags pa'i rdo rje'i mgur." In *Bod yul dmangs khrod kyi rtsa chen dpe rnying phyogs bsgrigs*, vol. 2, 675–748. Chengdu: Si khron mi rigs dpe skrun khang, 2015. BDRC W3CN8399.

Mi bkyod rdo rje. "Sku gsum ngo sprod kyi rnam par bshad pa mdo rgyud bstan pa mtha' dag gi e waṃ phyag rgya." In *Dpal rgyal ba karma pa sku 'phreng brgyad pa mi bskyod rdo rje'i gsung 'bum*, vols. 21–22. Lhasa: Karma Deleg, 2004. BDRC W8039.

Mi 'gyur rdo rje drag po nus ldan rtsal. "Rje karma pakshi zhal gzigs ma'i las byang bzhugs so." In *Rin chen gter mdzod chen mo*, edited by Kong sprul Blo gros mtha' yas, vol. 11, 815–28. New Delhi: Shechen Publications, 2007–08. BDRC W1KG14.

Mkha' spyod dbang po. "Chos kyi rje dpal ldan karma pa chen po'i rnam par thar pa bsam yas lha'i rnga chen." In *Karma pa sku phreng rim byon gyi gsung 'bum phyogs bsgrigs*, vol. 3, 249–339. Lhasa: Dpal brtsegs bod yig dpe rnying zhib 'jug khang, 2013. BDRC W3PD1288.

Namkhai Norbu. *Byang 'brog gi lam yig: A Journey into the Culture of Tibetan Nomads*. Arcidosso: Shang-Shung Edizioni, 1983. BDRC W00KG03605.

———. *Chos rgyal nam mkha'i nor bu'i gsung 'bum bzhugs so*. Xining: Mtsho sngon mi rigs dpe skrun khang, 2015. BDRC W3CN5660.

Nyang nyi ma 'od zer. *Chos 'byung me tog snying po sbrang rtsi'i bcud*. Lhasa: Bod ljongs mi dbang dpe skrun khang, 1988. BDRC W7972.

Padma dkar po. "Gdan sa chen po ra lung gi khyad par 'phags pa cung zad brjod pa ngo mtshar gyi gter." In *Collected Works (Gsuṅ-'bum) of Kun-mkhyen Padma-dkar-po*. Darjeeling: Kargyud Sungrab Nyamso Khang, 1973. BDRC W10736.

Rang byung rdo rje. "Dpal o rgyan pa'i rnam par thar pa bzhugs so." In *Karma pa rang byung rdo rje'i gsung 'bum*, vol. 4, 288–352. BDRC W30541.

———. *Karma pa rang byung rdo rje'i gsung 'bum*. Xining: Mkhan po lo yag bkra shis, 2006. BDRC W30541.

———. "Sku gsum ngo sprod." In *Karma pa rang byung rdo rje'i gsung 'bum*, vol. 11, 1–29. BDRC W30541.

———. "Thams cad mkhyen pa rin po che rang byung rdo rje rnam par thar pa tshigs su bcad pa zhugs pa'i dbu phyogs so." In *Karma pa rang byung rdo rje'i gsung 'bum*, vol. 4, 374–414. BDRC W30541.

Rin chen dpal bzang. *Mtshur phu dgon gyi dkar chag kung sal me long*. Beijing: Mi rigs dpe skrun khang, 1995. BDRC W20850.

Rta tshag Tshe dbang rgyal. *Dam pa'i chos kyi byung ba'i legs bshad lho rong chos 'byung ngam rta tshag chos 'byung zhes rtsom pa'i yul ming du chags pa'i ngo mtshar zhing dkon pa'i dpe khyad par can*. Lhasa: Bod ljong Bod yig dpe rnying dpe skrun khang, 1994. BDRC W27302.

Rus pa'i rgyan can. *Rnal 'byor gyi dbang phyug chen po mi la ras pa'i rnam mgur*. Xining: Mtsho sngon mi rigs dpe skrun khang, 1991. BDRC W21762.

Si tu chos kyi 'byung gnas. *Bka' brgyud gser phreng rnam thar zla ba chu shel gyi phreng ba*. Sarnath: Vajra Vidya Institute, 2004. BDRC W4CZ295072.

Situ-Paṇchen Chos-kyi-'byuṅ-gnas and 'Be-lo Tshe-dbaṅ-kun-khyab. *History of the Karma Bka-'brgyud-pa* [sic] *Sect: Being the Text of Sgrub brgyud Karma Kaṃ tshang brgyud pa rin po che'i rnam par thar pa rab 'byams nor bu zla ba chu śel gyi phreṅ ba*. New Delhi: D. Gyaltsan and Kesang Legshay, 1972. BDRC W23435.

Snga 'gyur rgyud 'bum phyogs bsgrigs. Beijing: Mi rigs dpe skrun khang, 2009. BDRC W1KG14783.

Tāranātha. "Slob dpon chen po padma 'byung gnas kyi rnam par thar pa gsal bar byed pa'i yi ge yid ches gsum ldan zhes bya ba bzhugs so: 'Di la slob dpon padma'i rnam thar rgya gar lugs zhes bya'o." In *Five Historical Works of Tāranātha*, 501–537. Tezu, Arunachal Pradesh: Tibetan Nyingmapa Monastery, 1974. BDRC W1KG10418.

Terchen Karma. *Bka' zab rdzogs chen po: rgyud rnams kun gyi gnad bsdus pa: ma 'ongs bsgyur du bsgrod pa'i thabs: sngon 'gro thos grol chen po dang: sdig chen dang rig gcer mthong pa: thod rgal snang bzhi mthar phyin bzhugs*. British Library, 19999.aa.71.

Thugs kyi rdo rje and Zur mang bstan sprul. "Gter chen rin po che mi 'gyur rdo rje'i rnam par thar pa skal ldan 'dren pa'i shing rta." In *The Lives of Two Lamas of Naṅ-Chen*. Bir: Kandro Tibetan Khampa Industrial Society, 1973. BDRC W00KG09218.

Tshal pa kun dga' rdo rje. *Deb ther dmar po.* Beijing: Mi rigs dpe skrun khang, 1981. BDRC W1KG5760.

Ye shes rgyal mtshan. "Rin po che kar ma pa rang byung rdo rje'i rnam thar bzhugs pa'i dbu phyogs lags soha." In *Bka' brgyud rnam thar rin chen gser gyi phreng ba.* BDRC W3CN674, scans 509–45.

———. *Rje grub thob chen po karma pakshi'i rnam par thar pa* (W1KG13822).

References

Berounský, Daniel. "Entering Dead Bodies and the Miraculous Power of the Kings: The Landmark of Karma Pakshi's Reincarnation in Tibet, Part 1." *Mongolo-Tibetica Pragensia '10: Ethnolinguistics, Sociolinguistics, Religion and Culture* 3, no. 2 (2010): 7–33.

———. "Entering Dead Bodies and the Miraculous Power of the Kings: The Landmark of Karma Pakshi's Reincarnation in Tibet, Part 2." *Mongolo-Tibetica Pragensia '11: Ethnolinguistics, Sociolinguistics, Religion and Culture* 4, no. 2 (2011): 7–29.

Birge, Bettina. *Marriage and the Law in the Age of Khubilai Khan: Cases from the Yuan Dianzhang.* Cambridge, MA: Harvard University Press, 2017.

Boyle, John Andrew. "The Seasonal Residences of the Great Khan Ögedei." In *The Mongol World Empire, 1206–1370*, 145–51. London: Variorum Reprints, 1977.

Chagmé, Karma. *A Spacious Path to Freedom: Practical Instructions on the Union of Mahamudrā and Atiyoga.* Translated by B. Alan Wallace. Ithaca, NY: Snow Lion, 1998.

Chögyam Trungpa. *The Sadhana of Mahamudra Sourcebook.* Boulder, CO: Vajradhatu Publications, 1979.

———. *The Tantric Path of Indestructible Wakefulness.* Vol. 3 of *The Profound Treasury of the Ocean of Dharma*, edited by Judith L. Lief. Boston: Shambhala, 2013.

Cleaves, Francis Woodman. "The Sino-Mongolian Inscription of 1240." *Harvard Journal of Asiatic Studies* 23 (1960–61): 62–75.

Dakpo Tashi Namgyal. *Moonbeams of Mahāmudrā.* Translated by Elizabeth M. Callahan. Boulder: Snow Lion, 2019.

Demiéville, Paul. "La situation religieuse en Chine au temps de Marco Polo." In *Oriente Poliano: Studi e conferenze tenute all'Is. M.E.O. in occasione del VII centenario della nascita di Marco Polo, 1254–1954*, edited by Étienne Balazs, 193–236. Rome: Istituto Italiano per il Medio ed Estremo Oriente, 1957.

Draszczyk, Martina. "Direct Introductions into the Three Embodiments, Supreme Key-Instructions of the Dwags po Bka' brgyud Tradition." *Revue d'Etudes Tibétaines* 45 (April 2018): 145–77.

Ducher, Cécile. *Building a Tradition: The Lives of Mar-pa the Translator*. Munich: Indus Verlag, 2017.

Gamble, Ruth. *Reincarnation in Tibetan Buddhism: The Third Karmapa and the Invention of a Tradition*. New York: Oxford University Press, 2018.

———. *The Third Karmapa, Rangjung Dorje: Master of Mahāmudrā*. Boulder: Shambhala, 2020.

Jackson, David P. *Patron and Painter: Situ Panchen and the Revival of the Encampment Style*. New York: Rubin Museum of Art, 2009.

Jackson, Peter, with David Morgan, trans. *The Mission of Friar William of Rubruck: His Journey to the Court of the Great Khan Möngke, 1253–1255*. London: Hakluyt Society, 1990.

Je Tukyi Dorje and Surmang Tendzin Rinpoche. *Chariot of the Fortunate: The Life of the First Yongey Mingyur Dorje*. Translated by Yeshe Gyamtso. Woodstock, NY: KTD Publications, 2006.

Kapstein, Matthew. "Religious Syncretism in 13th Century Tibet: The Limitless Ocean Cycle." In *Soundings in Tibetan Civilization: Proceedings of the 1982 Seminar of the International Association for Tibetan Studies held at Columbia University*, edited by Barbara Nimri Aziz and Matthew Kapstein, 358–371. New Delhi: Manohar Publications, 1985.

———. *The Tibetan Assimilation of Buddhism: Conversion, Contestation, and Memory*. Oxford: Oxford University Press, 2000.

———. "The Doctrine of Eternal Heaven: A Tibetan Defense of Mongol Imperial Religion." In *Mahāmudrā and the Bka'-brgyud Tradition*, edited by Roger R. Jackson and Matthew T. Kapstein, 259–315. Andiast, Switzerland: International Institute for Tibetan and Buddhist Studies, 2011.

Karma Choephel, David, and Michele Martin, trans. *The First Karmapa: The Life and Teachings of Dusum Khyenpa*. Woodstock, NY: KTD Publications, 2012.

Kersten. Peter. "Biographies of the First Karma-pa Dus-gsum-mkhyen-pa, Critical Text Edition and Translation of Two Biographical Works; and an Overview of the Dus-gsum-mkhyen-pa Collection." PhD diss., Université Paris Sciences et Lettres, 2018.

Kipling, Rudyard. *The Five Nations*. London: Methuen, 1903.

Li, Brenda. "A Critical Study of the Life of the 13th-Century Tibetan Monk U rgyan pa Rin chen dpal Based on His Biographies." PhD diss., University of Oxford, 2011.

Manson, Charles. "Introduction to the Life of Karma Pakshi (1204/6–1283)." *Bulletin of Tibetology* 45, no. 1 (2009): 25–52.

Münküyev, N. Ts. "A New Mongolian P'ai-Tzŭ from Simferopol." *Acta Orientalia Academiae Scientarium Hungaricae* 31, no. 2 (1977): 185–215.

Richardson, Hugh E. *A Corpus of Early Tibetan Inscriptions.* London: Royal Asiatic Society, 1985.

——. "The Karma-pa Sect: A Historical Note." In *High Peaks, Pure Earth: Collected Writings on Tibetan History and Culture*, edited by Michael Aris, 337–78. London: Serindia, 1998.

——. "Memories of Tshurphu." In *High Peaks, Pure Earth: Collected Writings on Tibetan History and Culture*, edited by Michael Aris, 730–33. London: Serindia, 1998.

Stein, R. A. *Tibetan Civilization.* Translated by John E. Stapleton Driver. London: Faber and Faber, 1972.

Taranatha. *The Life of Padmasambhava.* Translated and edited by Cristiana De Falco. Arcidosso, Italy: Shang Shung Institute, 2012.

Terton Karma Lingpa. *The Tibetan Book of the Dead.* Translated by Gyurme Dorje. New York: Penguin Books, 2005.

Tsang Nyön Heruka. *The Life of Marpa the Translator: Seeing Accomplishes All.* Translated by the Nālandā Translation Committee. Boston: Shambhala, 1995.

Tucci, Guiseppe. *The Tombs of the Tibetan Kings.* Rome: Istituto Italiano per il Medio ed Estremo Oriente, 1950.

van der Kuijp, Leonard W. J. "The Dalai Lamas and the Origins of Reincarnate Lamas." In *The Dalai Lamas: A Visual History*, edited by Martin Brauen, 15–31. Chicago: Serindia Publications, 2005.

Vitali, Roberto. "Glimpses of the History of the rGya Clan with Reference to Nyang stod, lHo Mon and Nearby Lands (7th–13th Century)." In *The Spider and the Piglet: Proceedings of the First International Seminar on Bhutan Studies*, edited by Karma Ura and Sonam Kinga, 6–20. Thimpu: Centre for Bhutan Studies, 2004.

Index

Drigung Monastery, 45, 46, 47
Drigung Til, 8
Drilung (valley), 152
Drogön Rechen, 14, 27, 33, 122, 160
drongjuk practice, 114–15
Drowo Lung, 13
Düsum Khyenpa, 13, 22, 24, 33, 78,
    150
  death of, 13, 40, 118
  doctrine of, 28
  elephant preincarnation, 59–60,
    77, 151–52
  future rebirths of, 62–63, 152
  hat of, 107, 108
  Karma Pakshi's recognition as, 12,
    44, 48
  Karma Pakshi's relationship to, 2,
    131, 215
  mahāmudrā lineage of, 16
  monasteries founded by, 13, 24, 30,
    38, 43, 47, 236n65
  Palden Lhamo and, 53
  prayer to, 178
  preincarnations of, 132
  relics of, 110
  Saraha and, 15
  secret name of, 247n175
  self-identification of Karma Pakshi
    with, 119
  as Siṃhanāda, 133, 134, 160–61, 171,
    250n197, 252n217
  statue, 102
  teachings, spread of, 50
  visions of, 13–14, 30, 47, 76
Dza River, 247n176
Dzogchen. See Great Perfection
    (Dzogchen)

Dzodzi Monastery, 123
Dzungar Mongols, 95

East Syriac Christians, 60
Effulgent Light Annihilating Poison, 80
ego, 148–49. See also twenty-one
    views of ego clinging
Eight Classes of Magical Net, 20
eightfold group of gods and
    demons, 34, 208
Elagan, 83, 174
Elchiqmish, 72
empowerments, 66, 221
  fourfold, 35, 39, 65, 81, 226
  Heruka, 75
  Jinasāgara, 107, 108
  at Karakorum, 45
  of Kubilai Khan (Hevajra), 105
  mahāmudrā and, 193
emptiness, 103, 125, 167–68, 192,
    251n205
enlightened attitude, 55. See also
    bodhicitta
equanimity, 17, 214
Esoteric Great Treasury, 4, 217–27
Essen, Gerd-Wolfgang, 240n104
Europe, 3–4, 44, 59, 123, 126,
    239n100
Everest, Mount, 50

faith, 152
  in consecrated artifacts, 100–101,
    209
  as direct perception, 158
  in Karma Pakshi, 84, 180–81
fear, 82, 113, 124, 173, 174, 175,
    187–88, 216

and Düsum Khyenpa, connection
between, 59–60, 62–63
empire of, 59
imperial encampment of, 61–62
initiation of, 45
invitation to Karma Pakshi, 58
Karma Pakshi's influence on,
66–67, 75–76
military expansion of, 69–70
patronage of, 76, 107, 203,
240n102, 240n104
religious politics of, 60–61
teachings received by, 18
Mongolia, 1, 3, 18, 37, 38, 43, 45–46,
89, 118, 123, 185
Mongolian Empire, 3, 62
in China, 1, 37, 69–70
civil war of, 197
expansion of, 65
invasions by, 27, 40, 44–45, 50–51,
59, 95
relay horse-riding system of, 58
succession battle in, 79–80
Tibetan ecclesiastical engagement
with, 53–54, 105, 106, 238n88
Mountain Dharma (Karma
Chakmé), 127
Mubarak-Shah, 72
Mukpo family, 9

Nāgārjuna, 149
nāgas, 51, 76, 208, 222
Namkha Ö, 137, 141, 145, 149, 163,
250n199
Namkhai Norbu, 91–92, 93
Namo, 61
Namrak hermitage, 19, 25

Nanda, 51, 53
Nara Tōdai-ji Daibutsu, 96
Nāropa, 33, 78, 107, 135, 140, 177,
199, 219, 251n204
Nāropa tradition, 25
Nénang Monastery. *See* Kampo
Nenang Monastery
Nénangpa, Lama, 118
Ngawang Lobsang Gyatso, Fifth
Dalai Lama, 2
nine vehicles, 163, 193, 195, 196, 197,
221–22, 224
nirmāṇakāya, 49, 103, 141, 223
emanations of, 132, 144, 166
power of, 225
pure land of, 77
scriptures of, 151
nirvana, 36, 194–95, 196
all dharmas as, 157
dharmakāya in, 103
identity of, 15
phenomena of, 18, 148, 154, 189,
191–92, 196
pure lands, 16
non-awareness, 25, 154
non-Buddhists
conversion of, 28, 72
faith in, 152
Ornament of the World and, 97,
204, 210
views and tenets, 44, 168, 192, 193,
220
*Nondual Means and Knowledge
Tantra*, 149
non-meditation, 16, 18, 19, 25, 195
Norlha, Lama, 36, 235n58
Nub Namkhai Nyingpo, 10

LIVES OF THE MASTERS

"Since the time of Buddha Shakyamuni himself, Buddhists have been accustomed to recollect the lives of great teachers and practitioners as a source of inspiration from which we may still learn. The Lives of the Masters series continues this noble tradition, recounting the stories, wisdom, and experience of many accomplished Buddhists over the last 2,500 years. I am sure readers will find the accounts in this series inspirational and encouraging."

HIS HOLINESS THE DALAI LAMA

"The lives of the most important Buddhist masters in history written by the very best of scholars in elegant and accessible prose—who could ask for more?"

JOSÉ CABEZÓN, *Professor of Tibetan Buddhist Studies,*
University of California, Santa Barbara

BOOKS IN THE SERIES

Atiśa Dīpaṃkara: Illuminator of the Awakened Mind
Dogen: Japan's Original Zen Teacher
Gendun Chopel: Tibet's Modern Visionary
Maitripa: India's Yogi of Nondual Bliss
S. N. Goenka: Emissary of Insight
The Second Karmapa Karma Pakshi: Tibetan Mahāsidda
The Third Karmapa Rangjung Dorje: Master of Mahāmudrā
Tsongkhapa: A Buddha in the Land of Snows
Xuanzang: China's Legendary Pilgrim and Translator

Please visit www.shambhala.com
for more information on forthcoming titles.